Rick Steves'

German

Phrase Book & Dictionary

Fifth Edition

**AVALON
TRAVEL**

Avalon Travel Publishing, 1400 65th Street, Suite 250, Emeryville, CA 94608, USA

Avalon Travel Publishing is an imprint of Avalon Publishing Group, Inc.

Printed in the United States of America by Worzalla.
Fifth edition. Third printing March 2006.

ISBN-10: 1-56691-519-8
ISBN-13: 978-1-56691-519-9

Europe Through the Back Door Managing Editor:
  Risa Laib
Europe Through the Back Door Editor:
  Cameron Hewitt
Avalon Travel Publishing Editor: Matt Orendorff
Translation: Julia Klimek, Martin Minich
Phonetics: Risa Laib, Cameron Hewitt
Production & Typesetting: Matt Orendorff
Cover Design: Kari Gim
Maps & Graphics: David C. Hoerlein, Zoey Platt
Photography: Rick Steves, Dominic Bonuccelli,
  Andrea Johnson
Front cover photos:
  foreground– © Anderson Ross/Getty Images/
Photodisc/2003; background– © Royalty-Free/CORBIS

Distributed to the book trade by
Publishers Group West, Berkeley, California

Other ATP travel guidebooks by Rick Steves

Rick Steves' Best of Europe
Rick Steves' Europe 101: History and Art for the Traveler
  (with Gene Openshaw)
Rick Steves' Europe Through the Back Door
Rick Steves' Mona Winks (with Gene Openshaw)
Rick Steves' Postcards from Europe
Rick Steves' France (with Steve Smith)
Rick Steves' Germany, Austria & Switzerland
Rick Steves' Great Britain
Rick Steves' Ireland (with Pat O'Connor)
Rick Steves' Italy
Rick Steves' Scandinavia
Rick Steves' Spain & Portugal
Rick Steves' Amsterdam, Bruges & Brussels
  (with Gene Openshaw)
Rick Steves' Florence (with Gene Openshaw)
Rick Steves' London (with Gene Openshaw)
Rick Steves' Paris
  (with Steve Smith and Gene Openshaw)
Rick Steves' Rome (with Gene Openshaw)
Rick Steves' Venice (with Gene Openshaw)
Rick Steves' Phrase Books: French, Italian, Portuguese,
Spanish, and French/Italian/German

For the latest on Rick's lectures, guidebooks, tours, and public television series, contact Europe Through the Back Door, Box 2009, Edmonds, WA 98020, tel. 425/771-8303, fax 425/771-0833, www.ricksteves.com, or e-mail: rick@ricksteves.com.

CONTENTS

Chatting 186–211

Dictionary 213–260

Tips for Hurdling the Language Barrier . 262–272

Illustrations

Maps

Hi, I'm Rick Steves.

I'm the only mono-lingual speaker I know who's had the nerve to design a series of European phrase books. But that's one of the things that makes them better. You see, after 25 summers of travel through Europe, I've learned first-hand (1) what's essential for communication in another country and (2) what's not. I've assembled these most important words and phrases in a logical, no-frills format, and I've worked with native Europeans and seasoned travelers to give you the simplest, clearest translations possible.

But this book is more than just a pocket translator. The words and phrases have been carefully selected to make you a happier, more effective budget traveler. The key to getting more out of every travel dollar is to get closer to the local people, and to rely less on entertainment, restaurants, and hotels that cater only to foreign tourists. This book will give you the linguistic four-wheel drive to navigate through German, Austrian, and Swiss culture—from ordering a meal at a locals-only Tirolean restaurant to discussing social issues, travel dreams, and your wurst memories with the family that runs the place. Long after your memories of castles and museums have faded, you'll still treasure the close encounters you had with your new European friends.

A good phrase book should help you enjoy your linguistic adventure—not just survive it—so I've added a healthy dose of humor. But please use these phrases carefully, in a self-effacing spirit. Remember that one ugly American can undo the goodwill built by dozens of culturally sensitive ones.

To get the most out of this book, take the time to internalize and put into practice my German pronunciation tips. I've spelled out the pronunciations as if you were reading English. Don't worry too much about memorizing grammatical rules, like which gender a particular noun is—toss sex out the window, and communicate!

German is the closest thing I'll ever have to a "second language." It takes only a few words to feel like I'm part of the greater Germanic family, greeting hikers in the Alps, commiserating over the crowds in Rothenburg, prosting in the beerhalls of Blindenpist, and slap-dancing in Tirol.

You'll notice that this book has a dictionary and a nifty menu decoder. You'll also find German tongue twisters, international words, telephone tips, and a handy tear-out cheat sheet. Tear it out and tuck it into your *dirndl* or *lederhosen* so you can easily use it to memorize key phrases during otherwise idle moments. As you prepare for your trip, you may want to take advantage of this year's edition of my *Rick Steves' Germany & Austria* and *Rick Steves' Switzerland* guidebooks.

My goal is to help you become a more confident, extroverted traveler. If this phrase book helps make that happen, or if you have suggestions for making it better, I'd love to hear from you. I personally read and value all feedback. My address is Europe Through the Back Door, P.O. Box 2009, Edmonds, WA 98020, tel. 425/771-8303, fax 425/771-0833, e-mail: rick@ricksteves.com.

Happy travels, and *Viel Glück* (good luck) as you hurdle the language barrier!

Rick Steves

GETTING
STARTED

Versatile, Entertaining German

...is spoken throughout Germany, Austria, and most
of Switzerland. In addition, German rivals English
as the handiest second language in Scandinavia, the
Netherlands, Eastern Europe, and Turkey.

German is kind of a "lego language." Be on the look-
out for fun combination words. A *Fingerhut* (finger hat) is a
thimble, a *Halbinsel* (half island) is a peninsula, a *Stinktier*
(stinky animal) is a skunk, and a *Dummkopf* (dumb head)
is... um... uh...

German has some key twists to its pronunciation:

CH sounds like the guttural CH in Scottish loch.
J sounds like Y in yes.
S can sound like S in sun or Z in zoo.
    But **S** followed by **CH** sounds like SH in shine.
V sounds like F in fun.
W sounds like V in volt.
Z sounds like TS in hits.
EI sounds like I in light.
EU sounds like OY in joy.
IE sounds like EE in seed.

1

German has a few unusual signs and sounds. The letter ß is not a letter B at all–it's interchangeable with "ss." Some of the German vowels are double-dotted with an umlaut. The ö has a sound uncommon in English. To make the ö sound, round your lips to say "o," but say "ee." The German *ch* has a clearing-your-throat sound. Say *Achtung!*

Here's a guide to the phonetics in this book:

ah like A in father.
ar like AR in far.
ay like AY in play.
ee like EE in seed.
eh like E in get.
ehr sounds like "air."
er like ER in mother.
ew pucker your lips and say "ee."
g   like G in go.
kh like the guttural CH in Achtung.
i   like I in hit.
ī   like I in light.
o   like O in cost.
oh like O in note.
or like OR in core.
oo like OO in moon.
ow like OW in now.
oy like OY in toy.
s   like S in sun.
u   like U in put.
uh like U in but.
ur like UR in purr.
ts like TS in hits. It's a small explosive sound.

In German, the verb is often at the end of the sentence–it's where the action is. Germans capitalize all nouns. Each noun has a sex, which determines which "the" you'll use (*der* man, *die* woman, and *das* neuter).

No traveler is expected to remember which is which. It's O.K. to just grab whichever "the" (*der, die, das*) comes to mind. In the interest of simplicity, we've occasionally left out the articles. Also for simplicity, we often drop the "please." Please use "please" (*bitte,* pronounced **bit**-teh) liberally.

Each German-speaking country has a distinct dialect. The Swiss speak a lilting Swiss-German around the home, but in schools and at work they speak and write in the same standard German used in Germany and Austria (called "High" German, or *Hochdeutsch*). The multilingual Swiss greet you with a cheery "*Gruetzi,*" (pron. **groyt**-see), thank you by saying "*Merci,*" (pron. **mehr**-see), and bid goodbye with "*Ciao*" (pron. chow). Both Austrians and Bavarians speak in a sing-song dialect, and greet one another with "*Grüss Gott*" (pron. grews goht) which means "May God greet you."

GERMAN
BASICS

While he used a tank instead of a Eurailpass, General Patton made it all the way to Berlin using only these phrases.

Meeting and Greeting

Good day.	Guten Tag.	**goo**-tehn tahg
Good morning.	Guten Morgen.	**goo**-tehn **mor**-gehn
Good evening.	Guten Abend.	**goo**-tehn **ah**-behnt
Good night.	Gute Nacht.	**goo**-teh nahkht
Hi. (informal)	Hallo.	**hah**-loh
Welcome!	Willkommen!	vil-**koh**-mehn
Mr.	Herr	hehr
Ms.	Frau	frow
Miss (under 18)	Fräulein	**froy**-līn
How are you?	Wie geht's?	vee gayts
Very well, thanks.	Sehr gut, danke.	zehr goot **dahng**-keh
And you?	Und Ihnen?	oont **ee**-nehn
My name is ___.	Ich heiße ___.	ikh **hī**-seh ___
What's your name?	Wie heißen Sie?	vee **hī**-sehn zee
Pleased to meet you.	Sehr erfreut.	zehr ehr-**froyt**
Where are you from?	Wo her kommen Sie?	voh hehr **koh**-mehn zee

4

I am / We are...	*Ich bin / Wir sind...*	ikh bin / veer zint
Are you...?	*Sind Sie...?*	zint zee
...on vacation	*...auf Urlaub*	...owf **oor**-lowp
...on business	*...auf Geschäftsreise*	...owf geh-**shehfts**-rī-zeh
See you later!	*Bis später!*	bis **shpay**-ter
So long! (informal)	*Tschüss!*	chewss
Goodbye.	*Auf Wiedersehen.*	owf **vee**-der-zayn
Good luck!	*Viel Glück!*	feel glewk
Have a good trip!	*Gute Reise!*	**goo**-teh **rī**-zeh

People use the greeting "*Guten Morgen*" (Good morning) until noon, and "*Guten Tag*" (Good day) switches to "*Guten Abend*" (Good evening) around 6 p.m.

Essentials

Good day.	*Guten Tag.*	**goo**-tehn tahg
Do you speak English?	*Sprechen Sie Englisch?*	**shprehkh**-ehn zee **ehng**-lish
Yes. / No.	*Ja. / Nein.*	yah / nīn
I don't speak German.	*Ich spreche nicht Deutsch.*	ikh **shprehkh**-eh nikht doych
I'm sorry.	*Es tut mir leid.*	ehs toot meer līt
Please.	*Bitte.*	**bit**-teh
Thank you.	*Danke.*	**dahng**-keh
Thank you very much.	*Vielen Dank.*	**fee**-lehn dahngk.
No problem.	*Kein Problem.*	kīn proh-**blaym**
Good.	*Gut.*	goot
Very good.	*Sehr gut.*	zehr goot
Excellent.	*Ausgezeichnet.*	ows-geht-**sīkh**-neht
You are very kind.	*Sie sind sehr freundlich.*	zee zint zehr **froynd**-likh
Excuse me. (to pass or get attention)	*Entschuldigung.*	ehnt-**shool**-dig-oong
It doesn't matter.	*Macht's nichts.*	mahkhts nikhts
You're welcome.	*Bitte.*	**bit**-teh

Sure.	*Sicher.*	**zikh**-er
O.K.	*In Ordnung.*	in **ord**-noong
Let's go.	*Auf geht's.*	owf gayts
Goodbye.	*Auf Wiedersehen.*	owf **vee**-der-zayn

Where?

Where is...?	*Wo ist...?*	voh ist
...the tourist information office	*...das Touristen-informations-büro*	dahs too-**ris**-tehn-in-for-maht-see-**ohns bew**-roh
...a cash machine	*...ein Bankomat*	**īn bahnk**-oh-maht
...the train station	*...der Bahnhof*	dehr **bahn**-hohf
...the bus station	*...der Busbahnhof*	dehr **boos**-bahn-hohf
...the toilet	*...die Toilette*	dee toh-**leh**-teh
men / women	*Herren / Damen*	**hehr**-ehn / **dah**-mehn

You'll find some German words are similar to English if you're looking for a *Bank, Hotel, Restaurant,* or *Supermarkt.*

How Much?

How much is it?	*Wie viel kostet das?*	vee feel **kohs**-teht dahs
Write it?	*Aufschreiben?*	**owf**-shrī-behn
Is it free?	*Ist es umsonst?*	ist ehs oom-**zohnst**
Included?	*Inklusive?*	in-kloo-**zee**-veh
Do you have...?	*Haben Sie...?*	**hah**-behn zee
Where can I buy...?	*Wo kann ich... kaufen?*	voh kahn ikh... **kow**-fehn
I'd like...	*Ich hätte gern...*	ikh **heh**-teh gehrn
We'd like...	*Wir hätten gern...*	veer **heh**-tehn gehrn
...this.	*...dies.*	deez
...just a little.	*...nur ein bißchen.*	noor īn **bis**-yehn
...more.	*...mehr.*	mehr
...a ticket.	*...eine Karte.*	**ī**-neh **kar**-teh
...a room.	*...ein Zimmer.*	īn **tsim**-mer
...the bill.	*...die Rechnung.*	dee **rehkh**-noong

How Many?

one	*eins*	īns
two	*zwei*	tsvī
three	*drei*	drī
four	*vier*	feer
five	*fünf*	fewnf
six	*sechs*	zehx
seven	*sieben*	**zee**-behn
eight	*acht*	ahkht
nine	*neun*	noyn
ten	*zehn*	tsayn

You'll find more to count on in the Numbers section (pages 15-16).

When?

At what time?	*Um wie viel Uhr?*	oom vee feel oor
open	*geöffnet*	geh-**urf**-neht
closed	*geschlossen*	geh-**shloh**-sehn
Just a moment.	*Moment.*	moh-**mehnt**
Now.	*Jetzt.*	yehtst
Soon.	*Bald.*	bahlt
Later.	*Später.*	**shpay**-ter
Today.	*Heute.*	**hoy**-teh
Tomorrow.	*Morgen.*	**mor**-gehn

Be creative! You can combine these phrases to say: "Two, please," or "No, thank you," or "Open tomorrow?" or "Please, where can I buy a ticket?" Please is a magic word in any language. If you want something and you don't know the word for it, just point and say, "*Bitte*" (Please). If you know the word for what you want, such as the bill, simply say, "*Rechnung, bitte*" (Bill, please).

BASICS

Struggling with German

Do you speak English?	*Sprechen Sie Englisch?*	**shprehkh**-ehn zee **ehng**-lish
A teeny weeny bit?	*Ein ganz klein bißchen?*	īn gahnts klīn **bis**-yehn
Please speak English.	*Bitte sprechen Sie Englisch.*	**bit**-teh **shprehkh**-ehn zee **ehng**-lish
You speak English well.	*Ihr Englisch ist sehr gut.*	eer **ehng**-lish ist zehr goot
I don't speak German.	*Ich spreche nicht Deutsch.*	ikh **shprehkh**-eh nikht doych
We don't speak German.	*Wir sprechen nicht Deutsch.*	veer **shprehkh**-ehn nikht doych
I speak a little German.	*Ich spreche ein bißchen Deutsch.*	ikh **shprehkh**-eh īn **bis**-yehn doych
Sorry, I speak only English.	*Es tut mir leid, ich spreche nur Englisch.*	ehs toot meer līt ikh **shprehkh**-eh noor **ehng**-lish
Sorry, we speak only English.	*Es tut mir leid, wir sprechen nur Englisch.*	ehs toot meer līt veer **shprehkh**-ehn noor **ehng**-lish
Does somebody nearby speak English?	*Spricht jemand in der Nähe Englisch?*	shprikht **yay**-mahnt in dehr **nay**-heh **ehng**-lish
Who speaks English?	*Wer kann Englisch?*	vehr kahn **ehng**-lish
What does this mean?	*Was bedeutet das?*	vas beh-**doy**-teht dahs
What is this in German / English?	*Wie heißt das auf Deutsch / Englisch?*	vee hīst dahs owf doych / **eng**-lish
Repeat?	*Noch einmal?*	nohkh **īn**-mahl
Please speak slowly.	*Bitte sprechen Sie langsam.*	**bit**-teh **shprehkh**-ehn zee **lahng**-zahm
Slower.	*Langsamer.*	**lahng**-zah-mer
I understand.	*Ich verstehe.*	ikh fehr-**shtay**-heh

I don't understand.	Ich verstehe nicht.	ikh fehr-**shtay**-heh nikht
Do you understand?	Verstehen Sie?	fehr-**shtay**-hehn zee
Write it?	Schreiben?	**shrī**-behn

Handy Questions

How much?	Wie viel?	vee feel
How many?	Wie viele?	vee **fee**-leh
How long...?	Wie lang...?	vee lahng
...is the trip	...dauert die Reise	**dow**-ert dee **rī**-zeh
How many minutes / hours?	Wie viele Minuten / Stunden?	vee **fee**-leh mee-**noo**-tehn / **shtoon**-dehn
How far?	Wie weit?	vee vīt
How?	Wie?	vee
Can you help me?	Können Sie mir helfen?	**kurn**-nehn zee meer **hehlf**-ehn
Can you help us?	Können Sie uns helfen?	**kurn**-nehn zee oons **hehlf**-ehn
Can I...?	Kann ich...?	kahn ikh
Can we...?	Können wir...?	**kurn**-nehn veer
...have one	...eins haben	īns **hah**-behn
...go free	...umsonst rein	oom-**zohnst** rīn
...borrow that for a moment	...das für ein Moment leihen	dahs fewr īn moh-**mehnt** **lī**-hehn
...borrow that for an hour	...das für ein Stunde leihen	dahs fewr īn **shtoon**-deh l ī-hehn
...use the toilet	...die Toilette benützen	dee toh-**leh**-teh beh-**newts**-ehn
What? (didn't hear)	Wie bitte?	vee **bit**-teh
What is this / that?	Was ist dies / das?	vahs ist deez / dahs
What is better?	Was ist besser?	vahs ist **behs**-ser
What's going on?	Was ist los?	vahs ist lohs
When?	Wann?	vahn
What time is it?	Wie spät ist es?	vee shpayt ist ehs
At what time?	Um wie viel Uhr?	oom vee feel oor

On time? / Late?	Pünktlich? / Spät?	**pewnkt**-likh / shpayt
How long will it take?	Wie lange dauert es?	vee **lahng**-eh **dow**-ert ehs
When does this open / close?	Wann ist hier geöffnet / geschlossen	vahn ist heer geh-**urf**-neht / geh-**shloh**-sehn
Is this open daily?	Ist es täglich offen?	ist ehs **tayg**-likh **oh**-fehn
What day is this closed?	An welchem Tag ist es geschlossen?	ahn **vehlkh**-ehm tahg ist ehs geh-**shloh**-sehn
Do you have...?	Haben Sie...?	**hah**-behn zee
Where is...?	Wo ist...?	voh ist
Where are...?	Wo sind...?	voh zint
Where can I find / buy...?	Wo kann ich... finden / kaufen?	voh kahn ikh... **fin**-dehn / **kow**-fehn
Where can we find / buy...?	Wo können wir... finden / kaufen?	vo **kurn**-ehn veer... **fin**-dehn / **kow**-fehn
Is it necessary?	Ist das nötig?	ist dahs **nur**-tig
Is it possible...?	Ist es möglich...?	ist ehs **mur**-glikh
...to enter	...hinein gehen	hin-**īn** gay-hehn
...to picnic here	...hier picknicken	heer **pik**-nik-ehn
...to sit here	...hier sitzen	heer **zit**-sehn
...to look	...ansehen	**ahn**-zay-hehn
...to take a photo	...ein Foto machen	īn **foh**-toh **mahkh**-ehn
...to see a room	...ein Zimmer sehen	īn **tsim**-mer **zay**-hehn
Who?	Wer?	vehr
Why?	Warum?	vah-**room**
Why not?	Warum nicht?	vah-**room** nikht
Yes or no?	Ja oder nein?	yah **oh**-der nīn

To prompt a simple answer, ask, "*Ja oder nein?*" (Yes or no?). To turn a word or sentence into a question, ask it in a questioning tone. An easy way to ask, "Where is the toilet?" is to say, "*Toilette?*"

Das Yin und Yang

cheap / expensive	billig / teuer	**bil**-lig / **toy**-er
big / small	groß / klein	grohs / klīn
hot / cold	heiß / kalt	hīs / kahlt
warm / cool	warm / kühl	varm / kewl
open / closed	geöffnet / geschlossen	geh-**urf**-neht / geh-**shloh**-sehn
entrance / exit	Eingang / Ausgang	**īn**-gahng / **ows**-gahng
push / pull	drücken / ziehen	**drewk**-ehn / **tsee**-hehn
arrive / depart	ankommen / abfahren	**ahn**-koh-mehn / **ahp**-fah-rehn
early / late	früh / spät	frew / shpayt
soon / later	bald / später	bahlt / **shpay**-ter
fast / slow	schnell / langsam	shnehl / **lahng**-zahm
here / there	hier / dort	heer / dort
near / far	nah / fern	nah / fayrn
indoors / outdoors	drinnen / draussen	**drin**-nehn / **drow**-sehn
good / bad	gut / schlecht	goot / shlehkht
best / worst	beste / schlechteste	**bes**-teh / **shlehkh**-tehs-teh
a little / lots	wenig / viel	**vay**-nig / feel
more / less	mehr / weniger	mehr / **vay**-nig-er
mine / yours	mein / Ihr	mīn / eer
this / that	dies / das	deez / dahs
everybody / nobody	jeder / keiner	**yay**-der / k**ī**-ner
easy / difficult	leicht / schwierig	līkht / **shvee**-rig
left / right	links / rechts	links / rehkhts
up / down	oben / unten	**oh**-behn / **oon**-tehn
beautiful / ugly	schön / häßlich	shurn / **hehs**-likh
nice / mean	nett / gemein	neht / geh-**mīn**
smart / stupid	klug / dumm	kloog / dum
vacant / occupied	frei / besetzt	frī / beh-**zehtst**
with / without	mit / ohne	mit / **oh**-neh

BASICS

Big Little Words

I	*ich*	ikh
you (formal)	*Sie*	zee
you (informal)	*du*	doo
we	*wir*	veer
he	*er*	ehr
she	*sie*	zee
they	*sie*	zee
and	*und*	oont
at	*bei*	bī
because	*weil*	vī l
but	*aber*	**ah**-ber
by (via)	*mit*	mit
for	*für*	fewr
from	*von*	fohn
here	*hier*	heer
if	*ob*	ohp
in	*in*	in
it	*es*	ehs
not	*nicht*	nikht
now	*jetzt*	yehtst
only	*nur*	noor
or	*oder*	**oh**-der
this / that	*dies / das*	deez / dahs
to	*nach*	nahkh
very	*sehr*	zehr

Very German Expressions

Ach so.	ahkh zoh	I see.
Achtung.	**ahkh**-toong	Attention. / Watch out.
Alles klar.	**ah**-lehs klar	Everything is clear.
Ausgezeichnet.	ows-geht-**sīkh**-neht	Excellent.
Bitte.	**bit**-teh	Please. / You're welcome.
		Can I help you?
Es geht.	ehs gayt	So-so.
Gemütlich.	geh-**mewt**-likh	Cozy.

Gemütlichkeit.	geh-**mewt**-likh-kīt	Coziness.
Genau.	geh-**now**	Exactly.
Halt.	hahlt	Stop.
Hoppla!	**hohp**-lah	Oops!
Kein Wunder.	kīn **voon**-der	No wonder.
Mach schnell!	mahkh shnehl	Hurry up!
Macht's nichts.	mahkhts nikhts	It doesn't matter.
Natürlich.	nah-**tewr**-likh	Naturally.
Prima.	**pree**-mah	Great.
Sonst noch etwas?	zohnst nohkh **eht**-vahs	Anything else?
Stimmt.	shtimt	Correct.
Warum nicht?	vah-**room** nikht	Why not?
Was ist los?	vahs ist lohs	What's up?

Gemütlich (the adjective) and *Gemütlichkeit* (the noun) refer to a special Bavarian or Tirolean coziness. A candle-lit dinner, a friendly pub, a strolling violinist under a grape arbor on a balmy evening...this is *gemütlich*.

COUNTING

Numbers

0	*null*	nool
1	*eins*	īns
2	*zwei*	tsvī
3	*drei*	drī
4	*vier*	feer
5	*fünf*	fewnf
6	*sechs*	zehx
7	*sieben*	**zee**-behn
8	*acht*	ahkht
9	*neun*	noyn
10	*zehn*	tsayn
11	*elf*	ehlf
12	*zwölf*	tsvurlf
13	*dreizehn*	**drī**-tsayn
14	*vierzehn*	**feer**-tsayn
15	*fünfzehn*	**fewnf**-tsayn
16	*sechzehn*	**zehkh**-tsayn
17	*siebzehn*	**zeeb**-tsayn
18	*achtzehn*	**ahkht**-tsayn
19	*neunzehn*	**noyn**-tsayn
20	*zwanzig*	**tsvahn**-tsig

21	*einundzwanzig*	**īn**-oont-tsvahn-tsig
22	*zweiundzwanzig*	**tsvī**-oont-tsvahn-tsig
23	*dreiundzwanzig*	**drī**-oont-tsvahn-tsig
30	*dreißig*	**drī**-sig
31	*einunddreißig*	**īn**-oont-drī-sig
40	*vierzig*	**feer**-tsig
41	*einundvierzig*	**īn**-oont-feer-tsig
50	*fünfzig*	**fewnf**-tsig
60	*sechzig*	**zehkh**-tsig
70	*siebzig*	**zeeb**-tsig
80	*achtzig*	**ahkht**-tsig
90	*neunzig*	**noyn**-tsig
100	*hundert*	**hoon**-dert
101	*hunderteins*	hoon-dert-**īns**
102	*hundertzwei*	hoon-dert-**tsvī**
200	*zweihundert*	**tsvī**-hoon-dert
1000	*tausend*	**tow**-zehnd
2000	*zweitausend*	**tsvī**-tow-zehnd
2001	*zweitausendeins*	**tsvī**-tow-zehnd-**īns**
2002	*zweitausendzwei*	**tsvī**-tow-zehnd-**tsvī**
2003	*zweitausenddrei*	**tsvī**-tow-zehnd-**drī**
2004	*zweitausendvier*	**tsvī**-tow-zehnd-**feer**
2005	*zweitausendfünf*	**tsvī**-tow-zehnd-**fewnf**
2006	*zweitausendsechs*	**tsvī**-tow-zehnd-**zehx**
2007	*zweitausendsieben*	**tsvī**-tow-zehnd-**zee**-behn
2008	*zweitausendacht*	**tsvī**-tow-zehnd-**ahkht**
2009	*zweitausendneun*	**tsvī**-tow-zehnd-**noyn**
2010	*zweitausendzehn*	**tsvī**-tow-zehnd-**tsayn**
million	*eine Million*	**ī**-neh mil-**yohn**
billion	*eine Milliarde*	**ī**-neh mil-**yar**-deh
number one	*Nummer eins*	**noo**-mer **īns**
first	*erste*	**ehr**-steh
second	*zweite*	**tsvī**-teh
third	*dritte*	**drit**-teh
once / twice	*ein Mal / zwei Mal*	īn mahl / tsvī mahl
a quarter	*ein Viertel*	īn **feer**-tehl
a third	*ein Drittel*	īn **drit**-tehl
half	*Halb*	hahlp

this much	*so viel*	zoh feel
a dozen	*ein Dutzend*	īn **doot**-tsehnd
some	*einige*	**ī**-ni-geh
enough	*genug*	geh-**noog**
a handful	*eine Hand voll*	**ī**-neh hahnt fohl
50%	*fünfzig Prozent*	**fewnf**-tsig proh-**tsehnt**
100%	*hundert Prozent*	**hoon**-dert proh-**tsehnt**

The number *zwei* (two) is sometimes pronounced "tsvoh" to help distinguish it from the similar sound of *eins* (one).

Remember the nursery rhyme about the four-and-twenty blackbirds? That's how Germans say the numbers from 21 to 99 (e.g., 59 = *neunundfünfzig* = nine-and-fifty).

COUNTING

Money

Where is a cash machine?	*Wo ist der Bankomat?*	voh ist dehr **bahnk**-oh-maht
My ATM card	*Meine Kontokarte*	**mī**-neh **kohn**-toh-kar-teh
has been...	*wurde...*	**voor**-deh
...demagnetized.	*...entmagnetisiert.*	ehnt-mahg-neh-teh-**zeert**
...stolen.	*...gestohlen.*	geh-**shtoh**-lehn
...eaten by the machine.	*...von der Maschine geschluckt.*	fohn dehr mahs-**shee**-neh geh-**shlookt**
Do you accept credit cards?	*Akzeptieren Sie Kreditkarten?*	ahk-tsehp-**teer**-ehn zee kreh-**deet**-kar-tehn
Can you change dollars?	*Können Sie Dollar wechseln?*	**kurn**-nehn zee **dohl**-lar **vehkh**-sehln
What is your exchange rate for dollars...?	*Was ist ihr Wechselkurs für Dollars...?*	vahs ist eer **vehkh**-sehl-koors fewr **dohl**-lars
...in traveler's checks	*...in Reiseschecks*	in **rī**-zeh-shehks
What is the commission?	*Wie viel ist die Kommission?*	vee feel ist dee koh-mis-see-**ohn**

COUNTING

Any extra fee?	*Extra Gebühren?*	**ehx**-trah geh-**bew**-rehn
Can you break this? (big bills into smaller bills)	*Können Sie dies wechseln?*	**kurn**-nehn zee deez **vehkh**-sehln
I would like...	*Ich hätte gern...*	ikh **heht**-teh gehrn
...small bills.	*...kleine Banknoten.*	**klī**-neh **bahnk**-noh-tehn
...large bills.	*...große Banknoten.*	**groh**-seh **bahnk**-noh-tehn
...coins.	*...Münzen.*	**mewn**-tsehn
€50	*fünfzig Euro*	**fewnf**-tsig **oy**-roh
Is this a mistake?	*Ist das ein Fehler?*	ist dahs īn **fay**-ler
This is incorrect.	*Das stimmt nicht.*	dahs shtimt nikht
Did you print these today?	*Haben Sie die heute gedruckt?*	**hah**-ben zee dee **hoy**-teh geh-**drookt**
I'm broke / poor / rich.	*Ich bin pleite / arm / reich.*	ikh bin **plī**-teh / arm / **rī**kh
I'm Bill Gates.	*Ich bin Bill Gates.*	ikh bin "Bill Gates"
Where is the nearest casino?	*Wo ist das nächste Kasino?*	voh ist dahs **nehkh**-steh kah-**see**-noh

Germany and Austria use the euro currency. Euros (€) are divided into 100 cents. Switzerland has held fast to its francs (Fr), which are divided into 100 centimes (c) or rappen (Rp). Use your common cents—cents and centimes are like pennies, and the euro and franc currency each have coins like nickels, dimes, and half-dollars.

KEY PHRASES: MONEY

euro (€)	*Euro*	**oy**-roh
money	*Geld*	gehlt
cash	*Bargeld*	**bar**-gehlt
credit card	*Kreditkarte*	kreh-**deet**-kar-teh
bank	*Bank*	bahnk
cash machine	*Bankomat*	**bahnk**-oh-maht
Where is a cash machine?	*Wo ist ein Bankomat?*	voh ist īn **bahnk**-oh-maht
Do you accept credit cards?	*Akzeptieren Sie Kreditkarten?*	ahk-tsehp-**teer**-ehn zee kreh-**deet**-kar-tehn

Money Words

euro (€)	Euro	**oy**-roh
cents	Cent	sehnt
money	Geld	gehlt
cash	Bargeld	**bar**-gehlt
cash machine	Bankomat	**bahnk**-oh-maht
bank	Bank	bahnk
credit card	Kreditkarte	kreh-**deet**-kar-teh
change money	Geld wechseln	gehlt **vehkh**-sehln
exchange	Wechsel	**vehkh**-sehl
buy / sell	kaufen / verkaufen	**kow**-fehn / fehr-**kow**-fehn
commission	Kommission	koh-mis-see-**ohn**
traveler's check	Reisescheck	**rī**-zeh-shehk
cash advance	Vorschuß in Bargeld	**for**-shoos in **bar**-gehlt
cashier	Kassierer	kahs-**seer**-er
bills	Banknoten	**bahnk**-noh-tehn
coins	Münzen	**mewn**-tsehn
receipt	Beleg	beh-**lehg**

Every cash mashine (*Bankomat*) is multilingual, but if you want to be adventuresome, *Bestätigung* means confirm, *Korrektur* means change or correct, and *Abbruch* is cancel. Your PIN number is a *Geheimnummer*.

Time

What time is it?	*Wie spät ist es?*	vee shpayt ist ehs
It's...	*Es ist...*	ehs ist
...8:00 in the morning.	*...acht Uhr morgens.*	ahkht oor **mor**-gehns
...16:00.	*...sechzehn Uhr.*	**zehkh**-tsayn oor
...4:00 in the afternoon.	*...vier Uhr nachmittags.*	feer oor **nahkh**-mit-tahgs
...10:30 in the evening. (literally half-eleven)	*...halb elf Uhr abends.*	hahlp ehlf oor **ah**-behnts

...a quarter past nine.	...Viertel nach neun.	**feer**-tehl nahkh noyn
...a quarter to eleven.	...Viertel vor elf.	**feer**-tehl for ehlf
...noon.	...Mittag.	**mit**-tahg
...midnight.	...Mitternacht	**mit**-ter-nahkht
...early / late.	...früh / spät.	frew / shpayt
...on time.	...pünktlich.	**pewnkt**-likh
...sunrise.	...Sonnenaufgang.	zoh-nehn-**owf**-gahng
...sunset.	...Sonnenuntergang.	zoh-nehn-**oon**-ter-gahng
It's my bedtime.	Es ist meine Zeit fürs Bett.	ehs ist **mī**-neh tsīt fewrs beht

Timely Expressions

I will / We will....	Ich bin / Wir sind...	ikh bin / veer zint
...be back at 11:20.	...um elf Uhr zwanzig zurück.	oom ehlf oor **tsvahn**-tsig tsoo-**rewk**
I will / We will...	Ich bin / Wir sind...	ikh bin / veer zint
...be there by 18:00.	...um achtzehn Uhr dort.	oom **ahkht**-tsayn oor dort
When is check-out time?	Wann muß ich das Zimmer verlassen?	vahn mus ikh dahs **tsim**-mer fehr-**lah**-sehn
When does this open / close?	Wann ist hier geöffnet / geschossen	vahn ist heer geh-**urf**-neht / geh-**shloh**-sehn

---

KEY PHRASES: TIME

minute	Minute	mee-**noo**-teh
hour	Stunde	**shtoon**-deh
day	Tag	tahg
week	Woche	**vohkh**-eh
What time is it?	Wie spät ist es?	vee shpayt ist ehs
It's...	Es ist...	ehs ist
...8:00.	...acht Uhr.	ahkht oor
...16:00.	...sechzehn Uhr.	**zehkh**-tsayn oor
When does this open / close?	Wann ist hier geöffnet / geschossen?	vahn ist heer geh-**urf**-neht / geh-**shloh**-sehn

COUNTING

When...?	Wann...?	vahn
...does this train / bus leave for ___	...geht der Zug / Bus nach ___	gayt dehr tsoog / boos nahkh ___
...does the next train / bus leave for ___	...geht der nächste Zug / Bus nach ___	gayt dehr **nehkh**-steh tsoog / boos nahkh ___
...doesthe train / bus arrive in ___	...kommt der Zug / Bus in ___ an	kohmt dehr tsoog / boos in ___ ahn
I want / We want...	Ich möchte / Wir möchten...	ikh **merkh**-teh / veer **merkh**-tehn
...to take the 16:30 train.	...den Zug um sechzehn Uhr dreißig nehmen.	dehn tsoog oom **zehkh**-tsayn oor **drī**-sig **nay**-mehn
Is the train / bus...?	Ist der Zug / Bus...?	ist dehr tsoog / boos
...early / late	...früh / spät	frew / shpayt
...on time	...pünktlich	**pewnkt**-likh

In Germany, Austria, and Switzerland, the 24-hour clock (or military time) is used by hotels, for the opening and closing hours of museums, and for train, bus, and boat schedules. Informally, Europeans use the same 12-hour clock we use.

About Time

minute	Minute	mee-**noo**-teh
hour	Stunde	**shtoon**-deh
in the morning	am Morgen	ahm **mor**-gehn
in the afternoon	am Nachmittag	ahm **nahkh**-mit-tahg
in the evening	am Abend	ahm **ah**-behnt
night	Nacht	nahkht
at 6:00 sharp	Punkt sechs Uhr	poonkt zehx oor
from 8:00 to 10:00	von acht bis zehn	fohn ahkht bis tsayn
in half an hour	in einer halben Stunde	in **ī**-ner **hahl**-behn **shtoon**-deh
in one hour	in einer Stunde	in **ī**-ner **shtoon**-deh
in three hours	in drei Stunden	in drī **shtoon**-dehn

anytime	jederzeit	yay-der-**tsīt**
immediately	jetzt	yehtst
every hour	jede Stunde	**yay**-deh **shtoon**-deh
every day	jeden Tag	**yay**-dehn tahg
last	letzte	**lehts**-teh
this	diese	**dee**-zeh
next	nächste	**nehkh**-steh
May 15	fünfzehnten Mai	**fewnf**-tsayn-tehn mī
high season	Hochsaison	**hohkh**-zay-zohn
low season	Nebensaison	**neh**-behn-zay-zohn
in the future	in Zukunft	in **tsoo**-koonft
in the past	in der Vergangenheit	in dehr fehr-**gahng**-ehn-hīt

The Day

day	Tag	tahg
today	heute	**hoy**-teh
yesterday	gestern	**geh**-stern
tomorrow	morgen	**mor**-gehn
tomorrow morning	morgen früh	**mor**-gehn frew
day after tomorrow	übermorgen	**ew**-ber-mor-gehn

The Week

week	Woche	**vohkh**-eh
last / this / next week	letzte / diese / nächste Woche	**lehts**-teh / **dee**-zeh / **nehkh**-steh **vohkh**-eh
Monday	Montag	**mohn**-tahg
Tuesday	Dienstag	**deen**-stahg
Wednesday	Mittwoch	**mit**-vohkh
Thursday	Donnerstag	**dohn**-ner-stahg
Friday	Freitag	**frī**-tahg
Saturday	Samstag, Sonnabend	**zahm**-stahg, **zohn**-ah-behnt
Sunday	Sonntag	**zohn**-tahg

The Month

month	Monat	**moh**-naht
January	Januar	**yah**-noo-ar
February	Februar	**fay**-broo-ar
March	März	mehrts
April	April	ah-**pril**
May	Mai	m ī
June	Juni	**yoo**-nee
July	Juli	**yoo**-lee
August	August	ow-**goost**
September	September	zehp-**tehm**-ber
October	Oktober	ohk-**toh**-ber
November	November	noh-**vehm**-ber
December	Dezember	day-**tsehm**-ber

For dates, take any number, add the sound "-ten" to the end, then say the month. June19 is *neunzehnten Juni*.

The Year

year	Jahr	yar
spring	Frühling	**frew**-ling
summer	Sommer	**zohm**-mer
fall	Herbst	hehrpst
winter	Winter	**vin**-ter

Holidays and Happy Days

holiday	Feiertag	**fī**-er-tahg
national holiday	staatlicher Feiertag	**shtaht**-likh-er **fī**-er-tahg
school holiday	Schulferien	**shool**-fer-een
religious holiday	religiöser	reh-lig-ee-**ur**-zer
	Feiertag	**fī**-er-tahg
Is today /	Ist heute /	ist **hoy**-teh /
tomorrow a	morgen ein	**mor**-gehn ī n
holiday?	Feiertag?	**fī**-er-tahg

Is a holiday coming up soon?	Ist bald ein Feiertag?	ist bahlt īn **fī**-er-tahg
When?	Wann?	vahn
What is the holiday?	Welcher Feiertag ist das?	**vehlkh**-er **fī**-er-tahg ist dahs
Merry Christmas!	Fröhliche Weihnachten!	**frur**-likh-eh **vī**-nahkh-tehn
Happy New Year!	Glückliches Neues Jahr!	**glewk**-likh-ehs **noy**-ehs yar
Easter	Ostern	**ohs**-tern
Happy anniversary!	Herzlichen Glückwunsch!	**hehrts**-likh-ehn **glewk**-voonsh
Happy birthday!	Herzlichen Glückwunsch zum Geburtstag!	**hehrts**-likh-ehn **glewk**-voonsh tsoom geh-**boorts**-tahg

Germans sing "Happy Birthday" to the tune we use, sometimes even in English. The German version means "On your birthday, best wishes": *Zum Geburtstag, viel Glück, Zum Geburtstag, viel Glück, Zum Geburtstag, liebe ___, Zum Geburtstag, viel Glück.*

Other German celebrations include *Karneval* (or *Fasching*), a week-long festival of parades and partying. It happens before Lent in February, and the centers of revelry are Köln (Germany), Mainz (Germany), and Basel (Switzerland). *Christi Himmelfahrt,* or the Ascension of Christ, comes in May, and doubles for Father's Day. You'll see men in groups on pilgrimages through the countryside, usually carrying beer or heading toward it.

Germany's national holiday is Oct. 3, Austria's is Oct. 26, and Switzerland's is Aug. 1.

TRAVELING

The German word for journey or trip is *Fahrt.* Many tourists enjoy collecting *Fahrts.* In Germany, you'll see signs for *Einfahrt* (entrance), *Rundfahrt* (round trip), *Rückfahrt* (return trip), *Panoramafahrt* (scenic journey), *Zugfahrt* (train trip), *Ausfahrt* (trip out), and throughout your trip, people will smile and wish you a *"Gute Fahrt."*

Flights

All airports have bilingual signage with the local language and always English. Also, nearly all airport service personnel and travel agents speak English these days. Still, these words and phrases could conceivably come in handy.

Making a Reservation

I'd like to... my reservation / ticket.	*Ich möchte meine Reservierung / Flugschein...*	ikh **murkh**-teh **mī**-neh reh-zer-**feer**-oong / **floog**-shīn
We'd like to... our reservation / ticket.	*Wir möchten unsere Reservierung / Flugschein...*	veer **murkh**-tehn **oon**-zer-eh reh-zer-**feer**-oong / **floog**-shīn

25

...confirm	...bestätigen.	beh-**shtay**-teh-gehn
...reconfirm	...nochmals bestätigen.	**nohkh**-mahls beh-**shtay**-teh-gehn
...change	...ändern.	**ehn**-dern
...cancel	...annulieren.	ah-nool-**eer**-ehn
aisle seat / window seat	Sitz am Gang / Sitz am Fenster	zits ahm gahng / zits ahm **fehn**-ster

At the Airport

Which terminal?	Welches Terminal?	**vehlkh**-ehs ter-mee-**nahl**
international flights	internationale Flüge	in-ter-naht-see-oh-**nah**-leh **flew**-geh
domestic flights	inländische Flüge	**in**-lehnd-ish-eh **flew**-geh
arrival	Ankunft	**ahn**-koonft
departure	Abflug	**ahp**-floog
baggage check	Gepäckaufgabe	geh-**pehk**-owf-gah-beh
baggage claim	Gepäckausgabe	geh-**pehk**-ows-gah-beh
Nothing to declare	Nichts zu deklarieren	nihkts tsoo dehk-lah-**reer**-ehn
I have only carry-on luggage.	Ich habe nur Handgepäck.	ikh **hah**-beh noor **hahnd**-geh-pehk
flight number	Flugnummer	**floog**-noo-mer
departure gate	Abflugtor	**ahp**-floog-tor
duty free	zollfrei	**tsohl**-frī
luggage cart	Gepäckwägelchen	geh-**pehk**-vehg-ehl-khehn
jet lag	Jetlag	"jet lag"

Getting to/from the Airport

Approximately how much is a taxi ride...?	Wie viel ungefähr ist die Taxifahrt...?	vee feel **oon**-geh-fehr ist dee **tahk**-see-fart
...to downtown	...zur Stadtmitte	tsoor **shtaht**-mit-teh
...to the train station	...zum Bahnhof	tsoom **bahn**-hohf
...to the airport	...zum Flughafen	tsoom **floog**-hah-fehn

Does a bus (or train) run...?	Fährt ein Bus (oder Zug)...?	fayrt īn boos (**oh**-der tsoog)
...from the airport to downtown	...vom Flughafen zur Stadtmitte	fohm **floog**-hah-fehn tsoor **shtaht**-mit-teh
...to the airport from downtown	...zum Flughafen von der Stadtmitte	tsoom **floog**-hah-fehn fohn dehr **shtaht**-mit-teh
How much is it?	Wie viel kostet das?	vee feel **kohs**-teht dahs
Where does it leave from...?	Von wo fährt er ab...?	fohn voh fayrt ehr ahp
Where does it arrive at...?	Wo kommt er an...?	voh kohmt ehr ahn
...at the airport	...am Flughafen	ahm **floog**-hah-fehn
...downtown	...in der Stadtmitte	in dehr **shtaht**-mit-teh
How often does it run?	Wie oft fährt er?	vee ohft fayrt ehr

Trains

The Train Station

Where is the...?	Wo ist der...?	voh ist dehr
...(central) train station	...(Haupt-)Bahnhof	(**howpt**-)**bahn**-hohf
German Railways	Deutsche Bahn (DB)	**doy**-cheh bahn (day bay)
Swiss Railways	Schweizer Bundesbahn (SBB)	**shvīt**-ser **boon**-dehs-bahn (ehs bay bay)
Austrian Railways	Österreichische Bundesbahn (ÖBB)	**urs**-ter-**rīkh**-is-sheh **boon**-dehs-bahn (ur bay bay)
train information	Zugauskunft	tsoog-**ows**-koonft
train	Zug	tsoog
high-speed train	Intercity, Schnellzug	"inter-city," **shnehl**-tsoog
highest-speed train	ICE	ee tsay ay
fast / faster	schnell / schneller	shnehl / **shnehl**-ler
arrival	Ankunft	**ahn**-koonft

departure	*Abfahrt*	**ahp**-fart
delay	*Verspätung*	fehr-**shpay**-toong
toilet	*Toilette*	toh-**leh**-teh
waiting room	*Wartesaal*	**var**-teh-zahl
lockers	*Schließfächer*	**shlees**-fehkh-er
baggage check room	*Gepäckaufgabe*	geh-**pehk**-owf-gah-beh
lost and found office	*Fundbüro*	**foond**-bew-roh
tourist information	*Touristen-information*	too-**ris**-tehn-in-for-maht-see-**ohn**
platform	*Bahnsteig*	**bahn**-shtīg
to the trains	*zu den Zugen*	tsoo dayn **tsoo**-gehn
track	*Gleis*	glīs
train car	*Wagen*	**vah**-gehn
dining car	*Speisewagen*	**shpī**-zeh-vah-gehn
sleeper car	*Liegewagen*	**lee**-geh-vah-gehn
conductor	*Schaffner*	**shahf**-ner

You'll encounter several types of trains in Germany. Along with the various local and milk-run trains, there are the:
• slow *RB* (*RegionalBahn*) and *RE* (*RegionalExpress*) trains,
• the medium-speed *IR* (*InterRegio*) trains,
• the fast *IC* (*InterCity*, domestic routes) and *EC* (*EuroCity*, international routes) trains, and
• the super-fast *ICE* trains (*InterCityExpress*).
Railpasses cover travel on all of these trains, except for the rare *Metropolitan* train between Köln and Hamburg.

KEY PHRASES: TRAINS		
(central) train station	*(Haupt-) Bahnhof*	**(howpt-) bahn**-hohf
train	*Zug*	tsoog
ticket	*Fahrkarte*	**far**-kar-teh
transfer (verb)	*umsteigen*	**oom**-shtī-gehn
supplement	*Zuschlag*	**tsoo**-shlahg
arrival	*Ankunft*	**ahn**-koonft
departure	*Abfahrt*	**ahp**-fart
platform	*Bahnsteig*	**bahn**-shtīg
track	*Gleis*	glīs
train car	*Wagen*	**vah**-gehn
A ticket to ___.	*Eine Fahrkarte nach ___.*	**ī**-neh **far**-kar-teh nahkh ___
Two tickets to ___.	*Zwei Fahrkarten nach ___.*	tsvī **far**-kar-tehn nahkh ___
When is the next train?	*Wann ist der nächste Zug?*	vahn ist dehr **nehkh**-steh tsoog
Where does the train leave from?	*Von wo fährt der Zug ab?*	fohn voh fayrt dehr tsoog ahp
Which train to ___?	*Welcher Zug nach ___?*	**vehlkh**-er tsoog nahkh ___

Getting a Ticket

Where can I buy a ticket?	*Wo kann ich eine Fahrkarte kaufen?*	voh kahn ikh **ī**-neh **far**-kar-teh **kow**-fehn
A ticket to ___.	*Eine Fahrkarte nach ___.*	**ī**-neh **far**-kar-teh nahkh ___
Where can we buy tickets?	*Wo können wir Fahrkarten kaufen?*	voh **kurn**-nehn veer **far**-kar-tehn **kow**-fehn
Two tickets to ___.	*Zwei Fahrkarten nach ___.*	tsvī **far**-kar-tehn nahkh ___
Is this the line for...?	*Ist das die Schlange für...?*	ist dahs dee **shlahng**-eh fewr
...tickets	*...Fahrkarten*	**far**-kar-tehn
...reservations	*...Reservierungen*	reh-zer-**feer**-oong-ehn

How much is a ticket to ___?	Wie viel kostet eine Fahrkarte nach ___?	vee feel **kohs**-teht **ī**-neh **far**-kar-teh nahkh ___
Is this ticket valid for ___?	Ist diese Fahrkarte gültig für ___?	ist **dee**-zeh **far**-kar-teh **gewl**-tig fewr
How long is this ticket valid?	Wie lange ist diese Fahrkarte gültig?	vee **lahng**-eh ist **dee**-zeh **far**-kar-teh **gewl**-tig
When is the next train?	Wann ist der nächste Zug?	vahn ist dehr **nehkh**-steh tsoog
Do you have a schedule for all trains departing today / tomorrow for ___?	Haben Sie einen Fahrplan für alle Züge heute / morgen nach ___?	**hah**-behn zee **ī**-nehn **far**-plahn fewr **ahl**-leh **tsew**-geh **hoy**-teh / **mor**-gehn nahkh
I'd like to leave...	Ich möchte... abfahren.	ikh **murkh**-teh... **ahp**-fah-rehn
We'd like to leave...	Wir möchten... abfahren.	veer **murkh**-tehn... **ahp**-fah-rehn
I'd like to arrive...	Ich möchte... ankommen.	ikh **murkh**-teh... **ahn**-koh-mehn
We'd like to arrive...	Wir möchten... ankommen.	veer **murkh**-tehn... **ahn**-koh-mehn
...by ___	... vor ___	for
...in the morning.	...am Morgen	ahm **mor**-gehn
...in the afternoon.	...am Nachmittag	ahm **nahkh**-mit-tahg
...in the evening.	...am Abend	ahm **ah**-behnt
Is there a...?	Gibt es einen...?	gipt ehs **ī**-nehn
...later train	...späterer Zug	**shpay**-ter-er tsoog
...earlier train	...früherer Zug	**frew**-her-er tsoog
...overnight train	...Nachtzug	**nahkht**-tsoog
...cheaper train	...billigere Zug	**bil**-lig-er-eh tsoog
...cheaper option	...billigere Möglichkeit	**bil**-lig-er-eh **murg**-likh-kī t
...local train	...Regionalzug	reh-gee-oh-**nahl**-tsoog
...express train	...Schnellzug	**shnehl**-tsoog

What track does the train leave from?	*Von welches Gleis fährt er ab?*	fohn **vehlkh**-ehs glī s fayrt ehr ahp
On time?	*Pünktlich?*	**pewnkt**-likh
Late?	*Spät?*	shpayt

Reservations, Supplements, and Discounts

Is a reservation required?	*Brauche ich eine Platzkarte?*	**browkh**-eh ikh **ī**-neh **plahts**-kar-teh
I'd like to reserve...	*Ich möchte... reservieren.*	ikh **murkh**-teh... reh-zer-**vee**-rehn
...a seat.	*...einen Sitzplatz*	**ī**-nehn **zits**-plahts
...a berth.	*...einen Liegewagenplatz*	**ī**-nehn **lee**-geh-vah-gehn-plahts
...a sleeper.	*...einen Schlafwagenplatz*	**ī**-nehn **shlahf**-vah-gehn-plahts
...the entire train.	*...den ganzen Zug*	dayn **gahn**-tsehn tsoog
We'd like to reserve...	*Wir möchten... reservieren.*	veer **murkh**-tehn... reh-zer-**vee**-rehn
...two seats.	*...zwei Sitzplätze*	tsvī **zits**-pleht-seh
...two couchettes.	*...zwei Liegewagenplätze*	tsvī **lee**-geh-vah-gehn-pleht-seh
...two sleepers.	*...zwei Schlafwagenplätze*	tsvī **shlahf**-vah-gehn-pleht-seh
Is there a supplement?	*Kostet das einen Zuschlag?*	**kohs**-teht dahs **ī**-nehn **tsoo**-shlahg
Does my railpass cover the supplement?	*Ist der Zuschlag in meinem Railpass enthalten?*	ist dehr **tsoo**-shlahg in m **ī**-nehm **rayl**-pahs ehnt-**hahl**-tehn
Is there a discount for...?	*Gibt es Ermäßigung für...?*	gipt ehs ehr-**may**-see-goong fewr
...youths	*...Jugendliche*	yoo-gehnd-**likh**-eh
...seniors	*...Senioren*	zehn-**yor**-ehn
...families	*...Familien*	fah-**mee**-lee-ehn

Ticket Talk

ticket window	Fahrscheine	far-**shī**-neh
reservations window	Reservierungen	reh-zer-**feer**-oong-ehn
national / international	Inland / Ausland	**in**-lahnt / **ows**-lahnt
ticket	Fahrkarte	**far**-kar-teh
one-way ticket	Hinfahrkarte	**hin**-far-kar-teh
roundtrip ticket	Rückfahrkarte	**rewk**-far-kar-teh
first class	erste Klasse	**ehr**-steh **klah**-seh
second class	zweite Klasse	**tsvī**-teh **klah**-seh
non-smoking	Nichtraucher	**nikht**-rowkh-er
validate	abstempeln	**ahp**-shtehm-pehln
schedule	Fahrplan	**far**-plahn
departure	Abfahrtszeit	**ahp**-farts-tsīt
direct	Direkt	dee-**rehkt**
transfer (verb)	umsteigen	**oom**-shtī-gehn
connection	Anschluß	**ahn**-shlus
with supplement	mit Zuschlag	mit **tsoo**-shlahg
reservation	Platzkarte	**plahts**-kar-teh
seat	Platz	plahts
window seat	Fensterplatz	**fehn**-ster-plahts
aisle seat	Platz am Gang	plahts ahm gahng
berth...	Liege...	**lee**-geh
...upper	...obere	**oh**-ber-eh
...middle	...mittlere	**mit**-leh-reh
...lower	...untere	**oon**-ter-eh
refund	Rückvergütung	**rewk**-fehr-gew-toong
reduced fare	verbilligte Karte	fehr-**bil**-lig-teh **kar**-teh

Changing Trains

Is it direct?	Direktverbindung?	dee-**rehkt**-fehr-bin doong
Must I transfer?	Muß ich umsteigen?	mus ikh **oom**-shtī-gehn
Must we transfer?	Müssen wir umsteigen?	**mew**-sehn veer **oom**-shtī-gehn

When? / Where?	*Wann? / Wo?*	vahn / voh
Do I / Do we change here for ___?	*Muß ich / Müssen wir hier umsteigen nach ___?*	mus ikh / **mew**-sehn veer heer **oom**-shtī-gehn nahkh
Where do I / do we change for ___?	*Wo muß ich / müssen wir umsteigen für ___?*	voh mus ikh / **mew**-sehn veer **oom**-shtī-gehn fewr
At what time?	*Um wie viel Uhr?*	oom vee feel oor
From what track does my / our connecting train leave ?	*Auf welchem Gleis fährt mein / unser Verbindungszug?*	owf **wehlkh**-ehm glīs fayrt mīn / **oon**-ser fehr-**bin**-doongs-tsoog
How many minutes in ___ to change trains?	*Wie viele Minuten zum Umsteigen in ___?*	vee **fee**-leh mee-**noo**-tehn tsoom **oom**-shtī-gehn in

On the Platform

Where is...?	*Wo ist...?*	voh ist
Is this...?	*Ist das...?*	ist dahs
...the train to ___	*...der Zug nach ___*	dehr tsoog nahkh ___
Which train to ___?	*Welcher Zug nach ___?*	**vehlkh**-er tsoog nahkh ___
Which train car to ___?	*Welcher Wagen nach ___?*	**vehlkh**-er **vah**-gehn nahkh ___
Where is first class?	*Wo ist die erste Klasse?*	voh ist dee **ehr**-steh **klah**-seh
...front / middle / back	*...vorne / mitte / hinten*	**for**-neh / **mit**-teh / **hin**-tehn
Where can I validate my ticket?	*Wo kann ich meine Fahrkarte abstempeln?*	voh kahn ikh **mī**-neh **far**-kar-teh **ahp**-shtehm-pehln

At the platform, you'll often see a sign that says *Etwa 10 Min. später.* This means that the train is running about (*etwa*) 10 minutes later (*später*) than expected.

On the Train

Is this seat free?	*Ist dieser Platz frei?*	ist **dee**-zer plahts frī
May I / May we...?	*Darf ich /*	darf ikh /
	Dürfen wir...?	**dewr**-fehn veer
...sit here	*...hier sitzen*	heer **zit**-sehn
...open the window	*...das Fenster öffnen*	dahs **fehn**-ster **urf**-nehn
...eat your meal	*...Ihre Mahlzeit*	**eer**-eh **mahl**-tsīt
	essen	**ehs**-sehn
Save my place?	*Halten Sie meinen*	**hahl**-tehn zee **mī**-nehn
	Platz frei?	plahts frī
Save our places?	*Halten Sie unsere*	**hahl**-tehn zee **oon**-zer-eh
	Plätze frei?	**pleht**-seh frī
That's my seat.	*Das ist mein Platz.*	dahs ist mīn plahts
These are our seats.	*Das sind unsere*	dahs zint **oon**-zer-eh
	Plätze.	**pleht**-seh
Where are you going?	*Wo hin fahren Sie?*	voh hin **far**-ehn zee
I'm going to ___.	*Ich fahre nach ___.*	ikh **far**-eh nahkh
We're going to ___.	*Wir fahren nach ___.*	veer **far**-ehn nahkh
Can you tell me / us when to get off?	*Können Sie mir / uns Bescheid sagen?*	**kurn**-nehn zee meer / oons beh-**shīt** zah-gehn
Where is a (good looking) conductor?	*Wo ist ein (hübscher) Schaffner?*	voh ist īn (**hewb**-sher) **shahf**-ner
Does this train stop in ___?	*Hält dieser Zug in ___?*	hehlt **dee**-zer tsoog in
When will it arrive in ___?	*Wann kommt er in ___ an?*	vahn kohmt ehr in ___ ahn
When will it arrive?	*Wann kommt er an?*	vahn kohmt ehr ahn

As you approach a station on the train, you will hear an announcement such as: *In wenigen Minuten erreichen wir in München* (In a few minutes, we will arrive in Munich).

Reading Train and Bus Schedules

German schedules use the 24-hour clock. It's like American time until noon. After that, subtract twelve and add p.m. So 13:00 is 1 p.m., 20:00 is 8 p.m., and 24:00 is midnight. One minute after midnight is 00:01.

Abfahrt	departure
Ankunft	arrival
auch	also
außer	except
bis	until
Feiertag	holiday
Gleis	track
jeden	every
nach	to
nicht	not
nur	only
Richtung	direction
Samstag	Saturday
Sonntag	Sunday
täglich (tgl.)	daily
tagsüber	days
über	via
verspätet	late
von	from
Werktags	Monday-Saturday (workdays)
Wochentags	weekdays
Zeit	time
Ziel	destination
1-5, 6, 7	Monday-Friday, Saturday, Sunday

36

Major Rail Lines in Germany

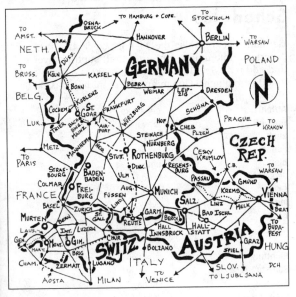

Going Places

Germany	*Deutschland*	**doych**-lahnd
Munich	*München*	**mewnkh**-ehn
Bavaria	*Bayern*	**bī**-ehrn
Black Forest	*Schwarzwald*	**shvahrts**-vahlt
Danube	*Donau*	**doh**-now
Austria	*Österreich*	**urs**-ter-rī kh
Vienna	*Wien*	veen
Switzerland	*Schweiz*	shvī tz
Belgium	*Belgien*	**behl**-gee-ehn
Czech Republic	*Tschechische Republik*	**shehkh**-i-sheh reh-poob-**leek**

TRAVELING

Prague	*Prag*	prahk
France	*Frankreich*	**frahnk**-rĩkh
Great Britain	*Großbritannien*	grohs-brit-**ahn**-ee-ehn
Greece	*Griechenland*	**greekh**-ehn-lahnd
Ireland	*Irland*	**ihr**-lahnd
Italy	*Italien*	i-**tah**-lee-ehn
Venice	*Venedig*	**veh**-neh-dig
Netherlands	*Niederlande*	**nee**-der-lahn-deh
Portugal	*Portugal*	**pohr**-too-gahl
Scandinavia	*Skandinavien*	shkahn-dee-**nah**-vee-ehn
Spain	*Spanien*	**shpahn**-ee-ehn
Turkey	*Türkei*	tewr-**kĩ**
Europe	*Europa*	oy-**roh**-pah
EU (European Union)	*EU*	ay oo
Russia	*Rußland*	**roos**-lahnd
Africa	*Afrika*	**ah**-free-kah
United States	*U.S.A.* (*Vereinigten Staaten*)	oo ehs ah (fehr-**ĩ**nig-tehn **shtah**-tehn)
Canada	*Kanada*	**kah**-nah-dah
world	*Welt*	vehlt

If you're using the *Rick Steves' Germany & Austria* or *Rick Steves' Switzerland* guidebooks, here are a few more place names:

Bacharach (Ger.)	**bahkh**-ah-rahkh
Jungfrau (Switz.)	**yoong**-frow
Kleine Scheidegg (Switz.)	**klĩ**-neh **shĩ**-dehg
Köln (Ger.)	kurln
Mosel (Ger.)	**moh**-zehl
Neuschwanstein (Ger.)	noysh-**vahn**-shtĩn
Reutte (Aus.)	**roy**-teh
Rothenburg (Ger.)	**roh**-tehn-boorg

Buses and Subways

At the Bus Station or Metro Stop

ticket	Fahrkarte	**far**-kar-teh
day ticket	Tageskarte	**tahg**-ehs-kar-teh
short-ride ticket	Kurzstrecke	**koorts**-streh-keh
city bus	Linienbus	**lee**-nee-ehn-boos
regional /	Regionalbus /	reh-gee-ohn-**ahl**-boos /
long-distance bus	Fernbus	**fayrn**-boos
bus stop	Bushaltestelle	**boos**-hahl-teh-**shtehl**-leh
bus station	Busbahnhof	**boos**-bahn-hohf
subway	U-Bahn	**oo**-bahn
subway station	U-Bahn-Station	**oo**-bahn-stah-tsee-ohn
subway map	U-Bahn-Streckenplan	**oo**-bahn-**shtrehk**-ehn-plahn

TRAVELING

KEY PHRASES: BUSES AND SUBWAYS

bus	Bus	boos
subway	U-Bahn	**oo**-bahn
ticket	Fahrkarte	**far**-kar-teh
How do I get to ___?	Wie komme ich zu ___?	vee **koh**-meh ikh tsoo
How do we get to ___?	Wie kommen wir zu ___?	vee **koh**-mehn veer tsoo
Which stop for ___?	Welche Haltestelle für ___?	**vehlkh**-eh **hahl**-teh-shtehl-leh fewr
Can you tell me / us when to get off?	Können Sie mir / uns Bescheid sagen?	**kurn**-nehn zee meer / oons beh-**shīt** zah-gehn

subway entrance	*U-Bahn-Eingang*	**oo**-bahn-**n̄**-gahng
subway stop	*U-Bahn-Haltestelle*	**oo**-bahn-**hahl**-teh-shtehl-leh
subway exit	*U-Bahn-Ausgang*	**oo**-bahn-**ows**-gahng
direct	*Direkt*	dee-**rehkt**
direction	*Richtung*	**rikh**-toong
connection	*Anschluß*	**ahn**-shlus
pickpocket	*Taschendieb*	**tahsh**-ehn-deep

Most big cities offer deals on transportation, such as one-day tickets, cheaper fares for youths and seniors, or a discount for buying a batch of tickets (which you can share with friends). If you're taking a short trip (usually 4 stops or fewer), buy a discounted *Kurzstrecke* ("short stretch" ticket). Major cities in Germany, such as Munich and Berlin, have a *U-Bahn* (subway) and an *S-Bahn* (urban rail system). If your Eurailpass is active on the day you're traveling, it covers the *S-Bahn* for free. On a map, *Standort* means "You are here."

Taking Buses and Subways

How do I get to ___?	*Wie komme ich zu ___?*	vee **koh**-meh ikh tsoo
How do we get to ___?	*Wie kommen wir zu ___?*	vee **koh**-mehn veer tsoo
How much is a ticket?	*Wie viel kostet eine Fahrkarte?*	vee feel **kohs**-teht īneh **far**-kar-teh
Where can I buy a ticket?	*Wo kaufe ich eine Fahrkarte?*	voh **kow**-feh ikh īneh **far**-kar-teh
Where can we buy tickets?	*Wo kaufen wir Fahrkarten?*	voh **kow**-fehn veer **far**-kar-tehn
One ticket, please.	*Eine Fahrkarte, bitte.*	īneh **far**-kar-teh, **bit**-teh
Two tickets.	*Zwei Fahrkarten.*	tsvī **far**-kar-teh
Is this ticket valid (for ___)?	*Ist diese Fahrkarte gültig (für ___)?*	ist **dee**-zeh **far**-kar-teh (**gewl**-tig fewr ___)

Is there a...?	Gibt es eine...?	gipt ehs Ī-neh
...one-day pass	...Tageskarte	**tahg**-ehs-kar-teh
...discount if I buy more tickets	...Preisnachlaß, wenn ich mehrere Fahrkarten kaufe	prīs-**nahkh**-lahs vehn ikh **meh**-reh-reh **far**-kar-tehn **kow**-feh
Which bus to ___?	Welcher Bus nach ___?	**vehlkh**-er boos nahkh
Does it stop at ___?	Hält er in ___?	hehlt ehr in
Which bus stop for ___?	Welche Haltestelle für ___?	**vehlkh**-eh **hahl**-teh-shtehl-leh fewr
Which metro stop for ___?	Welcher Halt für ___?	**vehlkh**-er hahlt fewr
Which direction for ___?	Welche Richtung nach ___?	**vehlkh**-eh **rikh**-toong nahkh
Must I transfer?	Muß ich umsteigen?	mus ikh **oom**-shtī-gehn
Must we transfer?	Müssen wir umsteigen?	**mew**-sehn veer **oom**-shtī-gehn
When is the...?	Wann fährt der... ab?	vahn fayrt dehr... ahp
...first / next / last	...erste / nächste / letzte	**ehr**-steh / **nehkh**-steh / **lehts**-teh
...bus / subway	...Bus / U-Bahn	boos / **oo**-bahn
What's the frequency per hour / day?	Wie oft pro Stunde / Tag?	vee ohft pro **shtoon**-deh / tahg
Where does it leave from?	Von wo fährt er ab?	fohn voh fayrt ehr ahp
What time does it leave?	Um wie viel Uhr fährt er ab?	oom vee feel oor fayrt ehr ahp
I'm going to ___.	Ich fahre nach ___.	ikh **far**-eh nahkh
We're going to ___.	Wir fahren nach ___.	veer **far**-ehn nahkh
Can you tell me / us when to get off?	Können Sie mir / uns Bescheid sagen?	**kurn**-nehn zee meer / oons beh-**shīt** zah-gehn

Taxis

Getting a Taxi

Taxi!	Taxi!	**tahk**-see
Can you call a taxi?	Können Sie mir ein Taxi rufen?	**kurn**-nehn zee meer īn **tahk**-see **roo**-fehn
Where can I get a taxi?	Wo finde ich ein Taxi?	voh fin-deh ikh īn **tahk**-see
Where can we get a taxi?	Wo finden wir ein Taxi?	voh fin-dehn veer īn **tahk**-see
Where is a taxi stand?	Wo ist ein Taxistand?	voh ist īn **tahk**-see-shtahnt
Are you free?	Sind Sie frei?	zint zee frī
Occupied.	Besetzt.	beh-**zehtst**
To ___, please.	Zu ___, bitte.	tsoo ___ **bit**-teh
To this address.	Zu dieser Adresse.	tsoo **dee**-zer ah-**dreh**-seh
Take me / us to ___.	Bringen Sie mich / uns zu ___.	**bring**-ehn zee mikh / oons tsoo
Approximately how much will it cost for a trip...?	Wie viel ungefähr kostet die Fahrt...?	vee feel **oon**-geh-fehr **kohs**-teht dee fart
...to ___	...zu ___	tsoo
...to the airport	...zum Flughafen	tsoom **floog**-hah-fehn
...to the train station	...zum Bahnhof	tsoom **bahn**-hohf
...to this address	...zu dieser Adresse	tsoo **dee**-zer ah-**dreh**-seh
No extra supplement?	Keine Zuschläge?	**kī**-neh **tsoo**-shleh-geh

TRAVELING

KEY PHRASES: TAXIS		
Taxi!	Taxi!	**tahk**-see
Are you free?	Sind Sie frei?	zint zee frī
To ___, please.	Zu ___, bitte.	tsoo ___ **bit**-teh
meter	Zähler	**tsay**-ler
Stop here.	Halten Sie hier.	**hahl**-tehn zee heer
Keep the change.	Stimmt so.	shtimt zoh

Too much.	Zu viel.	tsoo feel
Can you take ___ people?	Können Sie ___ Personen mitnehmen?	**kurn**-nehn zee ___ pehr-**zoh**-nehn **mit**-nay-mehn
Any extra fee?	Extra Gebühren?	**ex**-trah geh-**bew**-rehn
Do you have an hourly rate?	Haben Sie einen Stundenansatz?	**hah**-behn zee **ī**-nehn **shtoon**-dehn-ahn-zahts
How much for a one-hour city tour?	Wie viel für eine Stunde Stadtbesichtigung?	vee feel fewr **ī**-neh **shtoon**-deh **shtaht**-beh-**sikh**-ti-goong

Ride in style in a German taxi—usually a BMW or Mercedes. If you're having a tough time hailing a taxi, ask for the nearest taxi stand (*Taxistand*). The simplest way to tell a cabbie where you want to go is by stating your destination followed by "please" ("*Hofbräuhaus, bitte*"). Tipping isn't expected, but it's polite to round up. So if the fare is €19, round up to €20.

In the Taxi

The meter, please.	Den Zähler, bitte.	dayn **tsay**-ler **bit**-teh
Where is the meter?	Wo ist der Zähler?	voh ist dehr **tsay**-ler
I'm in a hurry.	Ich bin in Eile.	ikh bin in **ī**-leh
We're in a hurry.	Wir sind in Eile.	veer zint in **ī**-leh
Slow down.	Fahren Sie langsamer.	**fahr**-ehn zee **lahng**-zah-mer
If you don't slow down, I'll throw up.	Wenn Sie nicht langsamer fahren, muß ich kotzen.	vehn zee nikht **lahng**-zah-mer **far**-ehn mus ikh **koht**-sehn
Left / Right / Straight.	Links / Rechts / Geradeaus.	links / **rehkhts** / geh-rah-deh-**ows**
I'd like / We'd like to stop here briefly.	Ich möchte / Wir möchten hier kurz anhalten.	ikh **murkh**-teh / veer **murkh**-tehn heer koorts **ahn**-hahl-tehn
Please stop here for ___ minutes.	Bitte halten Sie hier für ___ Minuten.	**bit**-teh **hahl**-tehn zee heer fewr ___ mee-**noo**-tehn

Can you wait?	Können Sie warten?	**kurn**-nehn zee **var**-tehn
Crazy traffic, isn't it?	Verrückter Verkehr, nicht wahr?	fehr-**rewk**-ter fehr-**kehr**, nikht var
You drive like...	Sie fahren wie...	zee **far**-ehn vee
...a madman!	...ein Verrückter!	īn fehr-**rewk**-ter
...Michael Schumacher.	...Michael Schumacher.	"Michael Schumacher"
You drive very well.	Sie fahren sehr gut.	zee **far**-ehn zehr goot
Where did you learn to drive?	Wo haben Sie Auto fahren gelernt?	voh **hah**-behn zee **ow**-toh **far**-ehn geh-**lehrnt**
Stop here.	Halten Sie hier.	**hahl**-tehn zee heer
Here is fine.	Hier ist gut.	heer ist goot
At this corner.	An dieser Ecke.	ahn **dee**-zer **ehk**-eh
The next corner.	An der nächsten Ecke.	ahn dehr **nehkh**-stehn **ehk**-eh
My change, please.	Mein Wechselgeld, bitte.	mīn **vehkh**-sehl-gehlt **bit**-teh
Keep the change.	Stimmt so.	shtimt zoh
This ride is / was more fun than Disneyland.	Diese Fahrt ist / war lustiger als Disneyland.	**dee**-zer fart ist / var **loos**-ti-ger ahls "Disneyland"

Driving

Rental Wheels

car rental agency	Autovermietung	**ow**-toh-fehr-**mee**-toong
I'd like to rent a...	Ich möchte ein... mieten.	ikh **murkh**-teh īn... **mee**-tehn
We'd like to rent a...	Wir möchten ein... mieten.	veer **murkh**-tehn īn... **mee**-tehn
...car.	...Auto	**ow**-toh
...station wagon.	...Kombi	**kohm**-bee
...van.	...Kleinbus	**klīn**-boos
...motorcycle.	...Motorrad	**moh**-tor-raht
...motor scooter.	...Moped	**moh**-pehd

...tank.	...Panzer	**pahn**-tser
How much per...?	Wie viel pro...?	vee feel proh
...hour	...Stunde	**shtoon**-deh
...half day	...halben Tag	**hahl**-behn tahg
...day	...Tag	tahg
...week	...Woche	**vohkh**-eh
Unlimited mileage?	Unbegrenzte Kilometer?	oon-beh-**grents**-teh kee-loh-**may**-ter
When must I bring it back?	Wann muß ich es zurückbringen?	vahn mus ikh ehs tsoo-**rewk**-bring-ehn
Is there a...?	Gibt es eine...?	gipt ehs ī-neh
...helmet	...Helm	hehlm
...discount	...Ermäßigung	ehr-**may**-see-goong
...deposit	...Kaution	kowt-see-**ohn**
...insurance	...Versicherung	fehr-**zikh**-er-oong

At the Gas Station

TRAVELING

gas station	Tankstelle	**tahnk**-shtehl-leh
The nearest gas station?	Die nächste Tankstelle?	dee **nehkh**-steh **tahnk**-shtehl-leh
Self-service?	Selbstbedienung?	**zehlpst**-beh-dee-noong
Fill the tank.	Volltanken.	**fohl**-tahnk-ehn
Wash the windows.	Scheiben putzen.	**shī**-behn **poots**-ehn
I need...	Ich brauche...	ikh **browkh**-eh
We need...	Wir brauchen...	veer **browkh**-ehn
...gas.	...Benzin.	behn-**tseen**
...unleaded.	...Bleifrei.	**blī**-frī
...regular.	...Normal.	nor-**mahl**
...super.	...Super.	**zoo**-per
...diesel.	...Diesel.	**dee**-zehl
Check...	Sehen Sie nach...	**zay**-ehn zee nahkh
... the oil.	...dem Öl.	daym url
...the air in the tires.	...dem Luftdruck in Reifen.	daym **looft**-drook in **rī**-fehn
...the radiator.	...dem Kühler.	daym **kew**-ler
...the battery.	...der Batterie.	dehr bah-teh-**ree**
...the sparkplugs.	...den Zündkerzen.	dayn **tsewnt**-ker-tsehn

...the headlights.	...den Scheinwerfern.	dayn **shīn**-vehr-fern
...the tail lights.	...den Rücklichtern.	dayn **rewk**-likht-ern
...the directional signal.	...dem Blinker.	daym **blink**-er
...the brakes.	...den Bremsen.	dayn **brehm**-zehn
...the transmission fluid.	...dem Getriebeöl.	daym geh-**treeb**-eh-url
...the windshield wipers.	...den Scheibenwischern.	dayn **shī**-behn-vish-ern
...the fuses.	...den Sicherungen.	dayn **zikh**-eh-roong-ehn
...the fanbelt.	...dem Keilriemen.	daym **kīl**-ree-mehn
...my pulse.	...meinem Puls.	**mī**-nehm pools
...my husband / my wife.	...meinem Mann / meiner Frau.	**mī**-nehm mahn / **mī**-ner frow

Getting gas is a piece of *Strudel*. Regular is *normal* and super is *super*, and euros and liters replace dollars and gallons. If a euro is equal to a dollar and there are about four liters in a gallon, gas costing €1 a liter = $4 a gallon.

Car Trouble

accident	Unfall	**oon**-fahl
breakdown	Panne	**pah**-neh
dead battery	leere Batterie	**lehr**-eh baht-teh-**ree**
funny noise	komisches Geräusch	**koh**-mish-ehs geh-**roysh**
electrical problem	elektrische Schwierigkeiten	eh-**lehk**-trish-eh **shvee**-rig-kī-tehn
flat tire	Reifenpanne	**rī**-fehn-pah-neh
repair shop	Garage	gah-**rah**-zheh
My car won't start.	Mein Auto springt nicht an.	mīn **ow**-toh shpringt nikht ahn
My car is broken.	Mein Auto ist kaputt.	mīn **ow**-toh ist kah-**poot**
This doesn't work.	Das geht nicht.	dahs gayt nikht
It's overheating.	Es überhitzt.	ehs **ew**-ber-hitst
It's a lemon (useless box).	Es ist eine Schrottkiste.	ehs ist **ī**-neh **shroht**-kis-teh

I need a...	*Ich brauche einen...*	ikh **browkh**-eh **ī**-nehn
We need a...	*Wir brauchen einen...*	veer **browkh**-ehn **ī**-nehn
...tow truck.	*...Abschleppwagen.*	**ahp**-shlehp-vah-gehn
...mechanic.	*...Mechaniker.*	mehkh-**ahn**-i-ker
...stiff drink.	*...Schnaps.*	shnahps

For help with repair, look up "Repair" under Services.

Parking

parking lot	*Parkplatz*	**park**-plahts
parking garage	*Garage*	gah-**rah**-zheh
parking meter	*Parkuhr*	**park**-oor
parking clock (to put on dashboard)	*Parkscheibe*	**park**-shī-beh
Where can I park?	*Wo kann ich parken?*	voh kahn ikh **par**-kehn
Is parking nearby?	*Gibt es Parkplätze in der Nähe?*	gipt ehs **park**-pleht-seh in dehr **nay**-heh
Can I park here?	*Darf ich hier parken?*	darf ikh heer **par**-kehn
Is this a safe place to park?	*Ist dies ein sicherer Parkplatz?*	ist deez īn **zikh**-her-er **park**-plahts
How long can I park here?	*Wie lange darf ich hier parken?*	vee **lahng**-eh darf ikh heer **par**-kehn
Must I pay to park here?	*Kostet Parken hier etwas?*	**kohs**-teht **par**-kehn heer **eht**-vahs
How much per hour / day?	*Wie viel pro Stunde / Tag?*	vee feel proh **shtoon**-deh / tahg

Free but time-limited parking spaces use the "cardboard clock" (*Parkscheibe,* you'll usually find one in your rental car). Put the clock on your dashboard with your arrival time so parking attendants can see you've been there less than the posted maximum stay. At pay parking spaces, you'll pre-pay for the length of your stay. Find the parking meter (usually about one or two per block), pay for the amount of time you need, then put the ticket (*Parkschein*) on your dashboard. If you're not sure what to do, check the dashboards of the cars around you.

TRAVELING

Finding Your Way

I'm going on foot to ___.	Ich gehe nach ___.	ikh **gay**-heh nahkh
We're going on foot to ___.	Wir gehen nach ___.	veer **gay**-hehn nahkh
I'm going to ___. (using wheels)	Ich fahre nach ___.	ikh **fah**-reh nahkh
We're going to ___. (using wheels)	Wir fahren nach ___.	veer **fah**-rehn nahkh
How do I get to ___?	Wie komme ich nach ___?	vee **koh**-meh ikh nahkh ___
How do we get to ___?	Wie kommen wir nach ___?	vee **koh**-mehn veer nahkh ___
Do you have a...?	Haben Sie eine...?	**hah**-behn zee **ī**-neh
...city map	...Stadtplan	**shtaht**-plahn
...road map	...Straßenkarte	**shtrah**-sehn-kar-teh
How many minutes / hours...?	Wie viele Minuten / Stunden...?	vee **fee**-leh mee-**noo**-tehn / **shtoon**-dehn
...on foot	...zu Fuß	tsoo foos
...by bicycle	...mit dem Rad	mit daym raht
...by car	...mit dem Auto	mit daym **ow**-toh
How many kilometers to ___?	Wie viele Kilometer sind es nach ___?	vee **fee**-leh kee-loh-**may**-ter zint ehs nahkh ___
What's the...	Was ist der...	vahs ist dehr...
route to Berlin?	Weg nach Berlin?	vehg nahkh behr-**leen**
...most scenic	...schönste	**shurn**-steh
...fastest	...schnellste	**shnehl**-steh
...most interesting	...interessanteste	in-ter-ehs-**sahn**-tehs-teh
Point it out?	Zeigen Sie es mir?	**tsī**-gehn zee ehs meer
I'm lost. (if you're on foot)	Ich habe mich verlaufen.	ikh **hah**-beh mikh fehr-**lowf**-ehn

We're lost. (on foot)	Wir haben uns verlaufen.	veer **hah**-behn oons fehr-**lowf**-ehn
I'm lost. (if you're in a car)	Ich habe mich verfahren.	ikh **hah**-beh mikh fehr-**far**-ehn
We're lost. (by car)	Wir haben uns verfahren.	veer **hah**-behn oons fehr-**far**-ehn
Where am I?	Wo bin ich?	voh bin ikh
Where is...?	Wo ist...?	voh ist
The nearest...?	Der nächste...?	dehr **nehkh**-steh
Where is this address?	Wo ist diese Adresse?	voh ist **dee**-zeh ah-**drehs**-seh

Route-finding Words

city map	Stadtplan	**shtaht**-plahn
road map	Straßenkarte	**shtrah**-sehn-kar-teh
downtown	Zentrum, Stadtzentrum	**tsehn**-troom, **shtaht**-tsehn-troom
straight ahead	geradeaus	geh-rah-deh-**ows**
left	links	links
right	rechts	rehkhts
first	erste	**ehr**-steh
next	nächste	**nehkh**-steh
intersection	Kreuzung	**kroy**-tsoong
corner	Ecke	**ehk**-eh
block	Häuserblock	**hoy**-zer-blohk
roundabout	Kreisel	**krī**-zehl
ring road	Ringstraße	**ring**-shtrah-seh
stoplight	Ampel	**ahm**-pehl
(main) square	(Markt-)platz	(**markt**-)plahts
street	Straße	**shtrah**-seh
bridge	Brücke	**brew**-keh
tunnel	Tunnel	**too**-nehl
highway	Landstraße	**lahnd**-shtrah-seh
national highway	Fernstraße	**fayrn**-shtrah-seh
freeway	Autobahn	**ow**-toh-bahn

north	*Nord*	nord
south	*Süd*	zewd
east	*Ost*	ohst
west	*West*	vehst

The shortest distance between any two points in Germany is the *Autobahn.* The right to no speed limit is as close to the average German driver's heart as the right to bear arms is to many American hearts. To survive, never cruise in the passing lane. While all roads seem to lead to the little town of *Ausfahrt,* that is the German word for exit. The *Autobahn* information magazine, available at any *Autobahn Tankstelle* (gas station), lists all road signs, interchanges, and the hours and facilities available at various rest stops. Missing a turnoff can cost you lots of time and miles—be alert for *Autobahn Kreuz* (interchange) signs.

The Police

As in any country, the flashing lights of a patrol car are a sure sign that someone's in trouble. If it's you, try this handy phrase: *"Entschuldigung, ich bin Tourist"* (Sorry, I'm a tourist). Or, for the adventurous: *"Wenn es Ihnen nicht gefällt, wie ich Auto fahre, gehen Sie doch vom Gehweg runter."* (If you don't like how I drive, stay off the sidewalk.)

I'm late for my tour.	*Ich bin zu spät*	ikh bin tsoo shpayt
	für meine	fewr **mī**-neh
	Gruppenreise.	**groop**-ehn-**rī**-zeh
Can I buy your hat?	*Kann ich Ihren*	kahn ikh **eer**-ehn
	Hut kaufen?	hoot **kowf**-ehn
What seems to be the problem?	*Was ist los?*	vas ist lohs
Sorry, I'm a tourist.	*Engschuldigung,*	ehnt-**shool**-dig-oong
	ich bin tourist	ikh bin **too**-rist

Reading Road Signs

Alle Richtungen	Out of town (all destinations)
Ausfahrt	Exit
Autobahn Kreuz	Freeway interchange
Baustelle	Construction
Dreieck	"Three-corner" or fork
Einbahnstraße	One-way street
Einfahrt	Entrance
Fußgänger	Pedestrians
Gebühr	Toll
Langsam	Slow down
Nächste Ausfart	Next exit
Parken verboten	No parking
Stadtmitte	To the center of town
Stopp	Stop
Straßenarbeiten	Road workers ahead
Umleitung	Detour
Vorfahrt beachten	Yield
Zentrum	To the center of town

TRAVELING

KEY PHRASES: DRIVING

car	*Auto*	**ow**-toh
gas station	*Tankstelle*	**tahnk**-shtehl-leh
parking lot	*Parkplatz*	**park**-plahts
accident	*Unfall*	**oon**-fahl
left / right	*links / rechts*	links / rehkhts
straight ahead	*geradeaus*	geh-rah-deh-**ows**
downtown	*Zentrum*	**tsehn**-troom
How do I get to ___?	*Wie komme ich nach ___?*	vee **koh**-meh ikh nahkh
Where can I park?	*Wo kann ich parken?*	voh kahn ikh **par**-ken

Standard Road Signs

 STOP AND LEARN THESE ROAD SIGNS

Speed Limit (km/hr)

Yield

No Passing

End of No Passing Zone

One Way

Intersection

Main Road

Freeway

Danger

No Entry

No Entry for cars

All Vehicles Prohibited

Parking

No Parking

Customs

Peace

TRAVELING

Other Signs You May See

Belegt	No vacancy
Besetzt	Occupied
Bissiger Hund	Mean dog
Damen	Ladies
Drücken / Ziehen	Push / Pull
Einfahrt freihalten	Keep entrance clear
Eintritt frei	Free admission
Fahrrad	Bicycle
Gefahr	Danger
Geöffnet von... bis...	Open from... to...
Geöffnet	Open
Geschlossen	Closed
Herren	Men
Kein Eingang, Keine Einfahrt	No entry
Kein Trinkwasser	Undrinkable water
Keine Werbung	No soliciting
Lebensgefährlich	Extremely dangerous
Nicht rauchen	No smoking
Notausgang	Emergency exit
Ruhetag	Closed (quiet day)
Stammtisch	Reserved table for regulars
Toiletten	Toilet
Verboten	Forbidden
Vorsicht	Caution
WC	Toilet
Wegen Umbau geschlossen	Closed for restoration
Wegen Ferien geschlossen	Closed for vacation
Ziehen / Drücken	Pull / Push
Zimmer frei	Rooms available
Zu verkaufen	For sale
Zu vermieten	For rent or for hire
Zugang verboten	Keep out

TRAVELING

SLEEPING

Places to Stay

hotel	*Hotel*	hoh-**tehl**
small hotel	*Pension*	pehn-see-**ohn**
country inn	*Gasthaus, Gasthof*	**gahst**-hows, **gahst**-hohf
family-run hotel	*Familienbetrieb*	fah-**mee**-lee-ehn-beh-treeb
room in a home,	*Gästezimmer,*	**gehs**-teh-tsim-mer,
bed & breakfast	*Fremdenzimmer*	**frehm**-dehn-tsim-mer
youth hostel	*Jugendherberge*	**yoo**-gehnd-hehr-behr-geh
vacancy	*Zimmer frei*	**tsim**-mer frī
no vacancy	*belegt*	beh-**lehgt**

The word *garni* in a hotel name means "without restaurant."

Reserving a Room

I like to reserve rooms a few days in advance as I travel. But if my itinerary is set, I reserve before I leave home. To reserve from the U.S. by fax or e-mail, use the handy form in the Appendix (online at www.ricksteves.com/reservation).

Hello.	Guten Tag.	**goo**-tehn tahg
Do you speak English?	Sprechen Sie Englisch?	**shprehkh**-ehn zee **ehng**-lish
Do you have a room for...?	Haben Sie ein Zimmer für...?	**hah**-behn zee īn **tsim**-mer fewr
...one person	...eine Person	**ī**-neh pehr-**zohn**
...two people	...zwei Personen	tsvī pehr-**zoh**-nehn
...tonight	...heute Abend	**hoy**-teh **ah**-behnt
...two nights	...zwei Nächte	tsvī **naykh**-teh
...Friday	...Freitag	**frī**-tahg
...June 21	...einundzwanzigsten Juni	**īn**-oont-tsvahn-tsig-stehn **yoo**-nee
Yes or no?	Ja oder nein?	yah **oh**-der nīn
I'd like...	Ich möchte...	ikh **murkh**-teh
We'd like...	Wir möchten...	veer **murkh**-tehn
...a private bathroom	...eigenes Bad.	**ī**-geh-nehs baht
...your cheapest room.	...ihr billigstes Zimmer.	eer **bil**-lig-stehs **tsim**-mer
...___ bed(s) for ___ people in	...___ Bett(en) für ___ Personen in	beht-(tehn) fewr pehr-**zoh**-nehn in

KEY PHRASES: SLEEPING

I want to make / confirm a reservation.	Ich möchte eine Reservierung machen / bestätigen.	ikh **murkh**-teh **ī**-neh reh-zer-**feer**-oong **mahkh**-ehn / beh-**shtay**-teh-gehn
I'd like a room (for two people), please.	Ich möchte ein Zimmer (für zwei Personen), bitte.	ikh **murkh**-teh īn **tsim**-mer (fewr tsvī pehr-**zoh**-nehn) **bit**-teh
...with / without / and	...mit / ohne / und	mit / **oh**-neh / oont
...toilet	...Toilette	toh-**leh**-teh
...shower	...Dusche	**doo**-sheh
Can I see the room?	Kann ich das Zimmer sehen?	kahn ikh dahs **tsim**-mer **zay**-hehn
How much is it?	Wie viel kostet das?	vee feel **kohs**-teht dahs
Credit card O.K.?	Kreditkarte O.K.?	kreh-**deet**-kar-teh "O.K."

___ room(s).	___ Zimmer(n).	**tsim**-mer(n)
How much is it?	Wie viel kostet das?	vee feel **kohs**-teht dahs
Anything cheaper?	Etwas Billigeres?	**eht**-vahs **bil**-lig-er-ehs
I'll take it.	Ich nehme es.	ikh **nay**-meh ehs
My name is ___.	Ich heiße ___.	ikh **hī**-seh ___
I'll stay...	Ich bleibe...	ikh **blī**-beh
We'll stay...	Wir bleiben...	veer **blī**-behn
...for one night.	...für eine Nacht.	fewr **ī**-neh nahkht
...for ___ nights.	...für ___ Nächte.	fewr ___ **naykh**-teh
I'll come...	Ich komme...	ikh **koh**-meh
We'll come...	Wir kommen...	veer **koh**-mehn
...in the morning.	...am Morgen.	ahm **mor**-gehn
...in the afternoon.	...am Nachmittag.	ahm **nahkh**-mit-tahg
...in the evening.	...am Abend.	ahm **ah**-behnt
...in one hour.	...in einer Stunde.	in **ī**-ner **shtoon**-deh
...before 4:00 in the afternoon.	...vor vier Uhr abends.	for feer oor **ah**-behnts
...Friday before 6 p.m.	...Freitag vor sechs Uhr abends.	**frī**-tahg for zehx oor **ah**-behnts
Thank you.	Danke.	**dahng**-keh

Using a Credit Card

If you need to secure your reservation with a credit card, here's the lingo.

SLEEPING

Do you need a deposit?	Brauchen Sie eine Anzahlung?	**browkh**-ehn zee **ī**-neh **ahn**-tsahl-oong
Credit card O.K.?	Kreditkarte O.K.?	kreh-**deet**-kar-teh "O.K."
credit card	Kreditkarte	kreh-**deet**-kar-teh
debit card	Kontokarte	**kohn**-toh-kar-teh
The name on the card is ___.	Der name auf der Karte ist ___.	der **nah**-meh owf dehr **kar**-teh ist
The credit card number is...	Die Kreditkarten-nummer ist...	dee kreh-**deet**-kar-tehn-**noo**-mer ist
0	null	nool
1	eins	īns
2	zwei	tsvī

3	*drei*	dr ī
4	*vier*	feer
5	*fünf*	fewnf
6	*sechs*	zehx
7	*sieben*	**zee**-behn
8	*acht*	ahkht
9	*neun*	noyn
Valid until ___ .	*Gültig bis ___ .*	**gool**-tig bis
January	*Januar*	**yah**-noo-ar
February	*Februar*	**fay**-broo-ar
March	*März*	mehrts
April	*April*	ah-**pril**
May	*Mai*	mī
June	*Juni*	**yoo**-nee
July	*Juli*	**yoo**-lee
August	*August*	ow-g**oost**
September	*September*	zehp-**tehm**-ber
October	*Oktober*	ohk-**toh**-ber
November	*November*	noh-**vehm**-ber
December	*Dezember*	day-**tsehm**-ber
2003	*zweitausenddrei*	**tsvī**-tow-zehnd-**drī**
2004	*zweitausendvier*	**tsvī**-tow-zehnd-**feer**
2005	*zweitausendfünf*	**tsvī**-tow-zehnd-**fewnf**
2006	*zweitausendsechs*	**tsvī**-tow-zehnd-**zehx**
2007	*zweitausend-sieben*	**tsvī**-tow-zehnd-**zee**-behn
2008	*zweitausendacht*	**tsvī**-tow-zehnd-**ahkht**
2009	*zweitausendneun*	**tsvī**-tow-zehnd-**noyn**
2010	*zweitausendzehn*	**tsvī**-tow-zehnd-**tsayn**
Can I reserve with a credit card and pay in cash?	*Kann ich mit der Karte reservieren und bar zahlen?*	kahn ik mit dehr **kar**-teh reh-ser-**veer**-ehn und bar **tsah**-lehn
I have another card.	*Ich habe eine andere Karte.*	ik **hah**-beh ī-neh **ahn**-deh-reh **kar**-teh

SLEEPING

If your *Kreditkarte* (credit card) is not approved, you can say "*Ich habe eine andere Karte*" (I have another card)—if you do.

Das Alphabet

If phoning, you can use the code alphabet below to spell out your name if necessary. Unless you're giving the hotelier your name as it appears on your credit card, consider using a shorter version of your name to make things easier.

a	ah	*Anna*	**ah**-nah
ä	ay	*Ärger (anger)*	**ehr**-ger
b	bay	*Bertha*	**behr**-tah
c	tsay	*Cäsar*	**tseh**-zar
d	day	*Daniel*	**dah**-nee-ehl
e	ay	*Emil*	**eh**-meel
f	"f"	*Friedrich*	**freed**-rikh
g	gay	*Gustav*	**goo**-stahf
h	hah	*Heinrich*	**hīn**-rikh
i	ee	*Ida*	**ee**-dah
j	yot	*Jakob*	**yah**-kohp
k	kah	*Kaiser (emperor)*	**kī**-zer
l	"l"	*Leopold*	**lay**-oh-pohld
m	"m"	*Martha*	**mar**-tah
n	"n"	*Niklaus*	**nik**-lows
o	"o"	*Otto*	**oh**-toh
ö	ur	*Ökonom*	urk-oh-**nohm**
p	pay	*Peter*	**pay**-ter
q	koo	*Quelle*	**kveh**-leh
r	ehr	*Rosa*	**roh**-zah
s	"s"	*Sophie*	zoh-**fee**
t	tay	*Theodor*	**tay**-oh-dor
u	oo	*Ulrich*	**ool**-rikh
ü	ew	*Übel (evil)*	**ew**-behl
v	fow	*Viktor*	**veek**-tor
w	vay	*Wilhelm*	**vil**-hehlm
x	eeks	*Xaver*	**ksah**-ver
y	**ewp**-sil-lohn	*Ypsilon*	**ewp**-sil-lohn
z	tseht	*Zeppelin*	**tseh**-peh-lin
ß	**es**-tseht	*Ziss*	tsis

SLEEPING

Just the Fax, Ma'am

If you're booking a room by fax...

I want to send a fax.	Ich möchte einen Fax senden.	ikh **murkh**-teh **Ī**-nehn fahx **zehn**-dehn
What is your fax number?	Was ist Ihre Faxnummer?	vahs ist **eer**-eh **fahx**-noo-mer
Your fax number is not working.	Ihre Faxnummer funktioniert nicht.	**eer**-eh **fahx**-noo-mer foonk-tsee-ohn-**eert** nikht
Please turn on your fax machine.	Bitte stellen Sie Ihren Fax an.	**bit**-teh **shtehl**-lehn zee **eer**-ehn fahx ahn

Getting Specific

I'd like a room...	Ich möchte ein Zimmer...	ikh **murkh**-teh **ī**n **tsim**-mer
We'd like a room...	Wir möchten ein Zimmer...	veer **murkh**-tehn **ī**n **tsim**-mer
...with / without / and	...mit / ohne / und	mit / **oh**-neh / oont
...toilet	...Toilette	toh-**leh**-teh
...shower	...Dusche	**doo**-sheh
...shower down the hall	...Dusche im Gang	**doo**-sheh im gahng
...bathtub	...Badewanne	**bah**-deh-vah-neh
...double bed	...Doppelbett	**doh**-pehl-beht
...twin beds	...Einzelbetten	**ī**n-tsehl-beht-tehn
...balcony	...Balkon	bahl-**kohn**
...view	...Ausblick	**ows**-blick
...with only a sink	...nur mit Waschbecken	noor mit **vahsh**-behk-ehn
...on the ground floor	...im Erdgeschoß	im **ehrd**-geh-shohs
...television	...Fernsehen	**fehrn**-zay-hehn

SLEEPING

...telephone	...Telefon	tehl-eh-**fohn**
...air conditioning	...Klimaanlage	**klee**-mah-ahn-lah-geh
...kitchenette	...Kleinküche	**klīn**-kewkh-eh
Is there an elevator?	Gibt es einen Fahrstuhl?	gipt ehs **ī**-nehn **far**-shtool
Do you have a swimming pool?	Haben Sie einen Pool?	**hah**-behn zee **ī**-nehn pool
I arrive Monday, depart Wednesday.	Ich komme am Montag, und reise am Mittwoch ab.	ikh **koh**-meh ahm **mohn**-tahg oont **rī**-zeh ahm **mit**-vohkh ahp
We arrive Monday, depart Wednesday.	Wir kommen am Montag, und reisen am Mittwoch ab.	veer **koh**-mehn ahm **mohn**-tahg oont **rī**-zehn ahm **mit**-vohkh ahp
I'm desperate.	Ich bin am Verzweifeln.	ikh bin ahm fehr-**tsvī**-fehln
We're desperate.	Wir sind am Verzweifeln.	veer zint ahm fehr-**tsvī**-fehln
I'll sleep anywhere.	Ich kann irgendwo schlafen.	ikh kahn **ir**-gehnd-voh **shlah**-fehn
We'll sleep anywhere.	Wir können irgendwo schlafen.	veer **kurn**-nehn **ir**-gehnd-voh **shlah**-fehn
I have a sleeping bag.	Ich habe einen Schlafsack.	ikh **hah**-beh **ī**-nehn **shlahf**-zahk
We have sleeping bags.	Wir haben Schlafsäcke.	veer **hah**-behn **shlahf**-zehk-eh
Will you please call another hotel for me?	Rufen Sie bitte in einem anderen Hotel für mich an?	**roo**-fehn zee **bit**-teh in **ī**-nehm **ahn**-der-ehn hoh-**tehl** fewr meekh ah

SLEEPING

Families

Do you have a...?	Haben Sie ein...?	**hah**-behn zee īn
...family room	...Familienzimmer	fah-**mee**-lee-ehn-**tsim**-mer
...family discount	...Familienrabatt	fah-**mee**-lee-ehn-rah-**baht**
...discount for children	...Rabatt für Kinder	rah-**baht** fewr **kin**-der

I have / We have...	Ich habe / Wir haben...	ikh **hah**-beh / veer **hah**-behn
...one child, ___ months / years old.	...ein Kind, ___ Monate / Jahre alt.	īn kint, ___ moh-**nah**-teh / **yar**-eh ahlt
...two children, ___ and ___ years old.	...zwei Kinder, ___ und ___ Jahre alt.	tsvī **kin**-der, ___ oont ___ **yar**-eh ahlt
I'd like...	Ich hätte gern...	ikh **heht**-teh gehrn
We'd like...	Wir hätten gern...	veer **heht**-tehn gehrn
...a crib.	...ein Kinderbett.	īn **kin**-der-beht
...a small extra bed.	...ein kleines Extrabett.	īn **klī**-nehs **ehk**-strah-beht
...bunk beds.	...Kojen.	**koh**-yehn
babysitting service	Kinderaufsicht	**kin**-der-**owf**-zikht
Is a... nearby?	Ist ein... in der Nähe?	ist īn... in dehr **nay**-heh
...park	...Park	park
...playground	...Spielplatz	**shpeel**-plahts
...swimming pool	...Schwimmbad	**shvim**-baht

For fun, Germans call little boys *Lausbub* (kid with lice) and little girls *Göre* (brat).

Mobility Issues

Stairs are... for me / us / my husband / my wife.	Treppen sind für mich / uns / meinen Mann / meine Frau...	**treh**-pehn zint fewr mikh / oons / **mī**-nehn mahn / **mī**-neh frow
...impossible	...unmöglich.	oon-**murg**-likh
...difficult	...schwierig.	**shvee**-rig
Do you have...?	Haben Sie...?	**hah**-behn zee
...an elevator	...einen Lift	**ī**-nehn lift
...a ground floor room	...ein Zimmer im Erdgeschoß	īn **tsim**-mer im **ehrd**-geh-shohs
...a wheelchair-accessible room	...ein rollstuhl-gängiges Zimmer	īn **rohl**-shtool-**gayng**-ig-ehs **tsim**-mer

Confirming, Changing, and Canceling Reservations

You can use this template for your telephone call.

I have a reservation.	Ich habe eine Reservierung.	ikh **hah**-beh **ī**-neh reh-zer-**feer**-oong
We have a reservation.	Wir haben eine Reservierung.	veer **hah**-behn **ī**-neh reh-zer-**feer**-oong
My name is ___.	Ich heiße ___.	ikh **hī**-seh ___
I'd like to... my reservation.	Ich möchte meine Reservierung...	ikh **murkh**-teh **mī**-neh reh-zer-**feer**-oong
...confirm	...bestätigen	beh-**shtay**-teh-gehn
...reconfirm	...nochmals bestätigen.	**nohkh**-mahls beh-**shtay**-tig-ehn
...cancel	...annullieren	ah-nool-**eer**-ehn
...change	...ändern	**ayn**-dern
The reservation is / was for...	Die Reservierung ist / war für...	dee reh-zer-**feer**-oong ist / var fewr
...one person	...eine Person	**ī**-neh pehr-**zohn**
...two people	...zwei Personen	tsvī pehr-**zoh**-nehn
...today / tomorrow	...heute / morgen	**hoy**-teh / **mor**-gehn
...the day after tomorrow	...übermorgen	**ew**-ber-**mor**-gehn
...August 13	dreizehnten August	tsayn-tehn ow-**goost** drī
...one night / two nights	...eine Nacht / zwei Nächte	**ī**-neh nahkht / tsvī **naykh**-teh
Did you find my / our reservation?	Haben Sie meine / unsere Reservierung gefunden?	**hah**-behn zee **mī**-neh / **oon**-zer-eh reh-zer-**feer**-oong geh-**foon**-dehn
What is your cancellation policy?	Wie ist es mit einer Annulierung?	vee ist ehs mit **ī**-ner ah-nool-**eer**-oong
Will I be billed for the first night if I can't make it?	Werde ich für die erste Nacht belastet, wenn ich nicht kommen kann?	**vehr**-deh ikh fewr dee **ehr**-steh nahkht beh-**lah**-steht vehn ikh nikht **koh**-mehn kahn

SLEEPING

I'd like to arrive instead on ___.	*Ich möchte lieber am ___ kommen.*	ikh **murkh**-teh **lee**-ber ahm ___ **koh**-mehn
We'd like to arrive instead on ___.	*Wir möchten lieber am ___ kommen.*	veer **murkh**-tehn **lee**-ber ahm ___ **koh**-mehn
Is everything O.K.?	*Ist alles in Ordnung?*	ist **ahl**-lehs in **ord**-noong
Thank you. See you then.	*Vielen Dank. Bis dann.*	**fee**-lehn dahngk bis dahn
I'm sorry, I need to cancel.	*Ich bedaure, aber ich muß annullieren.*	ikh beh-**dow**-eh-reh **ah**-ber ikh moos ah-nool-**eer**-ehn

Nailing Down the Price

How much is...?	*Wie viel kostet...?*	vee feel **kohs**-teht
...a room for ___ people	*...ein Zimmer für ___ Personen*	īn **tsim**-mer fewr ___ pehr-**zoh**-nehn
...your cheapest room	*...Ihr billigstes Zimmer*	eer **bil**-lig-stehs **tsim**-mer
Breakfast included?	*Frühstück inklusive?*	**frew**-shtewk in-kloo-z**ee**-veh
Is half-pension required?	*Ist Halbpension Bedingung?*	ist **halb**-pehn-see-ohn beh-**ding**-oong
Complete price?	*Vollpreis?*	**fohl**-prīs
Is it cheaper if I stay three nights?	*Ist es billiger, wenn ich drei Nächte bleibe?*	ist ehs **bil**-lig-er vehn ikh drī **naykh**-teh **blī**-beh
I'll stay three nights.	*Ich werde drei Nächte bleiben.*	ikh **vehr**-deh drī **naykh**-teh **blī**-behn
We will stay three nights.	*Wir werden drei Nächte bleiben.*	veer **vehr**-dehn drī **naykh**-teh **blī**-behn
Is it cheaper if I pay cash?	*Ist es billiger, wenn ich bar zahle?*	ist ehs **bil**-lig-er vehn ikh bar **tsah**-leh
What is the cost per week?	*Was ist der Wochenpreis?*	vahs ist dehr **vohkh**-ehn-prīs

Choosing a Room

Can I see the room?	*Kann ich das Zimmer sehen?*	kahn ikh dahs **tsim**-mer **zay**-hehn
Can we see the room?	*Können wir das Zimmer sehen?*	**kurn**-nehn veer dahs **tsim**-mer **zay**-hehn
Show me / us another room?	*Zeigen Sie mir / uns ein anderes Zimmer?*	**tsī**-gehn zee meer / oons īn **ahn**-der-ehs **tsim**-mer
Do you have something...?	*Haben Sie etwas...?*	**hah**-behn zee **eht**-vahs
...larger / smaller	*...größeres / kleineres*	**grur**-ser-ehs / **klī**-ner-ehs
...better / cheaper	*...besseres / billigeres*	**behs**-ser-ehs / **bil**-lig-er-ehs
...brighter	*...helleres*	**hehl**-ler-ehs
...in the back	*...nach hinten hinaus*	nahkh **hin**-tehn hin-**ows**
...quieter	*...ruhigeres*	**roo**-i-ger-ehs
Sorry, it's not right for me / us.	*Tut mir leid, es ist nicht das Richtige für mich / uns.*	toot meer līt ehs ist nikht dahs **rikh**-tig-eh fewr mikh / oons
I'll take it.	*Ich nehme es.*	ikh **nay**-meh ehs
We'll take it.	*Wir nehmen es.*	veer **nay**-mehn ehs
My key, please.	*Mein Schlüssel, bitte.*	mīn **shlew**-sehl **bit**-teh
Sleep well.	*Schlafen Sie gut.*	**shlah**-fehn zee goot
Good night.	*Gute Nacht.*	**goo**-teh nahkht

Breakfast

When does breakfast start?	*Wann beginnt das Frühstück?*	vahn beh-**gint** dahs **frew**-shtewk
When does breakfast end?	*Wann endet das Frühstück?*	vahn **ehn**-deht dahs **frew**-shtewk

SLEEPING

| Where is breakfast served? | Wo wird Frühstück serviert? | voh virt **frew**-shtewk zer-**veert** |

Breakfast is normally included in the price of your room. For a list of breakfast words, see pages 82–83.

Hotel Help

I'd like...	Ich hätte gern...	ikh **heht**-teh gehrn
We'd like...	Wir hätten gern...	veer **heht**-tehn gehrn
...a / another	...ein / noch ein	īn / nohkh īn
...towel.	...Handtuch.	**hahnd**-tookh
...clean bath towel(s).	...sauberes Badetuch / saubere Badetücher.	**zow**-ber-ehs **bah**-deh-tookh / **zow**-ber-eh **bah**-deh-tewkh-er
...pillow.	...Kissen.	**kis**-sehn
...clean sheets.	...saubere Laken.	**zow**-ber-eh **lah**-kehn
...blanket.	...Decke.	**dehk**-eh
...glass.	...Glas.	glahs
...sink stopper.	...Abflußstöpsel.	**ahp**-floos-shturp-zehl
...soap.	...Seife.	**zī**-feh
...toilet paper.	...Klopapier.	**kloh**-pah-peer
...electrical adapter.	...Stromwandler.	**strohm**-vahnd-ler
...brighter light bulb.	...hellere Leuchtbirne.	**hehl**-eh-reh **loykht**-bir-neh
...lamp.	...Lampe.	**lahm**-peh
...chair.	...Stuhl.	shtool
...table.	...Tisch.	tish
...modem.	...Modem.	**moh**-dehm
...Internet access.	...Internetanschluß.	in-tehr-neht-**ahn**-shloos
...different room.	...anderes Zimmer.	**ahn**-der-ehs **tsim**-mer
...silence.	...Ruhe.	**roo**-heh
...to speak to the manager.	...mit dem Chef sprechen.	mit daym shehf **shprekh**-ehn
I've fallen and I can't get up.	Ich bin gefallen und kann nicht aufstehen.	ikh bin geh-**fahl**-lehn oont kahn nikht **owf**-shtay-hehn

How can I make the room...?	Wie kann ich das Zimmer... machen?	vee kahn ikh dahs **tsim**-mer...**mahkh**-ehn
...cooler / warmer?	...kühler /wärmer	**kewl**-er / **vehrm**-er
Where can I wash / hang my laundry?	Wo kann ich meine Wäsche waschen / aufhängen?	voh kahn ikh **mī**-neh **vehsh**-eh **vahsh**-ehn / **owf**-hehng-ehn
Is a... laundry nearby?	Ist ein Waschsalon... in der Nähe?	ist īn **vahsh**-sah-lohn in dehr **nay**-heh
...self-service	...mit Selbstbedienung	...mit zehlpst-beh-**dee**-noong
...full service	...mit Dienstleistung	mit **deenst**-līs-toong
I'd like / We'd like...	Ich möchte / Wir möchten...	ikh **murkh**-teh / veer **murkh**-tehn
...to stay another night.	...noch eine Nacht bleiben.	nokh **ī**-neh nahkht **blī**-behn
Where can I park?	Wo soll ich parken?	voh zohl ikh **par**-kehn
What time do you lock up?	Um wie viel Uhr schließen Sie ab?	oom vee feel oor **shlee**-sehn zee ahp
Please wake me at 7:00.	Wecken Sie mich um sieben Uhr, bitte.	**vehk**-ehn zee mikh oom **zee**-behn oor **bit**-teh
Where do you go to eat lunch / eat dinner / drink coffee?	Wo gehen Sie zum Mittag essen / Abend essen / Kaffee trinken?	voh **gay**-hehn zee tsoom **mit**-tahg **eh**-sehn / **ah**-behnt **eh**-sehn / kah-**fay trink**-ehn

Hotel Hassles

Come with me.	Kommen Sie mit mir.	**koh**-mehn zee mit meer
There is a problem in my room.	Es gibt ein Problem mit meinem Zimmer.	ehs gipt īn proh-**blaym** mit **mī**-nehm **tsim**-mer
It smells bad.	Es stinkt.	ehs shtinkt
bedbugs	Wanzen	**vahn**-tsehn
mice	Mäuse	**moy**-zeh
cockroaches	Kakerlaken	**kah**-ker-**lahk**-ehn
prostitutes	Freudenmädchen	**froy**-dehn-**mayd**-khehn

I'm covered with bug bites.	Ich bin mit Wanzenbissen übersät.	ikh bin mit **vahn**-tsehn-**bis**-sehn ew-ber-**zayt**
The bed is too soft / hard.	Das Bett ist zu weich / hart.	dahs beht ist tsoo vīkh / hart
I can't sleep.	Ich kann nicht schlafen.	ikh kahn nikht **shlah**-fehn
The room is too...	Das Zimmer ist zu...	dahs **tsim**-mer ist tsoo
...hot / cold.	...heiß / kalt.	hīs / kahlt
...noisy / dirty.	...laut / schmutzig.	lowt / **shmoot**-sig
I can't open / shut...	Ich kann... nicht öffnen / schliessen.	ikh kahn... nikht **urf**-nehn / **shlees**-ehn
...the door / the window.	...die Tür / das Fenster	dee tewr / dahs **fehn**-ster
Air conditioner...	Klimaanlage...	**klee**-mah-ahn-lah-geh
Lamp...	Lampe...	**lahm**-peh
Lightbulb...	Birne...	**bir**-neh
Electrical outlet...	Steckdose...	**shtehk**-doh-zeh
Key...	Schlüssel...	**shlew**-sehl
Lock...	Schloß...	shlohs
Window...	Fenster...	**fehn**-ster
Faucet...	Wasserhahn...	**vah**-ser-hahn
Sink...	Waschbecken...	**vahsh**-behk-ehn
Toilet...	Toilette...	toh-**leh**-teh
Shower...	Dusche...	**doo**-sheh
...doesn't work.	...ist kaputt.	ist kah-**poot**
There is no hot water.	Es gibt kein warmes Wasser.	ehs gipt kīn **var**-mehs **vahs**-ser
When is the water hot?	Wann wird das Wasser warm?	vahn virt dahs **vahs**-ser varm

Checking Out

When is check-out time?	Wann muß ich das Zimmer verlassen?	vahn mus ikh dahs **tsim**-mer fehr-**lah**-sehn
I'll leave...	Ich fahre... ab.	ikh **fah**-reh... ahp
We'll leave...	Wir fahren... ab.	veer **fah**-rehn... ahp

...today / tomorrow	...heute / morgen	**hoy**-teh / **mor**-gehn
...very early	...sehr früh	zehr frew
Can I pay now?	Kann ich jetzt zahlen?	kahn ikh yetzt **tsah**-lehn
Can we pay now?	Können wir jetzt zahlen?	**kurn**-nehn veer yetzt **tsah**-lehn
Bill, please.	Rechnung, bitte.	**rehkh**-noong **bit**-teh
Credit card O.K.?	Kreditkarte O.K.?	kreh-**deet**-kar-teh "O.K."
Everything was great.	Alles war gut.	**ahl**-lehs var goot
I slept like a bear.	Ich habe wie ein Bär geschlafen.	ikh **hah**-beh vee īn bayr geh-**shlahf**-ehn
Will you call my next hotel...?	Können Sie mein nächstes Hotel anrufen...?	**kurn**-nehn zee mīn **nehkh**-stehs hoh-**tehl ahn**-roo-fehn
...for tonight	...für heute Abend	fewr **hoy**-teh **ah**-behnt
...to make a reservation	...zum reservieren	tsoom reh-ser-**veer**-ehn
...to confirm a reservation	...zum bestätigen	tsoom beh-**shtay**-teh-gehn
I will pay for the call.	Ich bezahle für den Anruf.	ikh beh-**tsah**-leh fewr dayn **ahn**-roof
Can I...?	Kann ich...?	kahn ikh
Can we...?	Können wir...?	**kurn**-nehn veer
...leave baggage here until ___	...das Gepäck hier lassen bis ___	dahs geh-**pehk** heer **lah**-sehn bis ___

Camping

camping	Camping	**kahm**-ping
campsite	Zeltstelle	**tsehlt**-shtehl-leh
tent	Zelt	tsehlt
The nearest campground?	Der nächste Campingplatz?	dehr **nehkh**-steh **kahm**-ping-plahts
Can I...?	Kann ich...?	kahn ikh

Can we...?	Können wir...?	**kurn**-nehn veer
...camp here	...hier eine	heer **ī**-neh
for one night	Nacht zelten	nahkht **tsehl**-tehn
Are showers	Duschen	**doo**-shehn
included?	eingeschlossen?	**īn**-geh-shlohs-sehn

EATING

RESTAURANTS

Types of Restaurants

Here are several types of eateries and some variations you'll find per country:

Restaurant—Primarily fine dining with formal service
Ratskeller—Atmospheric restaurant cellar with food of varying quality
Gasthaus or *Gasthof*—Country inn serving fine meals
Gaststätte or *Gaststube*—Informal restaurant
Heurigen—Austrian wine bar that serves food (see "Wine," below)
Kneipe—German bar
Weinstübli or *Bierstübli*—Wine bar or tavern in Switzerland
Café or *Konditorei*—Pastry and coffee shop that sometimes serves light lunches (**Mittagessen**)
Schnell Imbiß—Small fast food stand

Finding a Restaurant

Where's a good...	*Wo ist hier ein gutes...*	voh ist heer īn **goo**-tehs...
restaurant nearby?	*Restaurant?*	rehs-tow-**rahnt**
...cheap	*...billiges*	**bil**-lig-ehs
...local-style	*...einheimisches*	īn-**hī**-mish-ehs
...untouristy	*...nicht für Touristen*	nikht fewr too-**ris**-tehn
	gedachtes	geh-**dahkh**-tehs
...vegetarian	*...vegetarisches*	vehg-eht-**ar**-ish-ehs
...fast food	*...Schnellimbiß*	shnehl-**im**-bis
...self-service	*...Selbstbedienungs-*	zehlpst-beh-**dee**-noongs-
buffet	*Buffet*	boo-fay
...Italian	*...italienisches*	i-tahl-**yehn**-ish-ehs
...Turkish	*...türkisches*	**tewrk**-ish-ehs
...Chinese	*...chinesisches*	khee-**nayz**-ish-ehs
beer garden	*Biergarten*	**beer**-gar-tehn
with terrace	*mit Terrasse*	mit tehr-**rahs**-seh
with a salad bar	*mit Salatbar*	mit **zah**-laht-bar
with candles	*bei Kerzenlicht*	bī **kehr**-tzehn-likht
romantic	*romantisch*	roh-**mahn**-tish
moderate price	*günstig*	**gewn**-stig
splurge	*zum Verwöhnen*	tsoom fehr-**vur**-nehn
Is it better than	*Ist es besser als*	ist ehs behs-ser ahls
McDonald's?	*McDonald's?*	"McDonald's"

German restaurants close one day a week. It's called *Ruhetag* (quiet day). Before tracking down a recommended restaurant, call to make sure it's open.

Getting a Table

When does this	*Wann ist hier*	vahn ist heer
open / close?	*geöffnet /*	geh-**urf**-neht /
	geschlossen?	geh-**shlohs**-sehn
Are you open...?	*Sind Sie... geöffnet?*	zint see... geh-**urf**-neht
...today / tomorrow	*...heute / morgen*	**hoy**-teh / **mor**-gehn
...for lunch / dinner	*...zum Mittagessen /*	tsoom **mit**-tahg-eh-sehn /
	Abendessen	**ah**-behnt-eh-sehn

EATING

Are reservations recommended?	Soll mann reservieren?	zohl mahn reh-zer-**feer**-ehn
I'd like...	Ich hätte gern...	ikh **heh**-teh gehrn
We'd like...	Wir hätten gern...	veer **heh**-tehn gehrn
...a table for one / two.	...einen Tisch für ein / zwei.	**ī**-nehn tish fewr **ī** n / tsvī
...to reserve a table for two people...	...einen Tisch für zwei reserviert...	**ī**-nehn tish fewr tsvī reh-ser-**veert**
...for today / tomorrow	...für heute / morgen	fewr **hoy**-teh / **mor**-gehn
...at 8 p.m.	...um zwanzig Uhr	oom **tsvahn**-tsig oor
My name is ___.	Ich heiße ___.	ikh **hī**-seh ___
I have a reservation for ___ people.	Ich haben eine Reservierung für ___ Personen.	ikh **hah**-behn **ī**-neh reh-zer-**feer**-oong fewr___pehr-**zohn**-ehn
I'd like to sit...	Ich möchte... sitzen.	ikh **murkh**-teh...**zit**-sehn
We'd like to sit...	Wir möchten... sitzen.	veer **murkh**-tehn... **zit**-sehn
...inside / outside.	...drinn / draussen	drin / **drow**-sehn
...by the window.	...beim Fenster	bī m **fehn**-ster
...with a view.	...mit Aussicht	mit **ows**-zikht
...where it's quiet.	...im Ruhigen	im **roo**-hig-ehn
non-smoking (if possible).	Nichtraucher (wenn mürglich).	**nikht**-rowkh-er (vehn **mur**-glikh)
Is this table free?	Ist dieser Tisch frei?	ist **dee**-zer tish frī
Can I sit here?	Kann ich hier sitzen?	kahn ikh heer **zit**-sehn
Can we sit here?	Können wir hier sitzen?	**kurn**-ehn veer heer **zit**-sehn

Germans eat meals about when we do. In many bars and restaurants, you'll see tables with little signs that say *Stammtisch* ("This table reserved for our regulars"). Don't sit there unless you're invited by a local.

EATING

KEY PHRASES: RESTAURANTS

Where's a good restaurant nearby?	Wo ist hier ein gutes Restaurant?	voh ist heer īn **goo**-tehs rehs-tow-**rahnt**
I'd like...	Ich hätte gern...	ikh **heh**-teh gehrn
We'd like...	Wir hätten gern...	veer **heh**-tehn gehrn
...a table for one / two.	...einen Tisch für ein / zwei.	**ī**-nehn tish fewr īn / tsvī
non-smoking (if possible).	Nichtraucher (wenn möglich).	**nikht**-rowkh-er (vehn **mur**-glikh)
Is this seat free?	Ist hier frei?	ist heer frī
Menu (in English), please.	Speisekarte (in Englisch), bitte.	**shpī**-zeh-kar-teh (in **ehng**-lish) **bit**-teh
Bill, please.	Rechnung, bitte.	**rehkh**-noong **bit**-teh
Credit card O.K.?	Kreditkarte O.K.?	kreh-**deet**-kar-teh "O.K."

The Menu

menu	Karte, Speisekarte	**kar**-teh, **shpī**-zeh-**kar**-teh
fixed-price meal	Touristenmenü	too-**ris**-tehn-meh-**new**
menu of the day	Tageskarte	**tah**-gehs-kar-teh
fast service special	Schnellbedienung	shnehl-beh-**dee**-noong
self-service	Selbstbedienung	sehlbst-beh-**dee**-noong
specialty of the house	Spezialität des Hauses	shpayt-see-ahl-ee-**tayt** dehs **how**-zehs
half portion	halbe Portion	**hahl**-beh por-tsee-**ohn**
breakfast	Frühstück	**frew**-shtewk
lunch	Mittagessen	**mit**-tahg-eh-sehn
dinner	Abendessen	**ah**-behnt-eh-sehn
appetizers	Vorspeise	**for**-shpī-zeh
cold plates	kalte Gerichte	**kahl**-teh geh-**rikh**-teh
sandwiches	Brotzeiten	**broht**-tsī-tehn
bread	Brot	broht
salad	Salat	zah-**laht**
soup	Suppe	**zup**-peh
first course	erster Gang	**ehr**-ster gahng
main course	Hauptgerichte	**howpt**-geh-rikh-teh
meat	Fleisch	flīsh

EATING

poultry	Geflügel	geh-**flew**-gehl
fish	Fisch	fish
seafood	Meeresfrüchte	**meh**-rehs-frewkh-teh
children's plate	Kinderteller	**kin**-der-tehl-ler
side dishes	Beilagen	**bī**-lah-gehn
vegetables	Gemüse	geh-**mew**-zeh
cheese	Käse	**kay**-zeh
dessert	Nachspeise	**nahkh**-shpī-zeh
munchies	zum Knabbern	tsoom **knahb**-bern
beverages	Getränke	geh-**trehnk**-eh
drink menu	Getränkekarte	geh-**trehnk**-eh-**kar**-teh
beer	Bier	beer
wine	Wein	vīn
cover charge	Eintritt	**īn**-trit
service included	Trinkgeld inklusive	**trink**-gehlt in-kloo-z**ee**-veh
service not included	Trinkgeld nicht inklusive	**trink**-gehlt nikht in-kloo-z**ee**-veh
hot / cold	warm / kalt	varm / kahlt
with / and / or / without	mit / und / oder / ohne	mit / oont / **oh**-der / **oh**-neh

Save money by ordering a *halbe Portion* (half portion) or a *Tageskarte* (menu of the day).

Ordering

waiter	Kellner	**kehl**-ner
waitress	Kellnerin	**kehl**-ner-in
I'm ready to order.	Ich möchte bestellen.	ikh **murkh**-teh beh-**shtehl**-lehn
We're ready to order.	Wir möchten bestellen.	veer **murkh**-tehn beh-**shtehl**-lehn
I'd like...	Ich möchte...	ikh **murkh**-teh
We'd like...	Wir möchten...	veer **murkh**-tehn
...just a drink.	...nur etwas zu trinken.	noor **eht**-vahs tsoo **trink**-ehn
...a snack.	...eine Kleinigkeit.	**ī**-neh **klī**-nig-kīt
...just a salad.	...nur einen Salat.	noor **ī**-nehn zah-**laht**

...a half portion.	...eine halbe Portion.	ī-neh **hahl**-beh por-tsee-**ohn**
...to see the menu.	...die Karte sehen.	dee **kar**-teh **zay**-hehn
...to order.	...bestellen.	beh-**shtehl**-lehn
...to pay.	...zahlen.	**tsahl**-ehn
...to throw up.	...mich übergeben.	mikh **ew**-ber-gay-behn
Do you have...?	Haben Sie...?	**hah**-behn zee
...an English menu	...eine Speisekarte in Englisch	ī-neh **shpī**-zeh-kar-teh in **ehng**-lish
...a lunch special	...ein Mittagsmenü	īn **mit**-tahgs-meh-**new**
What do you recommend?	Was schlagen Sie vor?	vahs **shlah**-gehn zee for
What's your favorite dish?	Was ist Ihr Lieblingsessen?	vahs ist eer **leeb**-lings-eh-sehn
Is it...?	Ist es...?	ist ehs
...good	...gut	goot
...expensive	...teuer	**toy**-er
...light	...leicht	līkht
...filling	...sättigend	**seht**-tee-gehnd
What is...?	Was ist...?	vahs ist
...that	...das	dahs
...local	...typisch	**tew**-pish
...fresh	...frisch	frish
...cheap and	...billig	**bil**-lig
What is fast?	Was geht schnell?	vahs gayt shnehl
Can we split this and have an extra plate?	Können wir das teilen und noch einen Teller haben?	**kurn**-nehn veer dahs **tī**-lehn oont nohkh ī-nehn **tehl**-ler **hah**-behn
I've changed my mind.	Ich habe es mir anders überlegt.	ikh **hah**-beh ehs meer **ahn**-ders ew-ber-**laygt**
Nothing with eyeballs.	Nichts mit Augen.	nihkts mit **ow**-gehn
Can I substitute (anything) for the ___?	Kann ich (etwas anderes) statt ___ haben?	kahn ikh (**eht**-vahs **ahn**-der-ehs) shtaht ___ **hah**-behn
Can I / Can we get it to go?	Kann ich / Können wir das mitnehmen?	kahn ikh / **kurn**-nehn veer dahs **mit**-nay-mehn
To go?	Zum Mitnehmen?	tsoom **mit**-nay-mehn

To get the waiter's attention, ask *"Bitte?"* (Please?).
This is the sequence of a typical restaurant experience:
The waiter gives you a menu (*Speisekarte*) and then
asks if you'd like something to drink (*Etwas zu trinken?*).
When ready to take your order, the waiter simply says,
"Bitte?" After the meal, he asks if the meal tasted good
(*Hat's gut geschmeckt?*), if you'd like dessert (*Möchten Sie
eine Nachspeise?*), and if you'd like anything else (*Sonst
noch etwas?*). You ask for the bill (*Die Rechnung, bitte*).

Tableware and Condiments

plate	Teller	**tehl**-ler
extra plate	Extrateller	**ehk**-strah-**tehl**-ler
napkin	Serviette	zer-vee-**eht**-teh
silverware	Besteck	beh-**shtehk**
knife	Messer	**mehs**-ser
fork	Gabel	**gah**-behl
spoon	Löffel	**lurf**-fehl
cup	Tasse	**tah**-seh
glass	Glas	glahs
carafe	Karaffe	kah-**rah**-feh
water	Wasser	**vah**-ser
bread	Brot	broht
large pretzels	Brezel	**breht**-sehl
butter	Butter	**boo**-ter
margarine	Margarine	mar-gah-**ree**-neh
salt / pepper	Salz / Pfeffer	zahlts / **pfehf**-fer
sugar	Zucker	**tsoo**-ker
artificial sweetener	Süßstoff	**sews**-shtohf
honey	Honig	**hoh**-nig
mustard...	Senf...	zehnf
...mild / sharp / sweet	...mild / scharf / süß	milt / sharf / zews
ketchup	Ketchup	"ketchup"
mayonnaise	Mayonnaise	mah-yoh-**nay**-zeh
toothpick	Zahnstocher	**tsahn**-shtohkh-er

The Food Arrives

Is it included?	Ist es inbegriffen?	ist ehs **in**-beh-grif-ehn
I did not order this.	Dies habe ich nicht bestellt.	deez **hah**-beh ikh nikht beh-**shtehlt**
We did not order this.	Dies haben wir nicht bestellt.	deez **hah**-behn veer nikht beh-**shtehlt**
Please heat this up?	Bitte aufwärmen?	**bit**-teh **owf**-vehr-mehn
A little.	Ein bißchen.	īn **bis**-yehn
More. / Another.	Mehr. / Noch ein.	mehr / nohkh īn
The same.	Das gleiche.	dahs **glīkh**-eh
Enough.	Genug.	geh-**noog**
Finished.	Fertig.	**fehr**-tig
I'm full.	Ich bin satt.	ikh bin zaht

After bringing the meal, your server might wish you a cheery
"Guten Appetit!" (pronounced goo-tehn ah-peh-**teet**).

Complaints

This is...	Dies ist...	deez ist
...dirty.	...schmutzig.	**shmut**-tsig
...greasy.	...fettig.	**feht**-tig
...salty.	...salzig.	**zahl**-tsig
...undercooked.	...zu wenig gekocht.	tsoo **vay**-nig geh-**kohkht**
...overcooked.	...zu lang gekocht.	tsoo lahng geh-**kohkht**
...inedible.	...nicht eßbar.	nikht **ehs**-bar
...cold.	...kalt.	kahlt
Do any of your customers return?	Kommen Ihre Kunden je zurück?	**koh**-mehn **eer**-eh **koon**-dehn yay tsoo-**rewk**
Yuck!	Igitt!	ee-**git**

Compliments

Yummy!	Mmmh!	mmm
Delicious!	Lecker!	**lehk**-er
Excellent!	Ausgezeichnet!	ows-geh-**tsīkh**-neht

It tastes very good!	Schmeckt sehr gut!	shmehkt zehr goot
I love German / this food.	Ich liebe deutsches / dieses Essen.	ikh **lee**-beh **doy**-chehs / **dee**-zehs **eh**-sehn
Better than mom's cooking.	Besser als bei Muttern.	**behs**-ser ahls bī **moo**-tern
My compliments to the chef!	Kompliment an den Koch!	kohmp-li-**mehnt** ahn dayn kohkh

Paying

The bill, please.	Die Rechnung, bitte.	dee **rehkh**-noong **bit**-teh
Together.	Zusammen.	tsoo-**zah**-mehn
Separate checks.	Getrennte Rechnung.	geh-**trehn**-teh **rehkh**-noong
Credit card O.K.?	Kreditkarte O.K.?	kreh-**deet**-kar-teh "O.K."
This is not correct.	Dies stimmt nicht.	deez shtimt nikht
Please explain.	Erklären Sie, bitte.	ehr-**klehr**-ehn zee **bit**-teh
Can you explain / itemize the bill?	Können Sie die Rechnung einzeln / erklären?	**kurn**-nehn zee dee **rehkh**-noong **īn**-tsehln / ehr-**klehr**-ehn
What if I wash the dishes?	Und wenn ich die Teller wasche?	oont vehn ikh dee **tehl**-ler **vah**-sheh
Is tipping expected?	Wird ein Trinkgeld erwartet?	virt īn **trink**-gehlt ehr-**var**-teht
What percent?	Wie viel Prozent?	vee feel proh-**tsehnt**
tip	Trinkgeld	**trink**-gehlt
Keep the change.	Stimmt so.	shtimt zoh
This is for you.	Dies ist für Sie.	deez ist fewr zee
Could I have a receipt, please?	Kann ich bitte einen Beleg haben?	kahn ikh **bit**-teh ī-nehn beh-**lehg hah**-behn

When you're ready for the bill, ask for the *Rechnung* (reckoning). The service charge is nearly always included. Tipping is not expected beyond that, though it's polite to round up to the next big coin. If you're uncertain whether to tip, ask another customer if tipping is expected (*Wird ein Trinkgeld erwartet?*). Rather than leave the tip on the

EATING

table, it's better style to say the total amount you want to pay (including the tip) when you give the waiter your money.

In Austria, a cover charge (*Gedeck*) is added at finer dining establishments. If the restaurant doesn't include a cover charge, the bread placed on your table usually costs extra. Ask to make sure you're not charged for food you don't want: "*Ist es inbegriffen?*" (Is it included?).

SPECIAL CONCERNS

In a Hurry

I'm in a hurry.	*Ich bin in Eile.*	ikh bin in **ī**-leh
We're in a hurry.	*Wir sind in Eile.*	veer zint in **ī**-leh
Will the food be ready soon?	*Ist das Essen bald bereit?*	ist dahs **eh**-sehn bahlt beh-**rīt**
I need / We need to be served quickly. Is that O.K.?	*Ich muß / Wir müssen schnell bedient werden. Geht das?*	ikh mus / veer **mews**-sehn shnehl beh-**deent vehr**-dehn. gayt dahs
I must / We must leave in 30 minutes / one hour.	*Ich muß / Wir müssen in dreißig Minuten / einer Stunde gehen.*	ikh mus / veer **mews**-sehn in **drī**-sig mee-**noo**-tehn / **ī**-ner **shtoon**-deh **gay**-hehn

Dietary Restrictions

I'm allergic to...	*Ich bin allergisch auf...*	ikh bin ah-**lehr**-gish **owf**
I / he / she cannot eat...	*Ich / er / sie darf kein...essen.*	ikh / ehr / zee darf kīn... **eh**-sehn
...dairy products.	*...Milchprodukte*	**milkh**-proh-dook-teh
...wheat.	*...Weizen*	vī-tsehn

...meat / pork.	...Fleisch / Schweinefleisch	flī sh / **shvī**-neh-flī sh
...salt / sugar.	...Salz / Zucker	zahlts / **tsoo**-ker
...shellfish.	...Meeresfrüchte	meh-rehs-**frewkh**-teh
...spicy foods.	...scharfe Gewürze	**shar**-feh geh-**vewr**-tseh
...nuts.	...Nüsse	**new**-seh
I'm a diabetic.	Ich bin Diabetiker.*	ikh bin dee-ah-**beht**-ik-er
I'd like a...	Ich hätte gern ein...	ikh **heh**-teh gehrn īn
We'd like a...	Wir hätten gern ein...	veer **heh**-tehn gehrn īn
...low-fat meal.	...wenig fettiges Gericht.	**veh**-nig **feht**-tig-ehs geh-**rikht**
...kosher meal.	...koscher Gericht.	**kohsh**-er geh-**rikht**
No salt / sugar.	Kein Salz / Zucker.	kī n zahlts / **tsoo**-ker
I eat only insects.	Ich esse nur Insekten.	ikh **ehs**-seh noor in-**zehkt**-ehn
No fat.	Ohne Fett.	**oh**-neh feht
Minimal fat.	Mit wenig Fett.	mit **vay**-nig feht
Low cholesterol.	Niedriges Cholesterin.	**nee**-dri-gehs koh-**lehs**-ter-in
No caffeine.	Koffeinfrei.	koh-fay-**in**-frī
No alcohol.	Kein Alkohol.	kī n **ahl**-koh-hohl
Organic.	Biologisch.	bee-oh-**loh**-gish
I'm a...	Ich bin...	ikh bin
...vegetarian.	...Vegetarier.*	veh-geh-**tar**-ee-er
...strict vegetarian.	...strenger Vegetarier.*	**shtrehng**-er veh-geh-**tar**-ee-er
...carnivore.	...Fleischesser.	**flī sh**-ehs-ser
...big eater.	...grosser Esser.	**groh**-ser **ehs**-ser
Is any meat or animal fat used in this?	Hat es Fleisch oder tierische Fette drin?	haht ehs flī sh **oh**-der **teer**-ish-eh **feht**-teh drin

* If you're female, add "in" to the end of these words if you're describing yourself, like this: *Diabetikerin* and *Vegetarierin*.

Children

Do you have...?	Haben Sie...?	**hah**-behn zee
...a children's portion	...eine Kinderportion	**ī**-neh **kin**-der-por-tsee-**ohn**
...a half portion	...eine halbe Portion	**ī**-neh **hahl**-beh por-tsee-**ohn**
...a high chair / booster seat	...einen Kinderhocker/ Kindersitz	**ī**-nehn **kin**-der-**hoh**-ker **kin**-der-zits
plain noodles / rice	Nudeln / Reis ohne alles	**noo**-dehln / rīs **oh**-neh **ahl**-lehs
with butter	mit Butter	mit **boo**-ter
no sauce	ohne Sauce	**oh**-neh **zoh**-seh
sauce / dressing on the side	Sauce / Salatsoße separat	**zoh**-seh /zah-**laht**-zoh-seh zeh-par-**aht**
pizza	Pizza	"pizza"
...cheese only	...nur Käse	noor **kay**-zeh
...pepperoni and cheese	...Salami und Käse	zah-**lah**-mee oont **kay**-zeh
jelly sandwich	Marmeladenbrot	mar-meh-**lah**-dehn-broht
toasted...	getoastet...	geh-**tohst**-eht
grilled...	gegrillt...	geh-**grilt**
...cheese sandwich	...Käsebrot	**kay**-zeh-broht
hot dog	frankfurter	**frahnk**-foort-er
hamburger	Hamburger	**hahm**-boor-ger
cheeseburger	Cheeseburger	**cheez**-boor-ger
French fries	Pommes frites, Pommes	pohm frits, **poh**-mehs
ketchup	Ketchup	"ketchup"
crackers	Kekse, Salzgebäck	**kehk**-seh, **zahlts**-geh-behk
Nothing spicy.	Nicht scharf gewürzt.	nikht sharf geh-**vewrtst**
Not too hot.	Nicht zu heiß.	nikht tsoo hīs
Don't let the food mix together on	Speisen auf Teller nicht	**shpī**-zehn owf **tehl**-ler nikht

the plate.	vermischen.	fehr-**mish**-ehn
He will / She will /	Er wird / Sie wird /	ehr virt / zee virt /
They will share	Sie werden unser	zee **vehr**-dehn **oon**-ser
our meal.	Essen teilen.	**eh**-sehn **tī**-lehn
Please bring the	Bitte schnell	**bit**-teh shnehl
food quickly.	servieren.	zer-**veer**-ehn
Can I / Can we	Kann ich / Können	kahn ikh / **kurn**-nehn
have an extra...?	wir ein	veer ī n
	zusätzliche...	tsoo-**zehts**-likh-eh...
	haben?	**hah**-behn
...plate	...Teller	**tehl**-ler
...cup	...Schale, Becher	**shah**-leh, **behkh**-er
...spoon / fork	...Löffel / Gabel	**lurf**-fehl / **gah**-behl
Can I / Can we	Kann ich / Können	kahn ikh / **kurn**-nehn
have two extra...?	wir zwei	veer tsvī
	zusätzliche...	tsoo-**zehts**-lish-eh...
	haben?	**hah**-behn
...plates	...Teller	**tehl**-ler
...cups	...Schalen, Becher	**shah**-lehn, **behkh**-er
...spoons / forks	...Löffel / Gabeln	**lurf**-fehl / **gah**-behln
A small milk	Eine kleine Portion	ī -neh klī-neh por-tsee-ohn
(in a plastic cup).	Milch (in einem	milkh (in ī-nehm plah-
	plastikbecher)	steek-behkh-er)
Straw(s).	Halm(e)	**hahlm**(-eh)
More napkins,	Mehr Servietten,	mehr zer-vee-**eht**-tehn
please.	bitte.	**bit**-teh
Sorry for the mess.	Entschuldigen Sie	ehnt-**shool**-dig-oong zee
	die Unordnung.	dee oon-**ord**-noong

WHAT'S COOKING

Breakfast

breakfast	Frühstück	**frew**-shtewk
bread	Brot	broht
roll	Brötchen, Semmel	**brurt**-khen, **zehm**-mehl
toast	Toast	tohst
butter	Butter	**boo**-ter
jelly	Marmelade	mar-meh-**lah**-deh
pastry	Kuchen, Gebäck	**kookh**-ehn, geh-**behk**
croissant	Gipfel	**gip**-fehl
omelet	Omelett	**ohm**-leht
egg / eggs	Ei / Eier	ī / ī-er
fried eggs	Spiegeleier	**shpee**-gehl-ī-er
scrambled eggs	Rühreier	**rew**-rī-er
soft boiled / hard boiled	weichgekocht / hartgekocht	**vīkh**-geh-kohkht / **hart**-geh-kohkht
ham	Schinken	**shink**-ehn
bacon	Speck	shpehk
cheese	Käse	**kay**-zeh
yogurt	Joghurt	**yoh**-gurt
cereal	Cornflakes	"cornflakes"
granola cereal	Müsli	**mews**-lee
milk	Milch	milkh
fruit juice	Fruchtsaft	**frookht**-zahft
orange juice (fresh)	Orangensaft (frischgepreßt)	oh-**rahn**-zhehn-zahft (frish-geh-**prehst**)
hot chocolate	heiße Schokolade	**hī**-seh shoh-koh-**lah**-deh
coffee / tea (see Drinking)	Kaffee / Tee	kah-**fay** / tay
Breakfast included?	Frühstück inklusive?	**frew**-shtewk in-kloo-**zee**-veh

Germans have an endearing and fun-to-mimic habit of greeting others in the breakfast room with a slow, miserable, *"Morgen"* (Morning). *Frühstück* is almost always included with your room and is your chance to fuel up for the day with pots of coffee, bread, rolls, cheese, ham, eggs, and sometimes local specialties. For a hearty cereal, try *Bircher Müsli,* a healthy mix of oats and nuts. If breakfast is optional, take a walk to the *Bäckerei-Konditorei* (bakery). Germany is famous for this special cultural attraction—more varieties of bread, pastries, and cakes than you ever imagined, baked fresh every morning and throughout the day. Sometimes a café is part of a *Konditorei.*

BEST OF THE WURST

Wurst mit...	voorst mit	sausage with...
...Kraut	krowt	...sauerkraut
...Brot und Senf	broht oont zehnf	...bread and mustard
Blutwurst	**bloot**-voorst	made from (gulp!) blood
Beinwurst	**bīn**-voorst	sausage made of smoked pork, herbs, and wine
Bockwurst	**bohk**-voorst	thick pork sausage (white)
Bosna	**bohs**-nah	sausage with onions and curry
Bratwurst	**braht**-voorst	thick pork sausage, grilled or fried
Burewurst	**boo**-reh-voorst	bratwurst boiled instead of grilled
Currywurst	**kuh**-ree-voorst	burewurst flavored with curry
Cervelat	sehr-veh-**la**	mild Swiss veal sausage
Cervelat Salat	sehr-veh-**la** zah-**laht**	served cold with onions, cheese, and salad dressing
Debreziner	deh-breh-**tseen**-er	thin, spicy sausage served in Austria

EATING

BEST OF THE WURST–continued

Jagdwurst	**yagt**-voorst	smoked pork with garlic and mustard
Käsekrainer	**kay**-zeh-krī-ner	sausage and cheese mixed
Leberkäse	**lay**-ber-kay-zeh	meatloaf of pork liver
Leberwurst	**lay**-ber-voorst	liverwurst
Mettwurst	**meht**-voorst	spicy, soft sausage spread
Nürnberger	**newrn**-behr-ger	fried, spiced pork and veal sausage
Stolzer Heinrich	**shtohlts**-er **hīn**-rikh	Bavarian fried pork sausage in beer sauce
Tirolerwurst	tee-**roh**-ler-voorst	Austrian smoked sausage
Weisswurst	**vīs**-voorst	very tender white boiled veal (Munich)
Wienerli / Frankfurter	**veen**-er-lee / **frahnk**-foort-er	thin frankfurter (hot dog)
Zwiebelwurst	**tsvee**-behl-voorst	liver and onion sausage

Snacks, Quick Lunches, and Appetizers

Bündnerfleisch	**bewnt**-ner-flī sh	air-dried beef, thinly sliced
Wurstplatte, Schlachtplatte (literally "slaughterplate")	**voorst**-plah-teh, **shlahkht**-plah-teh	assorted cold cuts (sausages, ham, liver paté, cow's tongue...)
Sauerkrautplatte	**zow**-er-krowt-**plah**-teh	assorted cold cuts with sauerkraut
Käsebrot	**kay**-zeh-broht	bread with cheese
Frikadelle	frik-ah-**dehl**-leh	large meatball / hamburger
Bauernomelette	**bow**-ern-ohm-leht	omelet with bacon and onion
Rollmops	**rohl**-mohps	pickled herring
Brezel	**breht**-sehl	pretzel
Toast mit Schinken und Käse	tohst mit **shink**-ehn oont **kay**-zeh	toast with ham and cheese

Say Cheese

cheese	Käse	**kay**-zeh
mild / sharp	mild / scharf	milt / sharf
cheese plate	Käseplatte,	**kay**-zeh-**plah**-teh,
	Käseteller	**kay**-zeh-**tehl**-ler
Can I try a taste?	Kann ich es	kahn ikh
	probieren?	**proh**-beer-ehn

Cheese Specialties

Allgäuer	**ahl**-goy-er	hard, mild cheese,
Bergkäse	**behrg**-kay-zeh	with holes
Altenburger	**ahlt**-ehn-boorg-er	soft, mild goat cheese
Appenzeller	**ah**-pehn-tsehl-ler	hard, sharp, tangy Swiss cow's milk cheese
Edelpilzkäse	**ay**-dehl-pilts-**kay**-zeh	mild blue cheese
Emmentaler	**ehm**-mehn-tah-ler	hard, mild Swiss cheese
Frischkäse	**frish**-kay-zeh	soft curd cheese with fresh herbs
Gorgonzola	gor-gohn-**tsoh**-lah	aged, blue-veined cheese
Gruyère	groo-**yehr**	strong-flavored, hard Swiss cheese
Limburger	**lim**-boorg-er	strong-smelling, herbed, soft cheese
Münster	**mewn**-ster	strong-tasting, hard cheese w/ caraway seed
Quark	kvark	smooth curd cheese, like thick yogurt
Tilsiter	**til**-sit-er	mild, semi-hard, and tangy cheese

The holes in Swiss cheese are made during fermentation—the more symmetrical the holes, the more expert the fermentation. Two of Switzerland's best-known specialties are cheese-based. *Käse Fondue* is Emmentaler and Gruyère cheese melted with white wine and garlic.

Eat this tasty, cheesy treat by dipping cubes of bread into it. Lose your bread in the pot and you have to kiss all the men (or women) at the table. *Raclette* is melted cheese from the Valais region. A special appliance slowly melts the bottom of the brick of cheese. Just scrape off a mound and eat it with potatoes, pickled onions, and gherkins.

Sandwiches

I'd like a sandwich.	Ich hätte gern ein Sandwich.	ikh **heh**-teh gehrn īn **zahnd**-vich
We'd like two sandwiches.	Wir hätten gern zwzi Sandwiche.	veer **heh**-tehn gehrn tvsī **zahnd**-vich-eh
toasted	getoastet	geh-**tohst**-eht
cheese	Käse	**kay**-zeh
chicken	Hähnchen	**hayn**-khehn
egg salad	Eiersalat	**ī**-er-zah-laht
fish	Fisch	fish
ham	Schinken	**shink**-ehn
jelly	Marmelade	mar-meh-**lah**-deh
peanut butter	Erdnußbutter	**ehrd**-noos-boo-ter
pork sandwich	Schweinefleisch Sandwich	**shvīn**-flī sh **zahnd**-vich
salami	Salami	zah-**lah**-mee
tuna	Thunfisch	**toon**-fish
turkey	Truthahn, Pute	**troot**-hahn, **poo**-teh
lettuce	Kopfsalat	**kohpf**-zah-laht
mayonnaise	Mayonnaise	mah-yoh-**nay**-zeh
tomatoes	Tomaten	toh-**mah**-tehn
mustard	Senf	zehnf
onions	Zwiebeln	**tsvee**-behln
Does this come cold or warm?	Wird das kalt oder warm serviert?	virt dahs kahlt **oh**-der varm zer-**veert**
Heated, please.	Erwärmt, bitte.	ehr-**vehrmt bit**-teh

KEY PHRASES: WHAT'S COOKING

food	Essen	**eh**-sehn
breakfast	Frühstück	**frew**-shtewk
lunch	Mittagessen	**mit**-tahg-eh-sehn
dinner	Abendessen	**ah**-behnt-eh-sehn
bread	Brot	broht
cheese	Käse	**kay**-zeh
soup	Suppe	**zup**-peh
salad	Salat	zah-**laht**
meat	Fleisch	flī sh
chicken	Hähnchen	**haynkh**-ehn
fish	Fisch	fish
fruit	Obst	ohpst
vegetables	Gemüse	geh-**mew**-zeh
dessert	Nachspeise	**nahkh**-shpī -zeh
Delicious!	Lecker!	**lehk**-er

If You Knead Bread

bread	Brot	broht
dark bread	dunkles Brot	**doon**-klehs broht
three-grain bread	Dreikornbrot	**drī**-korn-broht
rye bread	Roggenmischbrot	**roh**-gehn-mish-broht
dark rye bread	Schwarzbrot	**shvarts**-broht
whole grain bread	Vollkornbrot	**fohl**-korn-broht
light bread	Weißbrot	**vīs**-broht
wimpy white bread	Toast	tohst
French bread	Baguette	bah-**geht**
roll (Germany, Austria)	Brötchen, Semmel	**brurt**-khehn, **zehm**-mehl

There are hundreds of different kinds of local breads in Germany, Austria, and Switzerland. Add a visit to the neighborhood *Bäckerei* to your touring schedule and look for their specialties (*Spezialitäten*). *Stollen* (pron. **shtohl**-lehn) is a sweet Christmas bread with raisins and nuts, topped with powdered sugar.

EATING

Soups and Salads

soup (of the day)	Suppe (des Tages)	**zup**-peh (dehs **tahg**-ehs)
chicken broth...	Hühnerbrühe...	**hew**-ner-brew-heh
beef broth...	Rinderbrühe...	**rin**-der-brew-heh
...with noodles	...mit Nudeln	mit **noo**-dehln
...with rice	...mit Reis	mit rīs
stew	Eintopf	**īn**-tohpf
vegetable soup	Gemüsesuppe	geh-**mew**-zeh-zup-peh
spicy goulash soup	Gulaschsuppe	**goo**-lahsh-zup-peh
liver dumpling soup	Leberknödel- suppe	**lay**-ber-kuh-nur-dehl- zup-peh
split pea soup	Erbsensuppe	**ehrb**-sehn-zup-peh
oxtail soup	Ochsenschwanz- suppe	**okh**-sehn-shvants- zup-peh
cabbage and sausage soup	Bauernsuppe	**bow**-ern-zup-peh
Serbian-style bean soup	Serbische Bohnen- suppe	**zehr**-bi-sheh **boh**-nehn- zup-peh
salad	Salat	zah-**laht**
green salad	grüner Salat	**grew**-ner zah-**laht**
mixed salad	gemischter Salat	geh-**mish**-ter zah-**laht**
potato salad	Kartoffelsalat	kar-**tohf**-fehl-zah-laht
Greek salad	griechischer Salat	**greekh**-ish-er zah-**laht**
chef's salad...	gemischter Salat des Hauses...	geh-**mish**-ter zah-**laht** dehs **how**-zehs
small pieces of cold cuts mixed with pickles and mayonnaise	Fleischsalat	**flīsh**-zah-laht
...with ham and cheese	...mit Schinken und Käse	mit **shink**-ehn oont **kay**-zeh
...with egg	...mit Ei	mit ī
plate of various salads	Salatteller	zah-**laht**-tehl-ler

vegetable platter	*Gemüseplatte,*	geh-**mew**-zeh-plah-teh,
	Gemüseteller	geh-**mew**-zeh-tehl-ler
lettuce	*Salat*	zah-**laht**
tomato	*Tomate*	toh-**mah**-teh
onion	*Zwiebel*	**tsvee**-behl
cucumber	*Gurken*	**gur**-kehn
oil / vinegar	*Öl / Essig*	url / **ehs**-sig
salad dressing	*Salatsoße*	zah-**laht**-zoh-seh
dressing on	*Salatsoße*	zah-**laht**-zoh-seh
the side	*separat*	zeh-par-**aht**
What is in	*Was ist in*	vahs ist in
this salad?	*diesem Salat?*	**dee**-zehm zah-**laht**

In Germany, soup is often served as a first course to the large midday meal (*Mittagessen*). Typical German salads usually consist of a single ingredient with dressing, such as *Gurkensalat* (sliced cucumber marinated in a sweet vinaigrette) and *Tomatensalat* (tomatoes in vinaigrette with dill). For a meaty slad, try a Fleischsalat (**flish**-zah-laht)—chopped cold cuts mixed with pickles and mayonnaise.

The *Salatbar* (salad bar) is becoming a global phenomenon. You'll normally be charged by the size of the plate for one load. Choose a *Teller* (plate) that is *kleiner* (small), *mittlerer* (medium), or *großer* (large). Budget travelers eat a cheap and healthy lunch by grabbing a small plate and stacking it high.

Seafood

seafood	*Meeresfrüchte*	**meh**-rehs-**frewkh**-teh
assorted seafood	*gemischte*	geh-**mish**-teh
	Meeresfrüchte	**meh**-rehs-**frewkh**-teh
fish	*Fisch*	fish
clams	*Muscheln*	**moo**-shehln
cod	*Dorsch*	dorsh
herring	*Hering*	**hehr**-ing
pike	*Hecht*	hehkht
salmon	*Lachs*	lahkhs

trout	Forelle	foh-**rehl**-leh
tuna	Thunfisch	**toon**-fish
What's fresh today?	Was ist heute frisch?	vahs ist **hoy**-teh frish
Do you eat this part	Ißt man diesen Teil?	ist mahn **dee**-zehn tīl
Just the head, please	Nur den Kopf, bitte.	noor dayn kohpf **bit**-teh

Poultry

poultry	Geflügel	geh-**flew**-gehl
chicken	Hähnchen	**haynkh**-ehn
roast chicken	Brathähnchen	**braht**-hayn-khehn
duck	Ente	**ehn**-teh
turkey	Truthahn, Pute	**troot**-hahn, **poo**-teh
How long has this been dead?	Wie lange ist dieses tier schon tot?	vee **lahng**-eh ist **dee**-zehs teer shohn toht

Meat

meat	Fleisch	flīsh
bacon	Speck	shpehk
beef	Rindfleisch	**rint**-flīsh
beef steak	Beefsteak	**beef**-shtayk
brains	Hirn	hehrn
bunny	Kaninchen	kah-**neen**-khehn
cutlet	Kotelett	**koht**-leht
ham	Schinken	**shink**-ehn
lamb	Lamm	lahm
liver	Leber	**lay**-ber
mixed grill	Grillteller	**gril**-tehl-ler
organs	Innereien	in-neh-**rī**-ehn
pork	Schweinefleisch	**shvī**-neh-flīsh
roast beef	Rinderbraten	**rin**-der-brah-tehn
sausage	Wurst	voorst
tripe	Kutteln	**kut**-tehln
veal	Kalbfleisch	**kahlp**-flīsh

AVOIDING MIS-STEAKS

tenderloin	*Filet mignon*	"filet mignon"
T-bone	*T-bone*	**tay**-bohn
tenderloin of T-bone	*Lendenstück*	**lehn**-dehn-shtewk
raw	*roh*	roh
very rare	*blutig*	**bloo**-tig
rare	*rot*	roht
medium	*halbgar*	**hahlp**-gar
well-done	*gar,*	gar,
	durchgebraten	**durkh**-geh-brah-tehn
very well-done	*ganz gar*	gahnts gar
almost burnt	*fast verkohlt*	fahst fehr-**kohlt**

Main Course Specialties

Fleischtorte	**flĪsh**-tor-teh	meat pie
Geschnetzeltes	geh-**shneht**-sehl-tehs	strips of veal or chicken braised in a rich sauce and served with noodles or Rösti (Switz.)
Gulasch (suppe)	**goo**-lahsh (**zup**-peh)	spicy stew
Hasenpfeffer / Rehpfeffer	**hah**-zehn-**pfeh**-fer / **ray**-pfeh-fer	spicy rabbit / deer stew with mushrooms and onions (Aus. and Switz.)
Kohlroulade	**kohl**-roo-lah-deh	cabbage leaves stuffed with minced meat
Matjesfilet auf Hausfrauenart	maht-yehs-fi-**lay** owf **hows**-frow-ehn-art	herring filets sautéed with apples, onions, and sour cream (Ger.)
Maultaschen	**mowl**-tahsh-ehn	German ravioli filled with various fillings like veal, cheese, and spinach
Ratsherrentopf	**rahts**-hehr-rehn-tohpf	stew of roasted meat with potatoes
Rösti	**rur**-shtiee	Swiss hashbrowns often mixed with cheese, ham eggs, and/or vegetables

EATING

Schweinebraten	**shvīn**-eh-brah-tehn	roasted pork with gravy
Spargel	**shpar**-gehl	big, white asparagus in season in May, served as a cream soup or on a plate with cream sauce
Tafelspitz	**tah**-fehl-shpits	boiled beef with apple and horseradish sauce (Aus. and Switz.)
Tiroler Bauernschmaus	tee-**roh**-ler **bow**-ern-shmows	several types of meat served w/ sauerkraut, potatoes, and dumplings
Wiener Schnitzel	**vee**-ner **shnit**-sehl	breaded, fried veal cutlet—Viennese style

During fall hunting season in the Alps, venison
(*Wildbret*) and chamois (*Gämse*, a goat-like antelope)
are often featured on the menu.

Eating Italian in Germany

Italian restaurants provide a good budget break from
Wurst und *Kraut*. Here are the words you'll find on the
menu: *Spaghetti, Pizza, Tomaten, Schinken* (ham), *Käse*
(cheese), *Champignons* (mushrooms), *Paprika* (peppers),
Ei (egg), *Pepperoni* (small hot peppers), *Zwiebeln* (onions),
Artischocken (artichokes), *Basilikum* (basil), *Meeresfrnchte*
(seafood), *Muscheln* (clams), and *Vegetaria* (vegetarian).

How Food is Prepared

assorted	*gemischte*	geh-**mish**-teh
baked	*gebacken*	geh-**bah**-kehn
boiled	*gekocht*	geh-**kohkht**
braised	*geschmort*	geh-**shmort**
broiled	*ofengegrillt*	**ohf**-ehn-geh-grilt
cold	*kalt*	kahlt
cooked	*gekocht*	geh-**kohkht**
deep-fried	*frittiert*	frit-**eert**

fillet	*Filet*	fi-**lay**
fresh	*frisch*	frish
fried	*gebraten*	geh-**brah**-tehn
grilled	*gegrillt*	geh-**grilt**
homemade	*hausgemacht*	**hows**-geh-mahkht
hot	*heiß*	hīs
in cream sauce	*in Rahmsauce*	in **rahm**-zoh-seh
medium	*halbgar*	**hahlp**-gar
microwave	*Mikrowelle*	**mee**-kroh-vehl-leh
mild	*mild*	milt
mixed	*gemischte*	geh-**mish**-teh
poached	*pochierte*	pohkh-ee-**ehr**-teh
rare	*rot*	roht
raw	*roh*	roh
roast	*Braten*	**brah**-tehn
roasted	*geröstet*	geh-**rurs**-teht
sautéed	*pfannengebraten*	**pfahn**-nehn-geh **braht**-ehn
smoked	*geräuchert*	geh-**roykh**-ert
sour	*sauer*	**zow**-er
spicy hot	*scharf*	sharf
steamed	*gedünstet*	geh-**dewn**-steht
stuffed	*gefüllt*	geh-**fewlt**
sweet	*süß*	zews
topped with cheese	*mit Käseschicht*	mit **kay**-zeh-shnit
well-done	*gar*	gar
with rice	*mit Reis*	mit rīs

STYLES OF COOKING

Art	style of cooking
Bauern	farmer-style, with potatoes (good and hearty)
Französisch	French
Hausfrauen	housewife-style, with apples, onions, and sour cream
Hausgemacht	homemade
Italienisch	Italian
Jäger	hunter style, with mushrooms and gravy
Wiener	Viennese, breaded and fried

EATING

Side Dishes

green salad	grüner Salat	**grew**-ner zah-**laht**
mixed salad	gemischter Salat	geh-**mish**-ter zah-**laht**
potato salad	Kartoffelsalat	kar-**tohf**-fehl-zah-laht
potatoes	Kartoffeln	kar-**tohf**-fehln
roasted potatoes	Bratkartoffeln	**braht**-kar-tohf-fehln
mashed potatoes	Kartoffelbrei,	kar-**tohf**-fehl-brī
	Kartoffelstock	kar-**tohf**-fehl-shtohk
French fries	Pommes frites,	pom frits,
	Pommes	**poh**-mehs
potato pancake	Reibekuchen	**rī**-beh-kookh-ehn
hashbrowns	Rösti	**rur**-shtiee
rice	Reis	rī s
liver / bread...	Leber / Semmel...	**lay**-ber / **zehm**-mehl
...dumplings	...knödel	kuh-**nur**-dehl
sauerkraut	Sauerkraut	**zow**-er-krowt
noodles	Nudeln	**noo**-dehln
spaghetti	Spaghetti	shpah-**geh**-tee
boiled German-style noodles	Spätzle	**shpehts**-leh

Veggies

vegetables	Gemüse	geh-**mew**-zeh
mixed vegetables	gemischtes	geh-**mish**-tehs
	Gemüse	geh-**mew**-zeh
with vegetables	mit Gemüse	mit geh-**mew**-zeh
artichoke	Artischocke	art-i-**shoh**-keh
asparagus	Spargel	**shpar**-gehl
beans	Bohnen	**boh**-nehn
beets	rote Beete	**roh**-teh **bee**-teh
broccoli	Brokkoli	**brohk**-koh-lee
cabbage	Kohl	kohl
carrots	Karotten	kah-**roht**-tehn
cauliflower	Blumenkohl	**bloo**-mehn-kohl
corn	Mais	mī s
cucumber	Gurken	**goor**-kehn

eggplant	Auberginen	oh-ber-**zhee**-nehn
garlic	Knoblauch	kuh-**noh**-blowkh
green beans	grüne Bohnen	**grew**-neh **boh**-nehn
leeks	Lauch	lowkh
lentils	Linsen	**lin**-zehn
mushrooms	Pilze	**pilt**-seh
olives	Oliven	oh-**leev**-ehn
onions	Zwiebeln	**tsvee**-behln
peas	Erbsen	**ehrb**-zehn
pepper...	Paprika...	**pah**-pree-kah
...green / red / yellow	...grün / rot / gelb	grewn / roht / gehlp
pickles	Essiggurken	**ehs**-sig-goor-kehn
potatoes	Kartoffeln	kar-**tof**-fehln
radishes	Radieschen	rah-**dee**-shehn
spinach	Spinat	shpee-**naht**
tomatoes	Tomaten	toh-**mah**-tehn
zucchini	Zucchini	tsoo-**kee**-nee

Fruits

apple	Apfel	**ahp**-fehl
apricot	Aprikose	ahp-ri-**koh**-zeh
banana	Banane	bah-**nah**-neh
berries	Beeren	**behr**-ehn
blackberries	Brombeeren	**brohm**-behr-ehn
canteloupe	Melone	meh-**loh**-neh
cherry	Kirsche	**keer**-sheh
cranberries	Preiselbeeren	p **rī**-sehl-behr-ehn
date	Dattel	**daht**-tehl
fig	Feige	**fī**-geh
fruit	Obst	ohpst
grapefruit	Pampelmuse,	pahm-pehl-**moo**-zeh,
	Grapefruit	**grahp**-froot
grapes	Trauben	**trow**-behn
lemon	Zitrone	tsee-**troh**-neh
orange	Apfelsine,	ahp-fehl-**zee**-neh,
	Orange	oh-**rahn**-zheh
peach	Pfirsich	**pfeer**-zikh
pear	Birne	**beer**-neh
pineapple	Ananas	**ahn**-ahn-ahs

EATING

plum	Pflaume, Zwetsche	**pflow**-meh, **tsveht**-sheh
prune	Backpflaume	**bahk**-pflow-meh
raspberries	Himbeeren	**him**-behr-ehn
red currants	Johannis- beeren	yoh-**hahn**-nis- behr-ehn
strawberries	Erdbeeren	**ehrt**-behr-ehn
tangerine	Mandarine	mahn-dah-**ree**-neh
watermelon	Wassermelone	**vah**-ser-meh-loh-neh

Nuts

nut	Nuß	noos
almond	Mandel	**mahn**-dehl
chestnut	Kastanie	**kahs**-tah-nee
coconut	Kokosnuß	**koh**-kohs-noos
hazelnut	Haselnuß	**hah**-zehl-noos
peanut	Erdnuß	**ehrd**-noos
pistachio	Pistazien	pis-**tahts**-ee-ehn
walnut	Wallnuß	**vahl**-noos

Teutonic Treats

dessert	Nachspeise, Nachtisch	**nahkh**-shpī-zeh, **nahkh**-tish
strudel	Strudel	**shtroo**-dehl
cake	Kuchen	**kookh**-ehn
a piece of cake	ein Stück Kuchen	īn stewk **kookh**-ehn
sherbet	Sorbet	zor-**beht**
fruit cup	Früchtebecher	**frewkh**-teh-behkh-er
fruit salad	Obstsalat	**ohpst**-zah-laht
tart	Törtchen	**turt**-khehn
pie	Torte	**tor**-teh
cream	Sahne, Rahm	**zah**-neh, rahm
whipped cream	Schlagsahne	**shlahg**-zah-neh
chocolate	Schokolade	shoh-koh-**lah**-deh

chocolate mousse	Mousse	moos
pudding	Pudding	"pudding"
pastry	Gebäck	geh-**behk**
cookies	Kekse	**kayk**-zeh
candy	Bonbons	**bon**-bonz
low calorie	kalorienarm	kah-loh-**ree**-ehn-arm
homemade	hausgemacht	**hows**-geh-mahkht
We'll split one.	Wir teilen eine.	veer **tī**-lehn **ī**-neh
Two forks /	Zwei Gabeln /	tsvī **gah**-behln /
spoons, please.	Löffel, bitte.	**lurf**-fehl **bit**-teh
I shouldn't,	Ich sollte nicht,	ikh **zohl**-teh nikht
but...	aber...	**ah**-ber
Delicious!	Köstlich! Lecker!	**kurst**-likh / **lehk**-er
Heavenly.	Himmlisch.	**him**-lish
Death by	Tod durch	tohd durkh
chocolate.	Schokolade.	shoh-koh-**lah**-deh
Better than sex.	Besser als Sex.	**behs**-ser ahls zehx
A moment on	Ein Weilchen auf	īn **vīl**-khehn owf
the lips, forever	der Zunge, ewig	dehr **tsoong**-eh **eh**-vig
on the hips.	auf der Hüfte.	owf dehr **hewf**-teh
I'm in seventh	Ich bin im siebten	ikh bin im **zeeb**-tehn
heaven.	Himmel.	**him**-mehl

Ice Cream

ice cream	Eis	īs
scoop	Kugel	**koog**-ehl
cone	Waffel	**vah**-fehl
small bowl	Schale	**shah**-leh
chocolate	Schokolade	shoh-koh-**lah**-deh
vanilla	Vanille	vah-**nil**-leh
strawberry	Erdbeere	**ehrt**-behr-eh
lemon	Zitrone	tsee-**troh**-neh
rum-raisin	Malaga	**mah**-lah-gah
hazelnut	Haselnuß	**hah**-zehl-noos
Can I taste it?	Kann ich probieren?	kahn ikh **proh**-beer-ehn

EATING

Dessert Specialties

Apfelstrudel	**ahp**-fehl-**shtroo**-dehl	apples and raisins in puff pastry
Berliner	behr-**lee**-ner	raspberry-filled doughnut
Cremeschnitte	**krehm**-shnit-eh	flaky pastry layered w/ cream, topped w/ vanilla and chocolate icing
Germknödel	**gehrm**-ku-nur-dehl	sourdough dumplings
Kaiserschmarren	**kīz**-er-shmah-rehn	shredded pancakes w/ raisins, sugar, and cinnamon
Linzertorte	**lints**-er-tor-teh	almond cake w/ raspberry (Austria)
Mandelgipfel	**mahn**-dehl-gip-fehl	almond-filled croissant
Mohnkuchen	**mohn**-kookh-ehn	poppy-seed cake
Mohr im Hemd (literally "Moor in a shirt")	mor im hehmt	chocolate pudding w/ chocolate sauce
Nürnberger Lebkuchen	**newrn**-behr-ger **layb**-kookh-ehn	gingerbread in every shape and size (German Christmas specialty)
Pfannkuchen	**pfahn**-kookh-ehn	thin pancakes often served w/ berries and powdered sugar
Rissoles	**ree**-zohl	pear tarts
Rote Grütze	**roh**-teh **grew**-tseh	raspberry and currant pudding topped w/ cream
Sachertorte	**zahkh**-er-tor-teh	chocolate cake layered w/ chocolate cream
Salzburger Nockerl	**zalts**-boorg-er **nohk**-erl	fluffy baked pudding/flan
Schwarzwälder Kirschtorte	**shvarts**-vehl-der **keersh**-tor-teh	Black Forest cake—chocolate with cherries, cream, and rum
Streußelkuchen	**shtroy**-sehl-kookh-ehn	coffeecake squares w/ crumbled topping

Vermicell	vehr-mee-**sehl**	noodle-shaped chestnut mousse w/ rum and cream (Swiss)
Zwetschgenknödel	**tsvehtsh**-gehn-ku-nur-dehl	plum dumplings boiled, then fried in bread crumbs

Two great dessert specialties are Vienna's famous super-chocolate cake, *Sachertorte,* and Germany's Black Forest cherry cake, called *Schwarzwälder Kirschtorte.* This diet-killing chocolate cake with cherries and rum can be found all over Germany. For a little bit of Italy, try *Gelato* (Italian ice cream) at a *gelateria.*

In Germany at Christmas time, look for the spiced gingerbread, *Lebkuchen,* packaged inside tins shaped like cottages, bells, animals, and fanciful Christmas designs.

The Swiss changed the world in 1875 with their invention of milk chocolate. Nestlé, Suchard, and Lindt are the major producers and sometimes offer factory tours—and samples, of course. *Nußnougat Crème* (milk chocolate hazelnut) is a popular spread all over Europe, especially the Italian brand, Nutella. Anything dipped in Nutella becomes a tasty souvenir.

EATING

Drinking

Water and Juice

mineral water...	*Mineralwasser...*	min-eh-**rahl**-vah-ser
...with / without gas	*...mit / ohne Gas*	mit / **oh**-neh gahs
mixed with mineral water	*gespritzt*	geh-**shpritst**
tap water	*Leitungswasser*	**lī**-toongs-vah-ser
fruit juice	*Fruchtsaft*	**frookht**-zahft
100% juice (literally "pure")	*reiner Fruchtsaft*	**rī**-ner **frookht**-zahft
orange juice	*Orangensaft*	oh-**rahn**-zhehn-zahft
freshly squeezed	*frischgepreßt*	frish-geh-**prehst**
apple juice	*Apfelsaft*	**ahp**-fehl-zahft
grapefruit juice	*Grapefruitsaft*	**grahp**-froot-zahft
lemonade	*Limonade*	lee-moh-**nah**-deh
with / without...	*mit / ohne...*	mit / **oh**-neh
...sugar	*...Zucker*	**tsoo**-ker
...ice	*...Eis*	īs
glass / cup	*Glas / Tasse*	glahs / **tah**-seh
small / large	*kleine / große*	**klī**-neh / **groh**-seh
bottle	*Flasche*	**flah**-sheh
Is the water safe to drink?	*Ist das Trinkwasser?*	ist dahs **trink**-vahs-ser

On a menu, you'll find drinks listed under *Getränkekarte* (drink menu). If you ask for *Wasser* in a restaurant, you'll be served mineral water. Germans rarely drink tap water at the table; develop a taste for the inexpensive and classier *Mineralwasser*. Bubbly mineral water might be listed on menus or in stores as "*mit Kohlensäure*" (with carbon dioxide) or "*mit Sprudel*" (with bubbles). But when you're requesting it, the easy-to-remember "*mit Gas*" will do the trick. To get water without bubbles, look for *"ohne Kohlensäure / Sprudel / Gas."* If you have your heart set on free tap water, ask for *Leitungswasser* and be persistent.

Soda-lovers seek out the Fanta/Coke blend called *Mezzo Mix* or *Spezi*. *Rivella* is a dairy-based Swiss soft drink. To get a diet drink, use the word "light" instead of "diet" (for instance, Diet Coke is called "Coke Light").

Milk

milk	Milch	milkh
whole milk	Vollmilch	**fohl**-milkh
skim milk	Magermilch	**mah**-ger-milkh
fresh milk	frische Milch	**frish**-eh milkh
acidophilus	Acidophilus, Kefir	ah-**see**-doh-fi-lus, **keh**-feer
buttermilk	Buttermilch	**boo**-ter-milkh
chocolate milk	Schokomilch	**shoh**-koh-milkh
hot chocolate	heiße Schokolade, Kakao	**hī**-seh shoh-koh-**lah**-deh, **kah**-kow
Ovaltine (grain-based hot drink)	Ovomaltine	oh-voh-mahl-**tee**-neh
milkshake	Milchshake	**milkh**-shayk

KEY PHRASES: DRINKING

drink	Getränk-	geh-**traynk**-
(mineral) water	(Mineral-) Wasser	(min-eh-**rahl**-) **vah**-ser
tap water	Leitungswasser	**lī**-toongs-vah-ser
milk	Milch	milkh
juice	Saft	zahft
coffee	Kaffee	kah-**fay**
tea	Tee	tay
wine	Wein	vīn
beer	Bier	beer
Cheers!	Prost!	prohst

EATING

Coffee and Tea

coffee	*Kaffee*	kah-**fay**
espresso	*Espresso*	ehs-**prehs**-soh
cappuccino	*Cappuccino*	kah-poo-**chee**-noh
decaffeinated	*koffeinfrei, Haag*	koh-fay-**in**-frī , hahg
instant coffee	*Pulverkaffee, Nescafe*	pool-ver-kah-**fay**, "Nescafe"
black	*schwarz*	shvarts
with cream / milk	*mit Sahne / Milch*	mit **zah**-neh / milkh
with sugar	*mit Zucker*	mit **tsoo**-ker
iced coffee or	*Eiskaffee*	**īs**-kah-fay
coffee w/ ice cream		
hot water	*heißes Wasser*	**hī**-sehs **vah**-ser
tea / lemon	*Tee / Zitrone*	tay / tsee-**troh**-neh
tea bag	*Teebeutel*	**tay**-boy-tehl
iced tea	*Eistee*	**īs**-tay
herbal tea	*Kräutertee*	**kroy**-ter-tay
peppermint tea	*Pfefferminztee*	**pfeh**-fer-mints-tay
fruit tea	*Früchte Tee*	**frewkh**-teh tay
little pot	*Kännchen*	**kaynkh**-ehn
Another cup.	*Noch eine Tasse.*	nohkh **ī**-neh **tah**-seh

AUSTRIAN COFFEE LINGO

In Austria, coffee has a language of its own.

Brauner	**brown**-er	coffee w/ small pitcher of milk
Melange	meh-**lahnzh**	coffee with lots of milk
Mokka, Schwarzer	**moh**-kah, **shvart**-ser	black espresso
Obers	**oh**-bers	cream
Masagran	**mahs**-ah-grahn	iced coffee with maraschino liqueur
Wiener Eiskaffee	**veen**-er **īs**-kah-fay	coffee w/ vanilla ice-cream and whipped cream
Maria Theresia	mah-**ree**-ah teh-**ray**-zee-ah	coffee with orange liqueur

Wine

I would like...	*Ich hätte gern...*	ikh **heh**-teh gehrn
We would like...	*Wir hätten gern...*	veer **heh**-tehn gehrn
...a glass...	*...ein Glas...*	īn glahs
...an eighth liter...	*...ein Achtel...*	īn **ahkh**-tehl
...a quarter liter...	*...ein Viertel...*	īn **feer**-tehl
...a carafe...	*...eine Karaffe...*	ī-neh kah-**rah**-feh
...a half bottle...	*...eine halbe Flasche...*	ī-neh **hahl**-beh **flah**-sheh
...a bottle...	*...eine Flasche...*	ī-neh **flah**-sheh
...a five-liter jug...	*...einen fünf-Liter Krug...*	ī-nehn **fewnf**-lee-ter kroog
...a barrel...	*...ein Faß...*	īn fahs
...a vat...	*...ein Riesenfaß...*	īn **rī**-zeh-fahs
...of red wine.	*...Rotwein.*	**roht**-vīn
...of white wine.	*...Weißwein.*	**vīs**-vīn
...the wine list.	*...die Weinkarte.*	dee **vīn**-kar-teh

Three-quarters of German, Austrian, and Swiss wines are white. As you travel through wine-growing regions, you'll see *Probieren* signs inviting you in for a free (or nearly free) wine tasting.

White wines to look for in Germany are *Riesling* (fruity and fragrant), *Müller Thurgau* (best when young, smooth, and sweet), *Gewürztraminer* (intense and spicy), and *Grauburgunder* (soft, full-bodied white—known as *Pinot Gris* or *Grigio* in other countries). In Austria, consider *Grüner Veltliner* (dry, light), *Riesling, Pinot Blanc* (semi-dry, fruity nose), and *Heuriger* wine (new wine). In Switzerland, try the tart, white *Fendant* and the lovely, fruity *St. Saphorin* from the slopes above Lake Geneva.

Typically, you order a glass of wine by saying *Ein Viertel* (a quarter liter) or *Ein Achtel* (an eighth liter). In Switzerland, a *Pfiff* is two deciliters of red wine, and a *Bocalino* is a small, decorated ceramic jug with two deciliters of a light Swiss red wine called *Dole*.

EATING

Wine Words

wine	*Wein*	vīn
red wine	*Rotwein*	**roht**-vīn
white wine	*Weißwein*	**vīs**-vīn
rosé	*Rosé*	roh-**zay**
table wine	*Tafelwein*	**tah**-fehl-vīn
house wine	*Hausmarke*	**hows**-mar-keh
local	*einheimisch*	**īn**-hī-mish
of the region	*regional*	reh-gee-ohn-**ahl**
sparkling	*sprudelnd*	**shproo**-dehlnt
fruity	*fruchtig*	**frookh**-tig
light / heavy	*leicht / schwer*	līkht / shvehr
sweet	*süß, lieblich*	zews, **leeb**-likh
medium	*halbsüß*	**hahlp**-zews
semi-dry	*halbtrocken*	**hahlp**-trohk-ehn
dry	*trocken*	**trohk**-ehn
very dry	*sehr trocken*	zehr **trohk**-ehn
full-bodied	*vollmundig*	fohl-**moon**-dig
mature	*trinkreif*	**trink**-rīf
wine spritzer	*Wein gespritzt*	vīn geh-**shpritst**
cork	*Korken*	**kor**-kehn
corkscrew	*Korkenzieher*	**kor**-kehn-tsee-her
grapes	*Weintrauben*	**vīn**-trow-behn
vintage	*Weinlese*	**vīn**-lay-zeh
vineyard	*Weinberg*	**vīn**-behrg
wine-tasting	*Weinprobe*	**vīn**-proh-beh
What is a good year (vintage)?	*Welcher Jahrgang (Weinlese) ist gut?*	**vehlkh**-er **yar**-gahng (**vīn**-lay-zeh) ist goot
What do you recommend?	*Was empfehlen Sie?*	vahs ehmp-**fay**-lehn zee

Unfermented wine is called *Most*. Partially fermented wine is called *Federweißer* (pron. feh-der-vī-ser) in Germany, *Suuser* (pron. zoo-ser) in Switzerland, and *Sturm* (pron. shtoorm) in Austria. *Staubiger* (pron. shtow-big-er) is a cloudy, fully fermented Austrian wine.

EATING

Wine Labels

As with most European countries, Germany has a strict set of rules dictating how quality wine is produced: the higher the percentage of natural grape sugar, the higher the alcohol content, the higher the rating. You can identify the origin of German wine by the color or shape of the bottle: brown (Rhine), green (Mosel), or jug-shaped (Franconian). The *Weinsiegel* (wine seal) on the neck of the bottle is also color-coded—yellow for dry, green for semi-dry, and red for sweet. Switzerland and Austria produce less wine than Germany but follow similar standards. Listed below are terms to help you decipher all of the information on a German, Austrian, or Swiss wine label.

Kabinett	lightest and usually driest wine
Spätlese, Auslese, Beerenauslese, Trockenbeerenauslese, Eiswein	late harvest wines (listed in order of grape sugar content from high to highest)
Qualitätswein	mid-quality wine
QmP (Qualitätswein mit Prädikat)	highest quality wine
QbA (Qualitätswein bestimmter Anbaugebiete)	quality wine of a specific region
Sekt	sparkling champagne-like wine
Heuriger	new wine (Austria)
Landwein	country wine, dry to semi-dry
Tafelwein	table wine—lowest category

Beer

beer	*Bier*	beer
bar	*Kneipe* (Germany), *Beisl* (Austria), *Baiz* (Switzerland)	ku-**nī**-peh, **bī**-zehl, bīts
from the tap	*vom Faß*	fom fahs
bottle	*Flasche*	**flah**-sheh

light—but not "lite"	*Helles*	**hehl**-lehs
dark	*Dunkles*	**doonk**-lehs
local / imported	*einheimisch /*	**īn**-hī-mish /
	importiert	im-por-tee-**ehrt**
small / large	*kleines / großes*	**klī**-nehs / **groh**-sehs
half-liter	*Halbes*	**hahl**-behs
liter (Bavarian)	*Maß*	mahs
low calorie	*Light*	"light"
cold	*kalt*	kahlt
colder	*kälter*	**kehl**-ter

Germany is Europe's beer capital. Its beer is regulated by the German Purity law (*Reinheitsgebot*), the oldest food and beverage law in the world. Only four ingredients may be used in German beer: malt, yeast, hops, and water. Pils is a bottom-fermented, full beer and *Weizen* is wheat-based. *Malzbier* is the non-alcoholic malt beer that children drink. The barely alcoholic *Nährbier*, considered healthy and caloric, is for fattening up skinny kids. *Radler* (which means biker) is a refreshing mix of beer and lemonade, invented in Munich for cyclists on hot days. A *Berliner Weisse mit Schuß* is a wheat beer with a shot of fruit syrup. *Bockbier*, from Bavaria, is a strong amber called "liquid bread" and is consumed mostly at Easter and Christmas. *Märzen* is a light beer brewed in March (*März*), then stored for *Oktoberfest*.

Drink menus list exactly how many deciliters you'll get in your glass. A "5 dl" beer is half a liter, or about a pint. When you order beer, ask for "*Ein Halbes*" for a half liter or "*Ein Maß*" for a whole liter (about a quart). Some beer halls serve beer only by the liter! Children are welcome in beer halls.

In Austria, order "*ein Bier*" and you get a light, basic beer in a standard beer mug. Order a *Pils* and you get a more flavorful, stronger beer in a tulip glass. A *Dunkel* is the darkest, served in a straight, tall glass. In the German-speaking regions of Switzerland, a *Stange* is a *Pils* in a tall, fluted glass. The popular *Weizenbier*, which is poured slowly to build its frothy head thick and high, is served in a large rounded-top glass with a wedge of lemon.

Bar Talk

Let's go out for a drink.	Komm, wir gehen aus für ein Drink.	kohm veer **gay**-hehn ows fewr īn drink
May I buy you a drink?	Kann ich dir ein Drink spendieren?	kahn ikh deer īn drink shpehn-**deer**-ehn
My treat.	Ich lade ein.	ikh **lah**-deh īn
The next one's on me.	Die nächste Runde geht auf mich.	dee **nehkh**-steh **roon**-deh gayt owf mikh
What would you like?	Was hättest du gern?	vahs **heh**-tehst doo gehrn
I'll have a...	Ich nehme ein...	ikh **nay**-meh īn
I don't drink.	Ich trinke keinen Alcohol.	ikh **trink**-eh **kīn**-ehn **ahl**-koh-hohl
alcohol-free	alkoholfrei	**ahl**-koh-hohl-**frī**
What is the local specialty?	Was ist die Spezialität hier?	vahs ist dee **shpayt**-see-ahl-ee-**tayt** heer
What is a good man's / woman's drink?	Was ist ein gutes Männer-/Damen-Getränk?	vahs ist īn **goo**-tehs **meh**-ner / dah-mehn geh-**trehnk**
Straight.	Pur.	poor
With / Without...	Mit / Ohne...	mit / **oh**-neh
...alcohol.	...Alkohol.	**ahl**-koh-hohl
...ice.	...Eis.	īs
One more.	Noch eins.	nokh īns
Cheers!	Prost!	prohst
To your health!	Auf Ihre Gesundheit!	owf **eer**-eh geh-**zoond**-hīt
To you!	Zum Wohl!	tsoom vohl
Long life!	Langes Leben!	**lahng**-ehs **lay**-behn
I'm...	Ich bin...	ikh bin
...tipsy.	...beschwippst.	beh-**shvipst**
...a little drunk.	...ein bißchen betrunken.	īn **bis**-yehn beh-**trunk**-ehn
...blitzed.(literally "completely blue")	...völlig blau.	**furl**-lig blow

EATING

...a boozehound.	...Schnapshund.	**shnahps**-hoont
I'm hung over.	Ich hab' ein Kater.	ikh hahp īn **kah**-ter
(literally "I have		
a tomcat.")		

The bartender will often throw a coaster (*Bierdeckel*) down at your place and keep track of your bill by keeping a stroke tally on the coaster. To get your bill, hand the bartender your coaster.

Spirits

Apfelwein (especially popular in Frankfurt)	**ahp**-fehl-vīn	apple wine
Appenzeller	**ah**-pehn-tsehl-ler	digestive made from
Alpenbitter	**ahl**-pehn-bit-ter	65 different flowers and roots
Aprikosenlikör	ahp-ri-koh-zehn-li-kur	apricot liqueur
Eierlikör	ī-er-li-kur	eggnog-like liqueur
Glühwein	glew-vīn	hot spiced wine
Jägermeister	**yay**-ger-mī-ster	anise- and herb-flavored digestive
Jägertee(literally "hunter's tea")	**yay**-ger-tay	half tea and half brandy with rum
Kirsch	keersh	firewater from crushed cherry pits
Korn, Marc	korn, mark	grain-based Schnaps
Obstler	**ohpst**-ler	fruit brandy
Pflümli	**pflewm**-lee	plum Schnaps (Switzerland)
Schnaps	shnahps	high-alcohol brandy (firewater!)

For drinks at reasonable prices, do what the locals do. Visit an atmospheric *Weinstube* (wine bar) or *Biergarten* (beer garden) to have a drink and chat with friends.

EATING

Picnicking

At the Grocery

Self-service?	*Selbstbedienung?*	**zehlpst**-beh-dee-noong
Ripe for today?	*Jetzt reif?*	yehtst rīf
Does this need to be cooked?	*Muß man das kochen?*	mus mahn dahs **kohkh**-ehn
Can I taste it?	*Kann ich probieren?*	kahn ikh proh-**beer**-ehn
Fifty grams.	*Fünfzig Gramm.*	**fewnf**-tsig grahm
One hundred grams.	*Hundert Gramm.*	**hoon**-dert grahm
More. / Less.	*Mehr. / Weniger.*	mehr / **vay**-nig-er
A piece.	*Ein Stück.*	īn shtewk
A slice.	*Eine Scheibe.*	ī-neh **shī**-beh
Four slices.	*Vier Scheiben.*	feer **shī**-behn
Sliced.	*In Scheiben.*	in **shī**-behn
Half.	*Halb.*	hahlp
A small bag.	*Eine kleine Tüte.*	ī-neh **klīn**-eh **tew**-teh
A bag, please.	*Eine Tüte, bitte.*	īn **tew**-teh **bit**-teh
Can you make me / us...?	*Können Sie mir / uns... machen?*	**kurn**-nehn zee meer / oons... **mahkh**-ehn
...a sandwich	*...ein Sandwich*	īn **zahnd**-vich
...two sandwiches	*...zwei Sandwiche*	tsvī **zahnd**-vich-eh
To take out.	*Zum Mitnehmen.*	tsoom **mit**-nay-mehn
Can I use the microwave?	*Kann ich die Mikrowelle benutzen?*	kahn ikh dee mee-kroh-**vehl**-leh beh-**noot**-sehn
May I borrow a...?	*Kann ich ein... leihen?*	kahn ikh īn... **lī**-hehn
Do you have a...?	*Haben Sie ein...?*	**hah**-behn zee īn
Where can I buy / find a...?	*Wo kann ich ein... kaufen / finden?*	voh kahn ikh īn... **kow**-fehn / **fin**-dehn
...corkscrew	*...Korkenzieher*	**kor**-kehn-tsee-her
...can opener	*...Dosenöffner*	**doh**-zehn-urf-ner
Is there a park nearby?	*Gibt es einen Park in der Nähe?*	gipt ehs **ī**-nehn park in dehr **nay**-heh

| Where is a good place to picnic? | *Wo ist gut picknicken?* | voh ist goot **pik**-nik-ehn |
| Is picnicking allowed here? | *Darf man hier picknicken?* | darf mahn heer **pik**-nik-ehn |

Tasty Picnic Words

picnic	*Picknick*	**pik**-nik
open air market	*Markt*	markt
grocery store	*Lebensmittel-geschäft*	**lay**-behns-mit-tehl-geh-**shehft**
supermarket	*Supermarkt*	**zoo**-per-markt
delicatessen	*Feinkostgeschäft*	**fīn**-kohst-geh-**shehft**
bakery	*Bäckerei*	behk-eh-**rī**
pastry shop	*Konditorei, Patisserie*	kohn-dee-toh-**rī**, pah-tis-er-**ee**
cheese shop	*Käserei*	kay-zeh-**rī**
sandwich	*Sandwich*	**zahnd**-vich
bread	*Brot*	broht
roll	*Brötchen, Semmel*	**brurt**-khehn, **zehm**-mehl
ham	*Schinken*	**shink**-ehn
sausage	*Wurst*	voorst
cheese	*Käse*	**kay**-zeh
mustard...	*Senf...*	zehnf
mayonnaise...	*Mayonnaise...*	mah-yoh-**nay**-zeh
...in a tube	*...in der Tube*	in dehr **too**-beh
mild / sharp / sweet	*mild / scharf / süß*	milt / sharf / zews
yogurt	*Joghurt*	**yoh**-gurt
fruit	*Obst*	ohpst
juice	*Saft*	zaft
cold drinks	*kalte Getränke*	**kahl**-teh geh-**trehnk**-eh
plastic...	*Plastik...*	**plah**-stik
...spoon / fork	*...löffel / gabel*	**lurf**-fehl / **gah**-behl
paper...	*Papier...*	pah-**peer**
...plate / cup	*...teller / becher*	**tehl**-ler / **behkh**-er

EATING

Assemble your picnic at a *Markt* (open-air market) or *Supermarkt* (supermarket)—or get a fast snack at an *Obst* (fruit stand) or *Imbiß* (fast food stand).

At the grocery, you buy meat and cheese by the gram. One hundred grams is about a quarter pound, enough for two sandwiches. To weigh and price your produce, put it on the scale, push the photo or number (keyed to the bin it came from), and then stick your sticker on the food. To get real juice, look for 100% or *kein Zucker* on the label. *Drink* or *Trink* is pop. In Switzerland, *bio* means organically grown, and a *Bioläderli* is a store that sells organic products.

MENU
DECODER

German/English

This handy German-English decoder (followed by an English-German decoder) won't list every word on the menu, but it'll get you *Bratwurst* (pork sausage) instead of *Blutwurst* (blood sausage).

Abendessen	dinner
Achtel	eighth liter
Allgäuer Bergkäse	hard, mild cheese with holes
Altenburger	soft, mild goat cheese
Ananas	pineapple
Apfel	apple
Apfelsaft	apple juice
Apfelsine	orange
Apfelstrudel	apples and raisins in puff pastry
Appenzeller	sharp, hard Swiss cheese
Appenzeller Alpenbitter	digestive made from flower and roots
Aprikose	apricot
Artischocke	artichoke
Aubergine	eggplant

Bäckerei	bakery
Backpflaume	prune
Banane	banana
Bauern	farmer style—from the garden
Bauernsuppe	cabbage and sausage soup
Becher	small glass
Bedienung	service
Beere	berry
Beilagen	side dishes
Beinwurst	smoked pork, herb sausage
Berliner	raspberry-filled doughnut
Bier	beer
biologisch	organic
Birne	pear
Blumenkohl	cauliflower
Blutwurst	blood sausage
Bockbier	Bavarian amber beer
Bockwurst	white pork sausage
Bohnen	beans
Braten	roast
Brathähnchen	roast chicken
Bratwurst	pork sausage
Brezel	pretzel
Brokkoli	broccoli
Brombeere	blackberry
Brot	bread
Brötchen	roll
Brotzeit	snack
Bündnerfleisch	air-cured beef
Burewurst	boiled Bratwurst
Butterhörnchen	croissant
Champignon	mushroom
chinesisch	Chinese
Churer Fleischtorte	meat pie (Switz.)
Cremeschnitte	Napoleon
Currywurst	curry-flavored Burewurst
Dattel	date

Debreziner	spicy Hungarian sausage
Dorsch	cod
Dreikornbrot	three-grain bread
dunkel	dark
durchgebraten	well-done
Edelpilzkäse	mild blue cheese
Ei	egg
Eier	eggs
Eierlikör	eggnog-like liqueur
einheimisch	local
Eintopf	stew
Eintritt	cover charge
Eis	ice cream; ice
Eiskaffee	iced coffee, coffee with ice cream
Eistee	iced tea
Emmentaler	mild and hard Swiss cheese
Ente	duck
Erbsen	peas
Erbsensuppe	split pea soup
Erdbeere	strawberry
Erdnuß	peanut
erster Gang	first course
Essen	food
Essig	vinegar
Essiggurken	pickles
Feige	fig
Feinkostgeschäft	delicatessen
Fett	fat
Fisch	fish
Flasche	bottle
Fleisch	meat
Fleischsalat	cubed deli-meat salad
Forelle	trout
französisch	French
Frikadelle	large meatball, hamburger
frisch	fresh
frischgepreßt	freshly squeezed

Frischkäse	soft curd cheese with herbs
Frittaten	sliced pancakes
frittiert	deep-fried
Früchtebecher	fruit cup
fruchtig	fruity (wine)
Fruchtsaft	fruit juice
Frühstück	breakfast
Gang	course
ganz gar	very well-done
gar	well-done
Gas	carbonation
Gasthaus, Gasthof	country inn and restaurant
Gaststätte, Gaststube	informal restaurant
Gebäck	pastry
gebraten	baked
gedünstet	steamed
Geflügel	poultry
gefüllt	stuffed
gegrillt	grilled
gekocht	cooked
gemischt	mixed
gemischter Salat	mixed salad
Gemüse	vegetables
Gemüseplatte/-teller	vegetable platter
Gemüsesuppe	vegetable soup
geräuchert	smoked
Germknödel	sourdough dumplings
geröstet	roasted
geschmort	braised
Geschnetzeltes	meat slivers in a rich sauce with noodles or Rösti
gespritzt	with mineral water
Getränke	beverages
Getränkekarte	drink menu
Glas	glass
Glühwein	hot spiced wine
Graubrot	whole wheat bread

Grillteller	mixed grill
groß	big
grün	green
grüner Salat	green salad
Gruyère	strong-flavored Swiss cheese
Gulasch	spicy stew (goulash)
Gurken	cucumber
Gutsabfüllung	estate bottled (wine)
Hähnchen	chicken
halb	half
halbgar	medium
halbsüß	semi-sweet, medium (wine)
halbtrocken	semi-dry (wine)
hartgekocht	hard-boiled
Haselnuß	hazelnut
Hauptspeise	main course
Haus	house
Hausfrauen Art	housewife style—apples, onions, and sour cream
hausgemacht	homemade
heiß	hot
heiße Schockolade	hot chocolate
helles	light (beer)
Hering	herring
Heurigen	young wine, wine bar with food
Himbeere	raspberry
Honig	honey
Hühnerbrühe	chicken broth
importiert	imported
inklusive	included
Innereien	organs
italienisch	Italian
Jagdwurst	smoked pork, garlic, and mustard sausage
Jäger	hunter style—with mushrooms and gravy
Jägermeister	anise and herb digestive

Jägertee	tea with brandy and rum
Joghurt	yogurt
Johannisbeere	red currant
Kaffee	coffee
Kaiserschmarren	shredded pancakes with raisins, sugar, and cinnamon
Kakao	cocoa
Kalbfleisch	veal
kalt	cold
Kaninchen	bunny
Kännchen	small pot of tea
Karaffe	carafe
Karotte	carrot
Karte	menu
Kartoffel	potato
Kartoffelsalat	potato salad
Käse	cheese
Käse Fondue	melted Swiss cheeses eaten with cubes of bread
Käsebrot	cheese with bread
Käsekrainer	sausage mixed with cheese
Käseplatte/-teller	cheese platter
Käserei	cheese shop
Kastanie	chestnut
Kekse	cookies
Kinderteller	children's portion
Kirsche	cherry
klein	small
Kleinigkeit	snack
Kneipe	bar, tavern
Knoblauch	garlic
Knödel	dumpling
Kohl	cabbage
Kohlensäure	carbonation
Kohlroulade	stuffed cabbage leaves
Kokosnuß	coconut
Konditerei	pastry shop

Korkenzieher	corkscrew
koscher	kosher
köstlich	delicious
Kotelett	cutlet
Kraut	sauerkraut
Kräutertee	herbal tea
Kugel	scoop
Kutteln	tripe
Lamm	lamb
Leber	liver
Leberkäse	pork liver meatloaf
Leberknödelsuppe	liver dumpling soup
Leberwurst	liverwurst
Lebkuchen	gingerbread
leicht	light
lieblich	sweet (wine)
Limburger	strong-smelling, soft cheese with herbs
limonade	clear pop or lemonade
Linsen	lentils
Linzertorte	almond cake with raspberry
Mais	corn
Malaga	rum-raisin flavor
Malzbier	non-alcoholic kids' beer
Mandarine	tangerine
Mandel	almond
Mandelgipfli	almond croissant (Switz.)
Marmelade	jelly
Maß	liter of beer
Matjesfilet	herring filets
Maultaschen	ravioli
Meeresfrüchte	seafood
Melone	cantaloupe
Mettwurst	spicy, soft sausage spread
Miesmuscheln	mussels
Mikrowelle	microwave
Milch	milk
mild	mild

Mineralwasser	mineral water
mit	with
Mittagessen	lunch
Mohnkuchen	poppy-seed cake
Mohr im Hemd	chocolate pudding with chocolate sauce
Muscheln	clams
Müsli	granola cereal
Nachspeise	dessert
Nachtisch	dessert
Nudel	noodle
Obst	fruit
Obstler	fruit brandy
Obstsalat	fruit salad
Ochsenschwanzsuppe	oxtail soup
oder	or
ohne	without
Öl	oil
Oliven	olives
Omelett	omelet
Orange	orange
Orangensaft	orange juice
Pampelmuse	grapefruit
Paprika	bell pepper
Pfannekuchen	pancakes
Pfeffer	pepper
Pfefferminz	peppermint
Pfirsich	peach
Pflaume	plum
Pflümli	plum Schnaps
Pistazien	pistachio
pochieren	poached
Pommes (frites)	French fries
Preiselbeere	cranberry
Pute	turkey (north)
Quark	smooth curd cheese
Quittung	receipt

Raclette	melted cheese with vegetable side dishes (Switz.)
Radiesch	radish
Radler	beer and lemonade
Rahmsauce	cream sauce
Ratsheerentopf	roasted meats and potato stew
Ratskeller	cellar restaurant
Rinderbraten	roast beef
Rinderbrühe	beef broth
Rindfleisch	beef
Rissoles	pear tarts
Roggenmischbrot	rye bread
roh	raw
Rollmops	pickled herring
Rösti	hash browns (Switz.)
rote Beete	beets
Rote Grütze	raspberry and currant pudding
Rotwein	red wine
Rühreier	scrambled eggs
Sachertorte	chocolate cake layered with chocolate cream
Sahne	cream
Salat	salad
Salatsoße	salad dressing
Salatteller	plate of various salads
Salz	salt
Salzburger Nockerl	fluffy, baked pudding/flan
sättigend	filling
Sauce	sauce
Sauerbraten	braised beef
Schalentiere	shellfish
scharf	spicy
Scheibe	slice
Schinken	ham
Schlachtplatte	assorted cold meats
Schlagsahne	whipped cream
schnell	fast

Schnellimbiß	fast food
Schnitzel	thinly sliced pork or veal
Schokolade	chocolate
Schwarzbrot	dark rye bread
Schwarzwälder Kirschtorte	Black Forest cake—chocolate, cherries, and cream
Schweinebraten	roasted pork with gravy
Schweinefleisch	pork
sehr	very
Semmel	roll
Senf	mustard
Serbische Bohnensuppe	bean soup eaten in Austria
Sorbet	sherbet
Soße	sauce
Spargel	asparagus
Spätzle	German-style noodles
Speck	bacon
Spezialität	specialty
Spiegeleier	fried eggs
Spinat	spinach
Sprudel	carbonation (bubbles)
sprudelnd	sparkling
Stollen	Christmas bread with fruit and nuts
Stolzer Heinrich	pork sausage fried in beer
Streußelkuchen	coffeecake squares
Stück	piece
Suppe	soup
süß	sweet
Tafelspitz	boiled beef with apples and horseradish
Tafelwein	table wine
Tage	day
Tageskarte, Tagesgericht	menu of the day
Tasse	cup
Tee	tea
Teller	plate

Thunfisch	tuna
Tilsiter	mild, tangy, firm cheese
Tiroler Bauernschmaus	various meats with sauerkraut, potatoes, and dumplings
Tirolerwurst	Austrian smoked sausage
Tomaten	tomatoes
Törtchen	tart
Torte	cake
Traube	grape
trocken	dry
Truthahn	turkey (south)
typisch	local
und	and
Vanille	vanilla
Vegetarier	vegetarian
Vermicell	noodle-shaped chestnut mousse
Viertel	quarter liter
Vollkornbrot	dark bread, whole wheat
vollmundig	full-bodied (wine)
vom Faß	on tap (beer)
Vorspeise	appetizers
Waffel	cone
Wallnuß	walnut
Wasser	water
Wassermelone	watermelon
weichgekocht	soft-boiled
Wein	wine
Weinberg	vineyard
Weinkarte	wine list
Weinlese	vintage (wine)
Weinprobe	wine tasting
Weintrauben	grapes (wine)
weiß	white
Weißbrot	light bread
Weißwein	white wine
Weißwurst	boiled veal sausage
Weizen	wheat

Weizenbier	wheat beer
Wiener	Viennese style—breaded and fried
Wiener Schnitzel	breaded, pan-fried veal
Wienerli	thin frankfurter (hot dog)
Wurst	sausage
Zahnstocher	toothpick
Zitrone	lemon
Zucchini	zucchini
Zucker	sugar
zum Mitnehmen	"to go"
Zwetschge	plum
Zwetschgenknödel	fried plum dumplings
Zwiebel	onion
Zwiebelbraten	pot roast with onions
Zwiebelwurst	liver and onion sausage

English/German

almond	mandel
and	und
appetizers	Vorspeise
apple	Apfel
apple juice	Apfelsaft
apricot	Aprikose
artichoke	Artischocke
asparagus	Spargel
bacon	Speck
baked	gebraten
bakery	Bäckerei
banana	Banane
bar	Kneipe
beans	Bohnen
beef	Rindfleisch
beef broth	Rinderbrühe
beef, braised	Sauerbraten
beef, roast	Rinderbraten
beer	Bier
beer and lemonade	Radler
beer on tap	Bier vom Faß
beer, dark	dunkles
beer, light	helles
beer, non-alcoholic kids'	Malzbier
beer, wheat	Weizenbier
beets	rote Beete
bell pepper	Paprika
berry	Beere
beverages	Getränke
big	groß
blackberry	Brombeere
bottle	Flasche
bread	Brot

bread, dark rye	Schwarzbrot
bread, dark whole wheat	Vollkornbrot
bread, light	Weißbrot
bread, rye	Roggenmischbrot
bread, three-grain	Dreikornbrot
bread, whole wheat	Graubrot
breakfast	Frühstück
broccoli	Brokkoli
bunny	Kaninchen
cabbage	Kohl
cabbage leaves, stuffed	Kohlroulade
cake	Torte
cake, Black Forest	Schwarzwälder Kirschtorte
cake, chocolate, layered with chocolate cream	Sachertorte
cake, poppy-seed	Mohnkuchen
cantaloupe	Melone
carafe	Karaffe
carbonation	Gas, Kohlensäure, Sprudel
carrot	Karotte
cauliflower	Blumenkohl
cheese	Käse
cheese platter	Käseplatte, käseteller
cheese shop	Käserei
cheese with bread	Käsebrot
cherry	Kirsche
chestnut	Kastanie
chicken	Hähnchen
chicken broth	Hühnerbrühe
chicken, roast	Brathähnchen
children's portion	Kinderteller
Chinese	chinesisch
chocolate	Schokolade
clams	Muscheln
cocoa	Kakao
coconut	Kokosnuß

cod	Dorsch
coffee	Kaffee
coffee with ice cream or iced coffee	Eiskaffee
cold	kalt
cone	Waffel
cooked	gekocht
cookies	Kekse
corkscrew	Korkenzieher
corn	Mais
course	Gang
course, first	erster Gang
course, main	Hauptspeise
cover charge	Eintritt
cranberry	Preiselbeere
cream	Sahne
cream sauce	Rahmsauce
cream, whipped	Schlagsahne
croissant	Butterhörnchen
cucumber	Gurken
cup	Tasse
cutlet	Kotelett
dark	dunkel
date	Dattel
day	Tage
delicatessen	Feinkostgeschäft
delicious	köstlich
dessert	Nachspeise, Nachtisch
dinner	Abendessen
doughnut (raspberry-filled)	Berliner
drinks (menu)	Getränke(-karte)
dry	trocken
duck	Ente
dumpling	Knödel
dumplings, fried plum	Zwetschgenknödel
dumplings, sourdough	Germknödel

egg	Ei
eggs	Eier
eggs, fried	Spiegeleier
eggs, scrambled	Rühreier
eggplant	Aubergine
fast	schnell
fast food	Schnellimbiß
fat	Fett
fig	Feige
filling	sättigend
fish	Fisch
food	Essen
French	französisch
French fries	Pommes (frites)
fresh	frisch
freshly squeezed	frischgepreßt
fried or deep-fried	frittiert
fruit	Obst
fruit cup	Früchtebecher
fruity (wine)	fruchtig
full-bodied (wine)	vollmundig
garlic	Knoblauch
gingerbread	Lebkuchen
glass	Glas
glass, small	Becher
goulash (spicy stew)	Gulasch
granola cereal	Müsli
grape	Traube
grapefruit	Pampelmuse
grapes for wine	Weintrauben
green	grün
grill, mixed	Grillteller
grilled	gegrillt
half	halb
ham	Schinken
hard-boiled	hartgekocht

hashbrowns (Switz.)	Rösti
hazelnut	Haselnuß
herring	Hering
herring filets	Matjesfilet
herring, pickled	Rollmops
homemade	hausgemacht
honey	Honig
hot	heiß
hot chocolate	heiße Schockolade
house	Haus
ice cream	Eis
iced tea	Eistee
imported	importiert
included	inklusive
Italian	italienisch
jelly	Marmelade
juice, apple	Apfelsaft
juice, fruit	Fruchtsaft
juice, orange	Orangensaft
kosher	koscher
lamb	Lamm
lemon	Zitrone
lemonade (usually clear soda)	limonade
lentils	Linsen
light	leicht
light (beer)	helles
liter	Liter
liter of beer	Maß
liter, half	Halbes
liter, quarter	Viertel
liter, eighth	Achtel
liver	Leber
liverwurst	Leberwurst
local	einheimisch, typisch
lunch	Mittagessen
meat	Fleisch

medium (meat)	halbgar
menu	Karte
menu of the day	Tageskarte, Tagesgericht
microwave	Mikrowelle
mild	mild
milk	Milch
mineral water	Mineralwasser
mineral water, mixed with	gespritzt
mixed	gemischt
mushroom	Champignon
mussels	Miesmuscheln
mustard	Senf
noodle	Nudel
noodles, German-style	Spätzle
oil	Öl
olives	Oliven
omelet	Omelett
on tap (beer)	vom Faß
onion	Zwiebel
onion pot roast	Zwiebelbraten
or	oder
orange	Orange, Apfelsine
orange juice	Orangensaft
organic	biologisch
organs	Innereien
pancakes	Pfannekuchen
pancakes, shredded, with raisins, sugar, and cinnamon	Kaiserschmarren
pancakes, sliced	Frittaten
pastry	Gebäck
pastry shop	Konditerei
peach	Pfirsich
peanut	Erdnuß
pear	Birne
pear tarts	Rissoles
peas	Erbsen

pepper	Pfeffer
peppermint	Pfefferminz
pickles	Essiggurken
piece	Stück
pineapple	Ananas
pistachio	Pistazien
plate	Teller
plum	Pflaume, Zwetschge
poached	pochieren
pork	Schweinefleisch
pork, roasted, with gravy	Schweinebraten
potato	Kartoffel
poultry	Geflügel
pretzel	Brezel
prune	Backpflaume
rabbit	Kaninchen
radish	Radiesch
raspberry	Himbeere
ravioli	Maultaschen
raw	roh
receipt	Quittung
red currant	Johannisbeere
restaurant	Restaurant
restaurant, cellar	Ratskeller
restaurant, country inn	Gasthaus, Gasthof
restaurant, informal	Gaststätte, Gaststube
roast	Braten
roasted	geröstet
roll	Brötchen, Semmel
salad	Salat
salad dressing	Salatsoße
salad, cubed deli-meat	Fleischsalat
salad, fruit	Obstsalat
salad, green	grüner Salat
salad, mixed	gemischter Salat
salad, potato	Kartoffelsalat

salads, plate of various	Salatteller
salt	Salz
sauce	Soße, Sauce
sauce, cream	Rahmsauce
sauerkraut	Kraut
sausage	Wurst
sausage, blood	Blutwurst
sausage, boiled Bratwurst	Burewurst
sausage, boiled veal	Weißwurst
sausage, pork	Bratwurst
sausage, pork, fried in beer	Stolzer Heinrich
sausage, spicy Hungarian	Debreziner
sausage, thin frankfurter (hot dog)	Wienerli
sausage, white pork	Bockwurst
scoop	Kugel
seafood	Meeresfrüchte
semi-dry (wine)	halbtrocken
service	Bedienung
shellfish	Schalentiere
sherbet	Sorbet
side dishes	Beilagen
slice	Scheibe
small	klein
smoked	geräuchert
snack	Brotzeit, Kleinigkeit
soft-boiled	weichgekocht
soup	Suppe
soup, cabbage and sausage	Bauernsuppe
soup, oxtail	Ochsenschwanzsuppe
soup, split pea	Erbsensuppe
soup, vegetable	Gemüsesuppe
sparkling	sprudelnd
specialty	Spezialität
spicy	scharf
spinach	Spinat

steamed	gedünstet
stew	Eintopf
stew, spicy (goulash)	Gulasch
strawberry	Erdbeere
stuffed	gefüllt
sugar	Zucker
sweet	süß
sweet (wine)	süß, lieblich
tangerine	Mandarine
tart	Törtchen
tea	Tee
tea with brandy and rum	Jägertee
tea, herbal	Kräutertee
tea, iced	Eistee
tea, small pot	Kännchen
"to go"	zum Mitnehmen
tomatoes	Tomaten
toothpick	Zahnstocher
tripe	Kutteln
trout	Forelle
tuna	Thunfisch
turkey	Pute (north), Truthahn (south)
vanilla	Vanille
veal	Kalbfleisch
veal or pork, thinly sliced	Schnitzel
veal, breaded, pan-fried	Wiener Schnitzel
vegetable plate	Gemüseplatte, Gemüseteller
vegetables	Gemüse
vegetarian	Vegetarier
very	sehr
vinegar	Essig
vineyard	Weinberg
vintage (wine)	Weinlese
walnut	Wallnuß
water	Wasser
watermelon	Wassermelone

well-done	gar, durchgebraten
well-done, very	ganz gar
wheat	Weizen
whipped cream	Schlagsahne
white	weiß
wine	Wein
wine flavor, dry	trocken
wine flavor, fruity	fruchtig
wine flavor, full-bodied	vollmundig
wine flavor, semi-dry	halbtrocken
wine flavor, semi-sweet (medium)	halbsüß
wine flavor, sweet	süß, lieblich
wine grapes	Weintrauben
wine list	Weinkarte
wine tasting	Weinprobe
wine vintage	Weinlese
wine, hot spiced	Glühwein
wine, red	Rotwein
wine, table	Tafelwein
wine, white	Weißwein
wine, young	Heurigen
with	mit
without	ohne
yogurt	Joghurt
zucchini	Zucchini

ACTIVITIES

Sightseeing

Where?

Where is...?	*Wo ist...?*	voh ist
...the tourist information office	*...das Touristeninformationsbüro*	dahs too-**ris**-tehn-in-for-maht-see-**ohns**-bew-roh
...the best view	*...der beste Ausblick*	dehr **behs**-teh **ows**-blick
...the main square	*...der Hauptplatz*	dehr **howpt**-plahts

KEY PHRASES: SIGHTSEEING

Where is...?	*Wo ist...?*	voh ist
How much is it?	*Wie viel kostet das?*	vee feel **kohs**-teht dahs
What time does this...?	*Um wie viel Uhr ist hier...?*	oom vee feel oor ist heer
...open / close	*...geöffnet / geschlossen*	geh-**urf**-neht / geh-**shloh**-sehn
Do you have a guided tour?	*Haben Sie eine geführte Tour?*	**hah**-behn zee **ī**-neh geh-**fewr**-teh toor
When is the next tour in English?	*Wann ist die nächste Tour auf Englisch?*	vahn ist dee **nehkh**-steh toor owf **ehng**-lish

---

...the old town center	...die Altstadt	dee **ahlt**-shtaht
...the town hall	...das Rathaus	dahs **raht**-hows
...the museum	...das Museum	dahs moo-**zay**-um
...the castle	...die Burg	dee boorg
...the palace	...das Schloß	dahs shlohs
...the ruins	...die Ruine	dee roo-**ee**-neh
...an amusement park	...einen Vergnügungspark	**ī**-nehn fehrg-**new**-goongs-park
...the entrance / exit	...der Eingang / Ausgang	dehr **īn**-gahng / **ows**-gahng
...the toilet	...die Toilette	dee toh-**leh**-teh
Nearby is there a...?	Gibt es in der Nähe ein...?	gipt ehs in dehr **nay**-heh īn
...fair (rides, games)	...Kirmes	**keer**-mehs
...festival (music)	...Festival	fehs-tee-**vahl**

At the Sight

Do you have...?	Haben Sie...?	**hah**-behn zee
...information...	...Auskunft	**ows**-koonft
...a guidebook...	...einen Stadtführer / ein Reisebuch.	**ī**-nehn **shtaht**-fewr-er / īn **rī**-zeh-bookh
...in English	...auf Englisch	owf **ehng**-lish
Is it free?	Ist es umsonst?	ist ehs oom-**zohnst**
How much is it?	Wie viel kostet das?	vee feel **kohs**-teht dahs
Is the ticket good all day?	Gilt der Schein den ganzen Tag lang?	gilt dehr shīn dayn **gahn**-tsehn tahg lahng
Can I get back in?	Kann ich wieder hinein?	kahn ikh **vee**-der hin-**īn**
What time does this open / close?	Um wie viel Uhr ist hier geöffnet / geschlossen?	oom vee feel oor ist heer geh-**urf**-neht / geh-**shloh**-sehn
When is the last entry?	Wann ist letzter Einlaß?	vahn ist **lehts**-ter **īn**-lahs

Please

PLEASE let me / us in!	BITTE, lassen Sie mich / uns hinein!	**bit**-teh **lah**-sehn zee mikh / oons hin-**īn**
I've / We've...	Ich bin / Wir sind...	ikh bin / veer zint
...traveled all the way from ___.	...extra aus ___ gekommen.	**ehk**-strah ows ___ geh-**koh**-mehn
I must / We must...	Ich muß / Wir müssen...	ikh mus / veer **mew**-sehn
...leave tomorrow.	...morgen abreisen.	**mor**-gehn **ahp**-rī-zehn
I promise I'll / we'll be fast.	Ich verspreche, mich / uns zu beeilen.	ikh fehr-**shprehkh**-eh mikh / oons tsoo beh-**ī**-lehn
I promised my mother on her deathbed that I'd see this.	Ich habe meiner Mutter am Sterbebett versprochen, das zu sehen.	ikh **hah**-beh **mī**-ner **moo**-ter ahm **shtehr**-beh-beht fehr-**shprohkh**-ehn dahs tsoo **zay**-hehn
I've always wanted to see this.	Ich wollte das schon immer sehen.	ikh **vohl**-teh dahs shohn **im**-mehr **zay**-hen

Tours

Do you have...?	Haben Sie...?	**hah**-behn zee
...an audioguide	...einen Tonbandführer	**ī**-nehn **tohn**-bahnt-fewr-er
...a guided tour...	...eine geführte Tour...	**ī**-neh geh-**fewr**-teh toor
...a city walking tour...	...eine geführte Stadtbesichtigung...	**ī**-neh geh-**fewr**-teh shtaht-beh-**zikh**-tig-oong
...in English	...auf Englisch	owf **ehng**-lish
When is the next tour in English?	Wann ist die nächste Führung auf Englisch?	vahn ist dee **nehkh**-steh **few**-roong owf **ehng**-lish
Is it free?	Ist es umsonst?	ist ehs oom-**zohnst**
How much is it?	Wie viel kostet das?	vee feel **kohs**-teht dahs
How long does it last?	Wie lange dauert es?	vee **lahng**-eh **dow**-ert ehs

| Can I / Can we join a tour in progress? | Kann ich / Können wir mit der angefangenen Führung gehen? | kahn ikh / **kurn**-nehn veer mit dehr ahn-geh-**fahng**-ehn-ehn **few**-roong **gay**-hehn |

Entrance Signs

Erwachsene	adults
kombinierter Eintritt	combo-ticket
Führung	guided tour
Ausstellung	exhibit
Standort	you are here (on map)

Discounts

You may be eligible for a discount at tourist sights, in hotels, or on buses and trains—ask.

Is there a discount for...?	Gibt es Ermäßigung für...?	gipt ehs ehr-**may**-see-goong fewr
...youth	...Kinder	**kin**-der
...students	...Studenten	shtoo-**dehn**-tehn
...families	...Familien	fah-**meel**-yehn
...seniors	...Senioren	zehn-**yor**-ehn
...groups	...Gruppen	**groop**-ehn
I am...	Ich bin...	ikh bin
He / She is...	Er / Sie ist...	ehr / zee ist
...___ years old.	...___ Jahre alt.	___ **yah**-reh ahlt
...extremely old.	...extrem alt.	ehx-**trehm ahlt**

In the Museum

Where is...?	Wo ist...?	voh ist
I'd like to see...	Ich möchte gerne... sehen.	ikh **murkh**-teh **gehr**-neh... **zay**-hehn
We'd like to see...	Wir möchten gerne... sehen.	veer **murkh**-tehn **gehr**-neh... **zay**-hehn
Photo / Video O.K.?	Fotografieren / Videofilmen O.K.?	foh-toh-grah-**fee**-ehn / **Vee**-deh-oh-fil-mehn "O.K."

No flash.	Kein Blitz.	kīn blits
No tripod.	Stativ verboten.	shtah-**teef** fehr-**boh**-tehn
I like it.	Es gefällt mir.	ehs geh-**fehlt** meer
It's so...	Es ist so...	ehs ist zoh
...beautiful.	...schön.	shurn
...ugly.	...häßlich.	**hehs**-likh
...strange.	...seltsam.	**zehlt**-zahm
...boring.	...langweilig.	**lahng**-vī-lig
...interesting.	...interessant.	in-tehr-ehs-**sahnt**
...pretentious.	...angeberisch.	**ahn**-gay-ber-ish
...thought- provoking.	...Gedanken anregend.	geh-**dahnk**-ehn **ahn**-ray-gehnt
...B.S.	...Blödsinn.	**blurd**-zin
I don't get it.	Kapier' ich nicht.	kah-**peer** ikh nikht
Is it upside down?	Ist es verkehrt?	ist ehs fehr-**kehrt**
Who did this?	Wer hat das gemacht?	vehr haht dahs geh-**mahkht**
How old is this?	Wie alt ist das?	vee ahlt ist dahs
Wow!	Fantastisch! Toll!	fahn-**tahs**-tish / tohl
My feet have had it!	Meine Füße sind ganz plattgelaufen!	**mī**-neh **few**-seh zint gahnts **plaht**-geh-lowf-ehn
I'm exhausted!	Ich bin fix und fertig!	ikh bin fix oont **fehr**-tig
We're exhausted!	Wir sind fix und fertig!	veer zint fix oont **fehr**-tig

Be careful when planning your sightseeing. Many museums close one day a week, and many stop selling tickets 45 minutes or so before they close. Some sights are tourable only by groups with a guide. Individuals usually end up with the next German escort. To get an English tour, call in advance to see if one's scheduled. Individuals can often tag along with a large tour group.

Art and Architecture

art	Kunst	koonst
artist	Künstler	**kewnst**-ler
painting	Gemälde	geh-**mayl**-deh

self-portrait	Selbstporträt / Eigenbildnis	**zehlpst**-por-trayt / **ī**-gehn-bilt-nis
sculptor	Bildhauer	**bilt**-how-er
sculpture	Skulptur	skoolp-**toor**
architect	Architekt	**arkh**-i-tehkt
architecture	Architektur	arkh-i-tehk-**toor**
original	Original	oh-rig-ee-**nahl**
restored	restauriert	rehs-tow-**reert**
B.C.	vor Christus (v. Chr.)	for **kris**-tus
A.D.	nach Christus (n. Chr.)	nahkh **kris**-tus
century	Jahrhundert	yar-**hoon**-dert
style	Stil	shteel
copy by ___	Kopie von ___	koh-**pee** fohn ___
after the style of ___	im Stil von ___	im shteel fohn ___
from the	aus der	ows dehr
school of ___	Schule von ___	**shoo**-leh fohn ___
abstract	abstrakt	ahp-**strahkt**
ancient	altertümlich	ahl-ter-**tewm**-likh
Art Nouveau	Jugendstil	**yoo**-gehnd-shteel
Baroque	barock	bah-**rohk**
classical (music)	klassisch	**klah**-sish
classical period	klassizistisch	klah-sits-**is**-tish
Gothic	gothisch	**goh**-tish
Impressionist	impressionistisch	im-preh-see-oh-**nis**-tish
medieval	mittelalterlich	**mit**-tehl-ahl-ter-likh
modern	modern	moh-**dehrn**
neoclassical	neoklassizistisch	**nay**-oh-klah-sits-**is**-tish
Renaissance	Renaissance	**rehn**-ah-sahns
Romanesque	romanisch	roh-**mahn**-ish
Romantic	Romantik	roh-**mahn**-tik

Castles and Palaces

castle	Burg	boorg
palace	Schloß	shlohs
treasury	Schatzkammer	**shots**-kah-mer
hall	Saal	zahl

kitchen	Küche	**kewkh**-eh
cellar	Keller	**kehl**-ler
dungeon	Verlies	fehr-**lees**
castle keep	Wehr	vehr
moat	Burggraben	**boorg**-grah-behn
fortified wall	Burgmauer	**boorg**-mow-er
tower	Turm	toorm
fountain, well	Brunnen	**broon**-nehn
garden	Garten	**gar**-tehn
king / emperor	König / Kaiser	**kur**-nig / **kī**-zer
queen / empress	Königin/ Kaiserin	**kur**-nig-in / **kī**-zer-in
knights	Ritter	**rit**-ter

You'll see the words *Burg* (castle) and *Berg* (mountain) linked to the end of names (such as Rothenburg and Ehrenberg). Salzburg means "salt-castle."

Religious Words

cathedral	Kathedrale, Dom	kah-teh-**drah**-leh, dohm
church	Kirche	**keerkh**-eh
monastery	Kloster	**klohs**-ter
mosque	Moschee	moh-**shay**
synagogue	Synagoge	zin-ah-**goh**-geh
chapel	Kapelle	kah-**pehl**-leh
altar	Altar	ahl-**tar**
bells	Glocken	**glohk**-ehn
choir	Chor	kor
cloister	Kloster	**kloh**-ster
cross	Kreuz	kroyts
crypt	Krypte	**krip**-teh
dome	Kuppel	**kup**-pehl
organ	Orgel	**org**-ehl
pulpit	Kanzel	**kahnts**-ehl
relic	Reliquie	reh-**leek**-vee-eh
treasury	Schatzkammer	**shots**-kah-mer
saint	Heiliger	**hī**-lig-er
God	Gott	goht
Christian	christlich	**krist**-likh

Protestant	evangelisch	eh-vahn-**gay**-lish
Catholic	katholisch	kah-**toh**-lish
Jewish	jüdisch	**yew**-dish
Muslim	muselmanisch	moo-sehl-**mah**-nish
agnostic	agnostisch	ahg-**nohs**-tish
atheist	atheistisch	ah-tay-**is**-tish
When is the service?	Wann ist der Gottesdienst?	vahn ist dehr **goh**-tehs-deenst
Are there church concerts?	Gibt es Kirchenkon- zerte?	gipt ehs **keerkh**-ehn-kohn-**tsehr**-teh

Shopping

German Shops

Where is a...?	Wo ist ein...?	voh ist īn
antique shop	Antiquitäten- laden	ahn-tee-kvee-**tay**-tehn-**lah**-dehn
art gallery	Kunstgalerie	koonst-gah-leh-**ree**
bakery	Bäckerei	behk-eh-**rī**
barber shop	Herrenfrisör	hehr-rehn-friz-**ur**
beauty salon	Frisiersalon, Haarsalon	friz-**eer**-zah-lohn, **har**-zah-lohn
book shop	Buchladen	**bookh**-lah-dehn
camera shop	Photoladen	**foh**-toh-lah-dehn
cell phone shop	Natelladen	**nah**-tehl-lah-dehn
cheese shop	Käserei	kay-zeh-**rī**
clothing boutique	Kleiderladen	**klī**-der-lah-dehn
coffee shop	Kaffeeladen	**kah**-fay-lah-dehn
delicatessen	Feinkostgeschäft	**fīn**-kohst-geh-**shehft**
department store	Kaufhaus	**kowf**-hows
flea market	Flohmarkt	**floh**-markt
flower market	Blumenmarkt	**bloo**-mehn-markt
grocery store	Lebensmittel- geschäft	**lay**-behns-mit-tehl-geh-**shehft**

ACTIVITIES

hardware store	Eisenwaren-geschäft	ī-zehn-**vah**-rehn-geh-**shehft**
Internet café	Internetcafé	in-tehr-neht-kah-**fay**
jewelry shop	Schmuckladen	**shmook**-lah-dehn
launderette	Waschsalon	**vahsh**-zah-lohn
newsstand	Kiosk, Zeitungs-stand	**kee**-ohsk, **tsī**-toongs-shtahnt
office supplies	Bürobedarf	**bew**-roh-beh-darf
open-air market	Markt	markt
optician	Optiker	**ohp**-ti-ker
pastry shop	Zuckerbäcker, Konditorei	**tsoo**-ker-bayk-er kohn-dee-toh-**rī**
pharmacy	Apotheke	ah-poh-**tay**-keh
photocopy shop	Kopierladen	**koh**-pee-ehr-lah-dehn
shopping mall	Einkaufszentrum	**īn**-kowfs-tsehn-troom
souvenir shop	Souvenirladen	zoo-veh-**neer**-lah-den
supermarket	Supermarkt	**zoo**-per-markt
sweets shop	Süßwaren-geschäft	**zoos**-vah-rehn-geh-**shehft**
toy store	Spielzeugladen	**shpeel**-tsoyg-lah-dehn
travel agency	Reiseagentur	**rī**-zeh-ah-gehn-tur
used bookstore	Bücher aus zweiter Hand, Antiquariat	**bookh**-er ows **tsvī**-ter hahnt, ahn-teek-vah-**ree**-aht

---

KEY PHRASES: SHOPPING

Where can I buy...?	Wo kann ich... kaufen?	voh kahn ikh... **kow**-fehn
Where is a...?	Wo ist ein...?	voh ist īn
grocery store	Lebensmittel-geschäft	**lay**-behns-mit-tehl-geh-**shehft**
department store	Kaufhaus	**kowf**-hows
Internet café	Internetcafé	in-tehr-neht-kah-**fay**
launderette	Waschsalon	**vahsh**-zah-lohn
pharmacy	Apotheke	ah-poh-**tay**-keh
How much is it?	Wie viel kostet das?	vee feel **kohs**-teht dahs
I'm just browsing.	Ich sehe mich nur um.	ikh **zay**-heh mikh noor oom

| ...with books in English | ...mit englischen Büchern | mit **ehng**-lish-ehn **bookh**-ern |
| wine shop | Weinhandlung | **vīn**-hahnt-loong |

Many businesses close from 12:00 to 15:00 on weekday afternoons and all day on Sundays. Typical hours are Monday through Friday 9:00 to 18:00, Saturday 9:00 to 13:00. Some stores stay open Thursdays until 21:00.

Shop Till You Drop

opening hours	Öffnungszeiten	urf-noongs-**tsī**-tehn
sale	Ausverkauf	**ows**-fehr-kowf
special	Angebot	**ahn**-geh-boht
good value	preiswert	**prīs**-vehrt
I'd like...	Ich hätte gern...	ikh **heh**-teh gehrn
We'd like...	Wir hätten gern...	veer **heh**-tehn gehrn
Where can I buy...?	Wo kann ich... kaufen?	voh kahn ikh... **kow**-fehn
Where can we buy...?	Wo können wir... kaufen?	voh **kurn**-ehn veer... **kow**-fehn
How much is it?	Wie viel kostet das?	vee feel **kohs**-teht dahs
I'm just browsing.	Ich sehe mich nur um.	ikh **zay**-heh mikh noor oom
We're just browsing.	Wir sehen uns nur um.	veer **zay**-hehn oons noor oom
Do you have something cheaper?	Haben Sie etwas Billigeres?	**hah**-behn zee **eht**-vahs **bil**-lig-er-ehs
Better quality,	Bessere Qualität,	**behs**-ser-er kvah-lee-**tayt**
please.	bitte.	**bit**-teh
genuine / imitation	echt / imitation	ehkht / im-i-taht-see-**ohn**
Can I see more?	Kann ich mehr sehen?	kahn ikh mehr **zay**-hehn
Can we see more?	Können wir mehr sehen?	**kurn**-ehn veer mehr **zay**-hehn
This one.	Dieses.	**dee**-zehs

Can I try it on?	Kann ich es anprobieren?	kahn ikh ehs **ahn**-proh-beer-ehn
Do you have a mirror?	Haben Sie einen Spiegel?	**hah**-behn zee ī-nehn **shpee**-gehl
Too...	Zu...	tsoo
...big.	...groß.	grohs
...small.	...klein.	klīn
...expensive.	...teuer.	**toy**-er
It's too...	Es ist zu...	ehs ist tsoo
...short / long.	...kurz / lang.	koorts / lahng
...tight / loose.	...eng / weit.	ehng / vīt
...dark / light.	...dunkel / hell.	**doon**-kehl / hehl
What is it made of?	Was ist das für Material?	vahs ist dahs fewr mah-tehr-ee-**ahl**
Is it machine washable?	Ist es waschmaschinenfest?	ist ehs **vahsh**-mah-sheen-ehn-fehst
Will it shrink?	Läuft es ein?	loyft ehs īn
Is it color-fast?	Ist es farbenfest?	ist ehs **far**-behn-fehst
Credit card O.K.?	Kreditkarte O.K.?	kreh-**deet**-kar-teh "O.K."
Can you ship this?	Können Sie das versenden?	**kurn**-nehn zee dahs fehr-**zehn**-dehn
Tax-free?	Steuerfrei?	**shtoy**-er-frī
I'll think about it.	Ich denke drüber nach.	ikh **dehnk**-eh **drew**-ber nahkh
What time do you close?	Um wie viel Uhr schließen Sie?	oom vee feel oor **shlee**-sehn zee
What time do you open tomorrow?	Wann öffnen Sie morgen?	vahn **urf**-nehn zee **mor**-gehn

Street Markets

Did you make this?	Haben Sie das gemacht?	**hah**-behn zee dahs geh-**mahkht**
Is that your lowest price?	Ist das der günstigste Preis?	ist dahs dehr **gewn**-stig-steh prīs
Cheaper?	Billiger?	**bil**-ig-er
Good price.	Guter Preis.	**goo**-ter prīs

My last offer.	Mein letztes Angebot.	mīn **lehts**-tehs **ahn**-geh-boht
I'll take it.	Ich nehme es.	ikh **nay**-meh ehs
We'll take it.	Wir nehmen es.	veer **nay**-mehn ehs
I'm nearly broke.	Ich bin fast pleite.	ikh bin fahst **plī**-teh
We're nearly broke.	Wir sind fast pleite.	veer zint fahst **plī**-teh
My male friend...	Mein Freund...	mīn froynd
My female friend...	Meine Freundin...	**mī**-neh **froyn**-din
My husband...	Mein Mann...	mīn mahn
My wife...	Meine Frau...	**mī**-neh frow
...has the money.	...hat das Geld.	haht dahs gehlt

Clothes

For...	Für...	fewr
...a baby.	...ein Baby.	īn **bay**-bee
...a male / a female child.	...einen Buben / ein Mädchen.	**ī**-nehn **boo**-behn / īn **mayd**-khehn
...a male / a female teenager.	...einen Jungen / ein Fräulein.	**ī**-nehn **yoong**-ehn / īn **froy**-līn
...a man.	...einen Herren.	**ī**-nehn **hehr**-ehn
...a woman.	...eine Dame.	**ī**-neh **dah**-meh
bathrobe	Bademantel	**bah**-deh-mahn-tehl
bib	Latz	lahts
belt	Gurt	goort
bra	B. H. (Büstenhalter)	bay hah (**bewst**-ehn-hahl-ter)
clothing	Kleider	**klī**-der
dress	Kleid	klīt
flip-flops	Strandsandalen	**shtrahnt**-zahn-dah-lehn
gloves	Handschuhe	**hahnt**-shoo-heh
hat	Hut	hoot
jacket	Jacke	**yah**-keh
jeans	Jeans	"jeans"
nightgown	Nachthemd	**nahkht**-hehmt
nylons	Strümpfe	**shtrewmp**-feh
pajamas	Pyjama	pew-**jah**-mah

pants	Hosen	**hoh**-zehn
raincoat	Regenmantel	**ray**-gehn-mahn-tehl
sandals	Sandalen	zahn-**dah**-lehn
scarf	Schal	shahl
shirt...	Hemd...	hehmt
...long-sleeved	...mit langen Ärmeln	mit **lahng**-ehn **ehr**-mehln
...short-sleeved	...mit kurzen Ärmeln	mit **koorts**-ehn **ehr**-mehln
...sleeveless	...ohne Ärmel	**oh**-neh **ehr**-mehl
shoelaces	Schnürsenkel	**shnewr**-zehn-kehl
shoes	Schuhe	**shoo**-heh
shorts	kurze Hosen	**koorts**-eh **hoh**-zehn
skirt	Rock	rohk
sleeper (for baby)	Kindereinteiler	**kin**-der-**īn**-tī-ler
slip	Unterrock	**oon**-ter-rohk
slippers	Pantoffeln	pahn-**tohf**-ehln
socks	Socken	**zohk**-ehn
sweater	Pullover, Pulli	"pullover," **poo**-lee
swimsuit	Badeanzug	**bah**-deh-ahn-tsoog
tennis shoes	Tennisschuhe	**teh**-nis-shoo-heh
T-shirt	T-shirt, Hemdchen	**tay**-shirt, **hehmt**-khehn
underwear	Unterhosen	**oon**-ter-hoh-zehn
vest	Weste	**veh**-steh

Colors

black	schwarz	shvarts
blue	blau	blow (rhymes with cow)
brown	braun	brown
gray	grau	grow (rhymes with cow)
green	grün	grewn
orange	orange	oh-**rahn**-zheh
pink	rosa	**roh**-sah
purple	lila	**lee**-lah
red	rot	roht
white	weiß	vīs
yellow	gelb	gehlp

dark / light	dunkel / hell	**doon**-kehl / hehl
A lighter...	Eine hellere...	**ī**-neh **hehl**-er-eh
A brighter...	Eine farbigere...	**ī**-neh **far**-big-er-eh
A darker...	Eine dunklere...	**ī**-neh **doon**-kler-eh
...shade.	...Schattierung.	shaht-**eer**-oong

Materials

brass	Messing	**mehs**-sing
bronze	Bronze	**brohn**-seh
ceramic	Keramik	keh-**rah**-mik
copper	Kupfer	**koop**-fer
cotton	Baumwolle	**bowm**-voh-leh
glass	Glas	glahs
gold	Gold	gohlt
lace	Spitze	**shpit**-seh
leather	Leder	**lay**-der
linen	Leinen	**lī**-nehn
marble	Marmor	**mar**-mor
metal	Metall	meh-**tahl**
nylon	Nylon	**nee**-lohn
paper	Papier	pah-**peer**
pewter	Zinn	tsin
plastic	Plastik	**plah**-stik
polyester	Polyester	poh-lee-**ehs**-ter
porcelain	Porzellan	por-tsehl-**lahn**
silk	Seide	**zī**-deh
silver	Silber	**zil**-ber
velvet	Samt	zahmt
wood	Holz	hohlts
wool	Wolle	**voh**-leh

Jewelry

jewelry	Schmuck	shmook
bracelet	Armband	**arm**-bahnt
brooch	Brosche	**broh**-sheh
earrings	Ohrringe	**or**-ring-eh

necklace	*Halsband*	**hahls**-bahnt
ring	*Ring*	ring
Is this...?	*Ist das...?*	ist dahs
...sterling silver	*...echt Silber*	ehkht **zil**-ber
...real gold	*...echt Gold*	ehkht gohlt
...stolen	*...gestohlen*	geh-**shtoh**-lehn

Sports

Bicycling

bicycle	*Fahrrad, Velo (Switz.)*	**far**-raht, **feh**-loh
mountain bike	*Mountainbike*	"mountain bike"
I'd like to rent a bicycle	*Ich möchte ein Fahrrad mieten.*	ik **murkh**-teh īn **far**-raht **mee**-tehn
We'd like to rent two bicycles	*Wir möchten zwei Fahrräder mieten*	veer **murkh**-tehn tsvī **far**-ray-der **mee**-tehn
How much per...?	*Wie viel pro...?*	vee feel proh
...hour	*...Stunde*	**shtoon**-deh
...half day	*...halben Tag*	**hahl**-behn tahg
...day	*...Tag*	tahg
Is a deposit required?	*Brauchen Sie eine Anzahlung?*	**browkh**-ehn zee ī-neh **ahn**-tsahl-oong
deposit	*Anzahlung*	**ahn**-tsahl-oong
helmet	*Helm*	hehlm
lock	*Schloß*	shlohs
air / no air	*Luft / keine Luft*	looft / **kī**-neh looft
tire	*Reifen*	**rī**-fehn
pump	*Pumpe*	**poom**-peh
map	*Karte*	**kar**-teh
How many gears	*Wie viele Gänge?*	vee **fee**-leh **gayng**-eh
What is a...	*Was ist eine...*	vahs ist ī-neh...
route of about ___ kilometers?	*Strecke von etwas ___ Kilometer?*	**shtreh**-keh fohn **eht**-vahs ___ kee-loh-**may**-ter

...good	...gute	**goo**-teh
...scenic	...schöne	**shurn**-eh
...interesting	...interessante	in-tehr-ehs-**sahn**-teh
...easy	...leichte	**līkh**-teh
How many	Wie viele	vee **fee**-leh
minutes / hours	Minuten /	mee-**noo**-tehn /
by bicycle?	Stunden mit	**shtoon**-dehn mit
	dem Rad?	daym raht
I (don't) like hills.	Ich mag (keine)	ikh mahg (**kī**-neh)
	Hügel.	**hew**-gehl
I brake for	Ich bremse für	ikh **brehm**-zeh fewr
bakeries.	Bäckereien.	behk-eh-**rī**-ehn

Swimming and Boating

Where can I	Wo kann ich ein...	voh kahn ikh īn...
rent a...?	mieten?	**mee**-tehn
Where can we	Wo können wir ein...	voh **kurn**-ehn veer īn...
rent a...?	mieten?	**mee**-tehn
...paddleboat	...Wasserfahrrad	**vah**-ser-fah-raht
...rowboat	...Ruderboot	**roo**-der-boot
...boat	...Boot	boot
...sailboat	...Segelboot	**zay**-gehl-boot
How much per...?	Wie viel pro...?	vee feel proh
...hour	...Stunde	**shtoon**-deh
...half day	...halben Tag	**hahl**-behn tahg
...day	...Tag	tahg
beach	Strand	shtrahnt
nude beach	FKK-Strand	ehf-kay-kay-shtrahnt
Where's	Wo ist ein	voh ist īn
good beach?	guter Strand?	**goo**-ter shtrahnt
Is it safe for	Ist Schwimmen	ist **shvim**-mehn
swimming?	ohne Gefahr?	**oh**-neh geh-**far**
flip-flops	Sandalen	zahn-**dah**-lehn
pool	Schwimmbad	**shvim**-baht
snorkel and mask	Schnorchel	**shnorkh**-ehl
	und Maske	oont **mah**-skeh

sunglasses	*Sonnenbrille*	**zohn**-nehn-bril-leh
sunscreen	*Sonnenschutz*	**zohn**-nehn-shoots
surfboard	*Surfboard*	"surfboard"
surfer	*Wellenreiter*	**veh**-lehn-rī-ter
swimsuit	*Badeanzug*	**bah**-deh-ahn-tsoog
towel	*Badetuch*	**bah**-deh-tookh
waterskiing	*Wasserskifahren*	**vah**-ser-shi-**far**-ehn
windsurfing	*Windsurfen*	**vint**-zoorf-ehn

Germans are pioneers in the field of nudity—they're internationally known for letting it all hang out. Pretty much any beach in Germany can be topless, but if you want a true nude beach, look for *FKK*, which stands for *Freikörper Kultur* (Free Body Culture). You'll also stumble into plenty of nude sunbathers (more men than women) on sunny days at any big-city park or riverbank.

Sports Talk

sports	*Sport*	shport
game	*Spiel*	shpeel
championship	*Meisterschaft*	**mī**-ster-shahft
soccer	*Fußball*	**foos**-bahl
basketball	*Basketball,*	**bahs**-keht-bahl,
	Korbballspiel	**kor**-bahl-shpeel
hockey	*Hockey*	**hoh**-kee
American football	*Football*	**foot**-bahl
tennis	*Tennis*	**teh**-nees
golf	*Golf*	gohlf
skiing	*Skifahren*	**shee**-far-ehn
gymnastics	*Gymnastik*	gewm-**nah**-steek
Olympics	*Olympiade*	oh-lewm-pee-**ah**-deh
gold / silver / bronze...	*Gold-/Silber-/Ehren...*	gohlt / **zil**-ber / **eh**-rehn
...medal	*...Medaille*	**meh**-dahl-yeh

What sport athlete / team do you like?	*Sportler / Team haben Sie am liebsten?*	**shport**-ler / teem **hah**-behn zee ahm **leeb**-stehn
Where can I see a game?	*Wo kann ich ein Spiel sehen?*	voh kahn ikh īn shpeel **zay-h**ehn
jogging	*Jogging*	"jogging"
Where's a good place to jog?	*Wo geht man gut Jogging?*	voh gayt mahn goot "jogging"

Entertainment

What's happening tonight?	*Was ist heute abend los?*	vahs ist **hoy**-teh **ah**-behnt lohs
What do you recommend?	*Was empfehlen Sie?*	vahs ehmp-**fay**-lehn zee
Where is it?	*Wo ist es?*	voh ist ehs
How do I get there?	*Wie komme ich hin?*	vee **koh**-meh ikh hin
How do we get there?	*Wie kommen wir hin?*	vee **koh**-mehn veer hin
Is it free?	*Ist es umsonst?*	ist ehs oom-**zohnst**
Are there seats available?	*Gibt es noch Platz?*	gipt ehs nohkh plahts
Where can I buy a ticket?	*Wo kann ich eine Karte kaufen?*	voh kahn ikh **ī**-neh **kar**-teh **kowf**-ehn
Do you have tickets for today / tonight?	*Haben Sie Karten für heute Abend / heute Nacht?*	**hah**-behn zee **kar**-tehn fewr **hoy**-teh / **hoy**-teh **ah**-behnt
When does it start?	*Wann fängt es an?*	vahn fehngt ehs ahn
When does it end?	*Wann endet es?*	vahn **ehn**-deht ehs
Where's the best place to dance nearby?	*Wo geht man hier am besten Tanzen?*	voh gayt mahn heer ahm **behs**-tehn **tahn**-tsehn
Where do people stroll?	*Wo geht man hier Promenieren?*	voh gayt mahn heer proh-meh-**neer**-ehn

Entertaining Words

movie...	*Film...*	film
...original version	*...im Original*	im oh-rig-ee-**nahl**
...in English	*...auf Englisch*	owf **ehng**-lish
...with subtitles	*...mit Untertiteln*	mit **oon**-ter-tee-tehln
...dubbed	*...synchronisiert*	zewn-kroh-nee-**zeert**
music...	*Musik...*	moo-**zeek**
...live	*...live*	"live"
...classical	*...klassisch*	**klahs**-sish
...opera	*...Oper*	**oh**-per
...symphony	*...Symphonie*	zewm-foh-**nee**
...choir	*...Chor*	kor
folk music	*Volksmusik*	**fohlks**-moo-zeek
rock / jazz / blues	*Rock-N-Roll / Jazz / Blues*	"rock-n-roll" / "jazz" / "blues"
male singer	*Sänger*	**zehng**-er
female singer	*Sängerin*	**zehng**-er-in
concert	*Konzert*	kohn-**tsehrt**
show	*Vorführung*	**for**-few-roong
dancing	*Tanzen*	**tahn**-tsehn
folk dancing	*Volkstanz*	**fohlks**-tahnts
disco	*Disko*	**dis**-koh
bar with live music	*Bar mit Live-Musik*	bar mit "live" moo-**zeek**
nightclub	*Nachtklub*	**nahkht**-kloob
(no) cover charge	*(kein) Eintritt*	(kīn) **īn**-trit
sold out	*ausverkauft*	**ows**-fehr-kowft

Oktoberfest, the famous Munich beer festival, fills Bavaria's capital with the sounds of *"Prost!"*, carnival rides, sizzling *Bratwurst*, and oompah bands. The party starts the third Saturday in September and lasts for 16 days. The *Salzburger Festspiele* (Salzburg's music festival) treats visitors to the sound of music from late July to the end of August.

CONNECT

Phoning

I'd like to buy a...	Ich möchte eine... kaufen.	ikh **murkh**-teh ī-neh... **kow**-fehn
...telephone card.	...Telefonkarte	tehl-eh-**fohn**-kar-teh
...cheap international telephone card.	...billige internationale Telefonkarte	**bil**-lig-geh in-tehr-naht-see-oh-**nah**-leh tehl-eh-**fohn**-kar-teh
Where is the nearest phone?	Wo ist das nächste Telefon?	voh ist dahs **nehkh**-steh tehl-eh-**fohn**
It doesn't work.	Es ist außer Betrieb.	ehs ist **ow**-ser beh-**treep**
May I use your phone?	Darf ich Ihr Telefon benutzen?	darf ikh eer tehl-eh-**fohn** beh-**noot**-sehn
Can you talk for me?	Können Sie für mich sprechen?	**kurn**-nehn zee fewr mikh **shprehkh**-ehn
It's busy.	Besetzt.	beh-**zehtst**
Will you try again?	Noch einmal versuchen?	nohkh **īn**-mahl fehr-**zookh**-ehn
My name is ___.	Ich heiße ___.	ikh **hī**-seh
Sorry, I speak only a little German.	Tut mir leid, ich spreche nur ein bischen deutsch.	toot meer līt ikh **shprehkh**-eh noor īn **bis**-yehn doych
Speak slowly and clearly.	Sprechen Sie langsam und deutlich.	**shprehkh**-ehn zee **lahng**-zahm oont **doyt**-likh
Wait a moment.	Moment.	moh-**mehnt**

155

Telephone Words

telephone	*Telefon*	tehl-eh-**fohn**
telephone card	*Telefonkarte*	tehl-eh-**fohn**-kar-teh
cheap international	*billige internationale*	**bil**-lig-geh in-tehr-naht-
telephone card	*Telefonkarte*	see-oh-**nah**-leh
		tehl-eh-**fohn**-kar-teh
PIN code	*Geheimnummer*	geh-**hīm**-noo-mer
phone booth	*Telefonkabine*	tehl-eh-**fohn**-kah-bee-neh
out of service	*außer Betrieb*	**ow**-ser beh-**treep**
post office	*Post*	pohst
operator	*Vermittlung*	fehr-**mit**-loong
international	*internationale*	in-tehr-naht-see-oh-**nah**-leh
assistance	*Auskunft*	**ows**-koonft
international call	*Auslandsgespräch*	**ows**-lahnts-geh-shpraykh
collect call	*R-gespräch*	**ehr**-geh-shpraykh
credit card call	*Kreditkartenge-*	kreh-**deet**-kar-tehn-geh-
	spräch	shpraykh
toll-free	*gebührenfrei*	geh-**bew**-rehn-frī
fax	*Fax*	fahx
country code	*Landesvorwahl*	**lahn**-dehs-for-vahl
area code	*Vorwahl*	**for**-vahl
extension	*Intern*	in-**tehrn**
telephone book	*Telefonbuch*	tehl-eh-**fohn**-bookh
yellow pages	*gelbe Seiten*	**gehl**-beh **zī**-tehn

In Germany, it's polite to identify yourself by name at the beginning of every phone conversation. Telephone cards, sold at post offices and newsstands, are much handier than using coins for your calls. There are two kinds of phone cards: an insertable card (*Telefonkarte*) that you slide into a phone in a phone booth, and a cheaper-per-minute international phone card (*billige internationelle Telefonkarte*)—with a scratch-off PIN code—that you can use from any phone to make local or international calls (it's best to use these cards when calling from your hotel-room phone; rates soar if you use them with a pay phone).

At phone booths, you'll encounter these words:
Kartentelefon (accepts cards, sometimes coins), *Ganzein-schieben* (insert completely), *Bitte wählen* (please dial), and *Guthaben* (the value left on your card). If the number you're calling is out of service, you'll hear a recording: *"Kein Anschluß unter dieser Nummer."* For more tips, see "Let's Talk Telephones" on page 273 in the Appendix.

Cell Phones

Where is a cell phone shop?	*Wo is ein Natelladen?*	voh ist īn **nah**-tehl-lah-dehn
I'd like...	*Ich möchte...*	ikh **murkh**-teh
We'd like...	*Wir möchten...*	veer **murkh**-tehn
...a cell phone.	*...ein Handy.*	īn "handy"
...a chip.	*...eine Chipkarte.*	ī-neh **chip**-kar-teh
...to buy more time.	*...mehr Sprechzeit kaufen.*	mehr **shprehkh**-tsīt **kow**-fehn
How do you...?	*Wie kann man...?*	vee kahn mahn
...make calls	*...telefonieren*	teh-leh-fohn-**eer**-ehn
...receive calls	*...abnehmen*	**ahp**-nay-mehn
Will this work outside this country?	*Geht das im Ausland?*	gayt dahs im **ows**-lahnt
Where can I buy a chip for this this service / this phone?	*Wo kann ich einen Microchip kaufen für dieses Telefon / diesen Dienst?*	voh kahn ikh ī-nehn **meek**-roh-chip **kow**-fehn fewr **dee**-zehs teh-leh-**fohn** / **dee**-zehn deenst

Many travelers now buy cell phones in Europe to make both local and international calls. You'll pay under $100 for a "locked" phone that works only in the country you buy it in (includes about $20 worth of calls). You can buy additional time at a newsstand or cell phone shop. An "unlocked" phone is more expensive (over $100), but it works all over Europe: when you cross a border, buy a SIM card at a cell phone shop and insert the pop-out chip, which comes with a new phone number. Pricier tri-band phones (*Mehrkanal-Natel*) also work in North America.

E-mail and the Web

My e-mail address is ___.	Meine E-Mail-Adresse ist ___.	**mī**-neh **ee**-mayl-ah-**dreh**-seh ist ___
What's your e-mail address?	Was ist Ihre E-Mail-Adresse?	vahs ist **ee**-reh **ee**-mayl ah-**dreh**-seh
Can I use this computer to check my e-mail?	Darf ich diesen Computer benutzen um mein e-mail nachzulesen?	darf ikh **dee**-zehn kohm-**pew**-ter beh-**noot**-sehn oom mī n **ee**-mayl **nahkh**-tsoo-lay-zehn
Can we check our e-mail?	Können wir unser E-Mail nachlesen?	**kurn**-nehn veer **oon**-ser **ee**-mayl **nahkh**-lay-zehn
Where is there access to the Internet?	Wo gibt es einen Internet zugang?	voh gipt ehs **ī**-nehn **in**-tehr-neht **tsoo**-gahng
Where is an Internet café?	Wo ist ein Internetcafé?	voh ist ī n **in**-tehr-neht-kah-**fay**
How much for... minutes?	Wie viel für... Minuten?	vee feel fewr... mee-**noo**-tehn
...10	...zehn	tsayn
...15	...fünfzehn	**fewnf**-tsayn
...30	...dreißig	**drī**-sig
...60	...sechzig	**zehkh**-tsig
Help me, please.	Hilfen Sie mir, bitte.	**hil**-fehn zee meer **bit**-teh vee
How do I...	Wie...	vee
...start this?	...fange ich an?	**fahng**-eh ikh ahn
...send a file?	...sende ich einen Anhang?	**zehn**-deh ikh **ī**-nehn **ahn**-hahng
...print out a file?	...drucke ich einen Text?	**droo**-keh ikh **ī**-nehn tehkst
...make this symbol?	...mache ich dieses Symbol?	**mahkh**-eh ikh **dee**-zehs sewm-**bohl**

...type @?	...geht	gayt
	A-Affenschwanz?	ah-**ah**-fehn-shvants
This isn't working.	Das funktioniert	dahs foonk-tsee-ohn-**eert**
	nicht.	nikht

Web Words

e-mail	E-Mail	**ee**-mayl
e-mail address	E-Mail-Adresse	**ee**-mayl ah-**dreh**-seh
Web site	Internetseite	**in**-tehr-neht-**zī**-teh
Internet	Internet	**in**-tehr-neht
surf the Web	im Internet	im **in**-tehr-neht
	schwimmen	**shvim**-mehn
download	herunterladen	hehr-**oon**-ter-lah-dehn
@ sign	A-Affenschwanz	ah-**ah**-fehn-shvants
(literally "A-monkey tail")		
dot	Punkt	poonkt
hyphen (-)	Bindestrich	**bin**-deh-shtrikh
underscore (_)	Großstrich	**grohs**-shtrikh
modem	Modem	**moh**-dehm

On Screen

Ansicht	view	öffnen	open
bearbeiten	edit	Ordner	folder
drucken	print	Post	mail
löschen	delete	senden	send
Mitteilung	message	speichern	save

KEY PHRASES: E-MAIL AND THE WEB

e-mail	E-Mail	**ee**-mayl
Internet	Internet	**in**-tehr-neht
Where is the	Wo ist das	voh ist dahs
nearest Internet	nächste	**naykh**-steh
café?	Internetcafé?	**in**-tehr-neht-kah-**fay**
I'd like to check	Ich möchte mein	ikh **murkh**-teh mī n
my e-mail.	E-Mail nachlesen.	**ee**-mayl **nahkh**-lay-zehn

Mailing

Where is the post office?	*Wo ist die Post?*	voh ist dee pohst
Which window for...?	*An welchem Schalter ist...?*	ahn **vehlkh**-ehm **shahl**-ter ist
Is this the line for...?	*Ist das die Schlange für...?*	ist dahs dee **shlahng**-eh fewr
...stamps	*...Briefmarken*	**breef**-mar-kehn
...packages	*...Pakete*	pah-**kay**-teh
To the U.S.A.....	*In die U. S. A....*	in dee oo ehs ah
...by air mail.	*...mit Luftpost.*	mit **looft**-pohst
...by surface mail.	*...per Schiff.*	pehr shif
...slow and cheap.	*...langsam und billig.*	**lahng**-zahm oont **bil**-lig
How much is it?	*Wie viel kostet das?*	vee feel **kohs**-teht dahs
How much to send a letter / postcard to ___?	*Wie viel ist ein Brief / Postkarte nach ___?*	vee feel ist īn breef / **pohst**-kar-teh nahkh ___
I need stamps for ___ postcards to...	*Ich brauche Briefmarken für ___ Postkarten nach...*	ikh **browkh**-eh **breef**-mar-kehn fewr ___ **pohst**-kar-tehn nahkh
...America / Canada.	*...Amerika / Kanada.*	ah-**mehr**-ee-kah / **kah**-nah-dah
Pretty stamps, please.	*Hübsche Briefmarken, bitte.*	**hewb**-sheh **breef**-mar-kehn **bit**-teh
I always choose the slowest line.	*Ich wähle immer die langsamste Schlange.*	ikh **vay**-leh **im**-mer dee **lahng**-zahm-steh **shlahng**-eh
How many days will it take?	*Wie viele Tage braucht das?*	vee **fee**-leh **tahg**-eh browkht dahs

In Germany, you can often get stamps at a *Kiosk* (news-stand) or *Tabak* (tobacco shop). As long as you know which stamps you need, this is a great convenience. At the post office, the window labeled *"Alle Leistungen"* handles everything.

German mailboxes often come in pairs: the box for local mail is labeled with its range of zip codes, and the other box (labeled *Andere PLZ*) is for everything else.

Licking the Postal Code

German		
German Postal Service	*Deutsche Bundespost*	**doy**-cheh **boon**-dehs-pohst
post office	*Post(-amt)*	**pohst** (-ahmt)
stamp	*Briefmarke*	**breef**-mar-keh
postcard	*Postkarte*	**pohst**-kar-teh
letter	*Brief*	breef
envelope	*Umschlag*	**oom**-shlahg
package	*Paket*	pah-**kayt**
box	*Karton / Schachtel*	kar-**tohn** / **shahkh**-tehl
string	*Schnur*	shnoor
tape	*Klebeband*	**klay**-beh-bahnd
mailbox	*Briefkasten*	**breef**-kahs-tehn
airmail	*Luftpost*	**looft**-pohst
express mail	*Eilpost*	**īl**-pohst
slow and cheap	*langsam und billig*	**lahng**-zahm oont **bil**-lig
book rate	*Büchersendung*	**bewkh**-er-zehn-doong
weight limit	*Gewichtsbe-grenzung*	geh-**vikhts**-beh-grehn-tsoong
registered	*Einschreiben*	**īn**-shrī-behn
insured	*versichert*	fehr-**zikh**-ert
fragile	*zerbrechlich*	tsehr-**brehkh**-likh
contents	*Inhalt*	**in**-hahlt
customs	*Zoll*	tsohl
to / from	*nach / von*	nahkh / fohn
address	*Adresse*	ah-**dreh**-seh
zip code	*Postleitzahl*	**pohst**-līt-sahl
general delivery	*postlagernd*	**pohst**-lahg-ernt

CONNECT

KEY PHRASES: MAILING

post office	Post (-amt)	**pohst** (-ahmt)
stamp	Briefmarke	**breef**-mar-keh
postcard	Postkarte	**pohst**-kar-teh
letter	Brief	breef
airmail	Luftpost	**looft**-pohst
Where is the post office?	Wo ist die Post?	voh ist dee pohst
I need stamps for __ postcards / letters to America.	Ich brauche Briefmarken für __ Postkarten / Briefe nach Amerika.	ikh **browkh**-eh **breef**-mar-kehn fewr __ **pohst**-kar-tehn / **breef**-eh nahkh ah-**mehr**-ee-kah

HELP!

Help!	*Hilfe!*	**hil**-feh
Help me!	*Helfen Sie mir!*	**hehl**-fehn zee meer
Call a doctor!	*Rufen Sie einen Arzt!*	**roo**-fehn zee **ī**-nehn artst
Call...	*Rufen Sie...*	**roo**-fehn zee
...the police.	*...die Polizei.*	dee poh-leet-**sī**
...an ambulance.	*...den Krankenwagen.*	dayn **krahnk**-ehn-vah-gehn
...the fire department.	*...die Feuerwehr.*	dee **foy**-er-vehr
I'm lost. (on foot)	*Ich habe mich verlaufen.*	ikh **hah**-beh mikh fehr-**lowf**-ehn
We're lost. (on foot)	*Wir haben uns verlaufen.*	veer **hah**-behn oons fehr-**lowf**-ehn

---

KEY PHRASES: HELP!

accident	*Unfall*	**oon**-fahl
emergency	*Notfall*	**noht**-fahl
police	*Polizei*	poh-leet-**sī**
Help!	*Hilfe!*	**hil**-feh
Call a doctor / the police!	*Rufen Sie einen Arzt / die Polizei!*	**roo**-fehn zee **ī**-nehn artst / dee poh-leet-**sī**
Stop, thief!	*Halt, Dieb!*	hahlt deep

I'm lost. (by car)	Ich habe mich verfahren.	ikh **hah**-beh mikh fehr-**far**-ehn
We're lost. (by car)	Wir haben uns verfahren.	veer **hah**-behn oons fehr-**far**-ehn
Thank you for your help.	Danke für Ihre Hilfe.	**dahng**-keh fewr **ee**-reh **hil**-feh
You are very kind.	Sie sind sehr freundlich.	zee zint zehr **froynd**-likh

Theft and Loss

Stop, thief!	Halt, Dieb!	hahlt deep
I've been robbed.	Ich bin beraubt worden.	ikh bin beh-**rowbt vor**-dehn
We've been robbed.	Wir sind beraubt worden.	veer zint beh-**rowbt vor**-dehn
A thief took...	Ein Dieb hat... genommen.	īn deep haht... geh-**noh**-mehn
Thieves took...	Die Diebe haben... genommen.	dee **dee**-beh **hah**-behn... geh-**noh**-mehn
I've lost...	Ich habe... verloren.	**hah**-beh... fehr-**lor**-ehn
...my money.	...mein Geld	mīn gehlt
...my passport.	...meinen Paß	**mī**-nehn pahs
...my ticket.	...meine Fahrkarte / Flugkarte	**mī**-neh **far**-kar-teh / **floog**-kar-teh
...my baggage.	...mein Gepäck	mīn geh-**pehk**
...my purse.	...meine Handtasche	**mī**-neh **hahnt**-tahsh-eh
...my wallet.	...meine Brieftasche	**mī**-neh **breef**-tahsh-eh
...my faith in humankind.	...meinen Glauben an die Menschheit	**mī**-nehn **glow**-behn ahn dee **mehnsh**-hīt
We've lost our...	Wir haben unsere... verloren.	veer **hah**-behn **oon**-zer-eh... fehr-**lor**-ehn
...passports.	...Pässe	**peh**-seh
...tickets.	...Fahrkarten / Flugkarten	**far**-kar-tehn / **floog**-kar-tehn
...baggage.	...Gepäck	geh-**pehk**

HELP!

| I want to contact my embassy. | Ich möchte meine Botschaft kontaktieren. | ikh **murkh**-teh **mī**-neh **boht**-shahft kohn-tahk-**tee**-rehn |
| I need to file a police report for my insurance. | Ich muß einen Polizeireport für meine Versicherung erstellen. | ikh mus **ī**-nehn poh-leet-**sī**-reh-port fewr **mī**-neh fehr-**zikh**-er-oong ehr-**shteh**-lehn |

See the Appendix (page 275) for information on U.S. embassies in Germany, Austria, and Switzerland.

Helpful Words

ambulance	Krankenwagen	**krahnk**-ehn-vah-gehn
accident	Unfall	**oon**-fahl
injured	verletzt	fehr-**lehtst**
emergency	Notfall	**noht**-fahl
emergency room	Notfallaufnahme	noht-fahl-**owf**-nah-meh
fire	Feuer	**foy**-er
police	Polizei	poh-leet-**sī**
smoke	Rauch	rowkh
thief	Dieb	deep
pickpocket	Taschendieb	**tahsh**-ehn-deep

Help for Women

Leave me alone.	Lassen Sie mich in Ruhe.	**lah**-sehn zee mikh in **roo**-heh
I want to be alone.	Ich möchte alleine sein.	ikh **murkh**-teh ah-**lī**-neh zīn
I'm not interested.	Ich habe kein Interesse.	ikh **hah**-beh kīn in-tehr-**ehs**-seh
I'm married.	Ich bin verheiratet.	ikh bin fehr-**hī**-rah-teht
I'm a lesbian.	Ich bin lesbisch.	ikh bin **lehz**-bish
I have a contagious	Ich habe eine ansteckende	ikh **hah**-beh ī-neh **ahn**-shtehk-ehn-deh

disease.	*Krankheit.*	**krahnk**-hīt
You are bothering me.	*Sie sind mir lästig.*	zee zint meer **lehs**-tig
He is bothering me.	*Er belästigt mich.*	ehr beh-**lehs**-tigt mikh
Don't touch me.	*Fassen Sie mich nicht an.*	**fah**-sehn zee mikh nikht ahn
You're disgusting.	*Sie sind eklig.*	zee zint **ehk**-lig
Stop following me.	*Hör auf, mir nachzulaufen.*	hur owf meer **nahkh**-tsoo-**lowf**-ehn
Stop it!	*Hören Sie auf!*	**hur**-ehn zee owf
Enough!	*Das reicht!*	dahs rīkht
Go away.	*Gehen Sie weg.*	**gay**-ehn zee vayg
Get lost!	*Hau ab!*	how ahp
Drop dead!	*Verschwinde!*	fehr-**shvin**-deh
I'll call the police.	*Ich rufe die Polizei.*	ikh **roo**-feh dee poh-leet-**sī**

HELP!

SERVICES

Laundry

Is a... laundry nearby?	Ist ein Waschsalon... in der Nähe?	ist īn **vahsh**-zah-lohn... in dehr **nay**-heh
...self-service	...mit Selbstbedienung	mit zehlpst-beh-**dee**-noong
...full service	...mit Dienstleistung	mit **deenst**-līs-toong
Help me, please.	Hilfen Sie mir, bitte.	**hil**-fehn zee meer **bit**-teh
How does this work?	Wie funktioniert das?	vee foonk-tsee-ohn-**eert** dahs
Where is the soap?	Wo ist das Waschmittel?	voh ist dahs **vahsh**-mit-tehl
Are these yours?	Sind das Ihre?	zint dahs **ee**-reh
This stinks.	Das stinkt.	dahs shtinkt
Smells like...	Riecht wie...	rī kht vee
...spring time.	...Frühling.	**frew**-ling
...a locker room.	...Turnhalle.	**toorn**-hah-leh
...cheese.	...Käse.	**kay**-zeh
I need change.	Ich brauche Kleingeld.	ikh **browkh**-eh **klīn**-gehlt
Same-day service?	Noch am selben Tag?	nohkh ahm **zehl**-behn tahg
By when do I need to drop off my clothes?	Bis wann kann ich meine Wäsche vorbeibringen?	bis vahn kahn ikh **mī**-neh **veh**-sheh for-**bī**-bring-ehn

When will my clothes be ready?	*Wann wird meine Wäsche fertig sein?*	vahn virt **mī**-neh **veh**-sheh **fehr**-tig zīn
Dried?	*Getrocknet?*	geh-**trohk**-neht
Folded?	*Gefaltet?*	geh-**fahl**-teht
Hey there, what's spinning?	*Hey, worum dreht's sich?*	hay **voh**-room drayts zikh

Clean Words

full-service laundry	*Waschsalon mit Dienstleistung*	**vahsh**-zah-lohn mit **deenst**-līs-toong
self-service laundry	*Waschsalon mit Selbstbedienung*	**vahsh**-zah-lohn mit zehlpst-beh-**dee**-noong
wash / dry	*waschen / trocknen*	**vahsh**-ehn / **trohk**-nehn
washer / dryer	*Waschmaschine / Trockner*	**vahsh**-mahs-shee-neh / **trohk**-ner
detergent	*Waschmittel*	**vahsh**-mit-tehl
token	*Zahlmarke, Jeton*	**tsahl**-mar-keh, **yeh**-tohn
whites	*Helles*	**hehl**-lehs
colors	*Buntwäsche*	**boont**-vah-sheh
delicates	*Feinwäsche*	**fīn**-vah-sheh
handwash	*von Hand waschen*	fohn hahnt **vah**-shehn

Haircuts

Where is a barber / hair salon?	*Wo ist ein Herrenfrisör / Frisiersalon?*	voh ist īn heh-rehn-friz-**ur** / friz-**eer**-zah-lohn
I'd like...	*Ich möchte...*	ikh **murkh**-teh
...a haircut.	*...meine Haare schneiden.*	**mī**-neh **hah**-reh **shnī**-dehn
...a permanent.	*...eine Dauerwelle.*	**ī**-neh **dow**-er-veh-leh
...just a trim.	*...nur stutzen.*	noor **shtoot**-sehn
Cut about this much off.	*Etwa so viel kürzen.*	**eht**-vah zo feel **kewrt**-sehn

Cut my bangs here.	Meine Stirnhaare hier kürzen.	**mī**-neh **shteern**-hah-reh heer **kewrt**-sehn
Longer / shorter here.	Hier länger / kürzer.	heer **layng**-er / **kewrt**-ser
I'd like my hair...	Ich möchte meine Haare..	ikh **murkh**-teh **mī**-neh **hah**-reh
...short.	...kurz.	koorts
...colored.	...gefärbt.	geh-**fayrbt**
...shampooed.	...gewaschen.	geh-**vahsh**-ehn
...blow dried.	...getrocknet.	geh-**trohk**-neht
It looks good.	Es sieht gut aus.	ehs zeet goot ows

Repair

These handy lines can apply to any repair, whether it's a ripped rucksack, broken camera, or bad haircut.

This is broken.	Das hier ist kaputt.	dahs heer ist kah-**poot**
Can you fix it?	Können Sie das reparieren?	**kurn**-nehn zee dahs reh-pah-**reer**-ehn
Just do the essentials.	Machen Sie nur das Nötigste.	**mahkh**-ehn zee noor dahs **nur**-tig-steh
How much will it cost?	Wie viel kostet das?	vee feel **kohs**-teht-dahs
When will it be ready?	Wann ist es fertig?	vahn ist ehs **fehr**-tig
I need it by ___.	Ich brauche es bis ___.	ikh **browkh**-eh ehs bis
We need it by ___.	Wir brauchen es bis ___.	veer **browkh**-ehn ehs bis
Without it, I'm...	Ohne bin ich...	**oh**-neh bin ikh
...helpless.	...hilflos.	**hilf**-lohs
...a mess. (literally "all thrown up in the air.")	...aufgeschmissen.	**owf**-geh-shmis-sehn
...done for.	...erledigt.	ehr-**lay**-digt

SERVICES

Filling Out Forms

Herr / Frau / Fräulein	Mr. / Mrs. / Miss
Vorname	first name
Name (Familienname)	name (last name)
Adresse	address
Wohnort	address / city
Straße	street
Stadt	city
Staat	state
Land	country
Nationalität	nationality
Herkunft / Reiseziel	origin / destination
Alter	age
Geburtsdatum	date of birth
Geburtsort	place of birth
Geschlecht	sex
männlich / weiblich	male / female
verheiratet / ledig	married / single
geschieden / verwittwet	divorced / widowed
Beruf	profession
Erwachsener	adult
Kind / Junge / Mädchen	child / boy / girl
Kinder	children
Familie	family
Unterschrift	signature

When filling out dates, do it European-style: day/month/year.

SERVICES

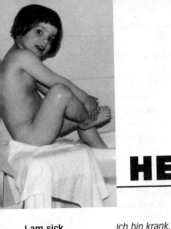

HEALTH

I am sick.	Ich bin krank.	ikh bin krahnk
I feel (very) sick.	Ich fühle mich (sehr) schlecht.	ikh **few**-leh mikh (zehr) shlehkht
My husband / My wife...	Mein Mann / Meine Frau...	mīn mahn / **mī**-neh frow
My son / My daughter...	Mein Sohn / Meine Tochter...	mīn zohn / **mī**-neh **tohkh**-ter
My male friend / My female friend...	Mein Freund / Meine Freundin...	mīn froynt / **mī**-neh **froyn**-din
...feels (very) sick.	...fühlt sich (sehr) schlecht.	fewlt zikh (zehr) shlehkht

---

KEY PHRASES: HEALTH

doctor	Arzt	artst
hospital	Krankenhaus	**krahn**-kehn-hows
pharmacy	Apotheke	ah-poh-**tay**-keh
medicine	Medikament	meh-dee-kah-**mehnt**
I am sick.	Ich bin krank.	ikh bin krahnk
I need a doctor (who speaks English).	Ich brauche einen Arzt (der Englisch spricht).	ikh **browkh**-eh ī-nehn artst (dehr **ehng**-lish shprikht)
It hurts here.	Hier tut es weh.	heer toot ehs vay

It's urgent.	*Es ist dringend.*	ehs ist **dring**-ehnt
I need a doctor...	*Ich brauche einen Arzt...*	ikh **browkh**-eh **ī**-nehn artst
We need a doctor...	*Wir brauchen einen Arzt...*	veer **browkh**-ehn **ī**-nehn artst
...who speaks English.	*...der Englisch spricht.*	dehr **ehng**-lish shprikht
Please call a doctor.	*Bitte rufen Sie einen Arzt.*	**bit**-teh **roo**-fehn zee **ī**-nehn artst
Could a doctor come here?	*Kann der Arzt hier kommen?*	kahn dehr artst heer **koh**-mehn
I am...	*Ich bin...*	ikh bin
He / She is...	*Er / Sie ist...*	ehr / zee ist
...allergic to penicillin / sulfa.	*...allergisch auf Penizillin / Sulfa.*	ah-**lehr**-gish owf pehn-ee-tsee-**leen** / **zool**-fah
I am diabetic.	*Ich bin Diabetiker.*	ikh bin dee-ah-**beht**-ee-ker
I have cancer.	*Ich habe Krebs.*	ikh **hah**-beh krehbs
I had a heart attack ___ years ago.	*Ich hatte einen Herzschlag vor ___ Jahren.*	ikh **hah**-teh **ī**-nehn **hayrts**-shlahg for ___ **yah**-rehn
It hurts here.	*Hier tut es weh.*	heer toot ehs vay
I feel faint.	*Ich fühle mich schwach.*	ikh **few**-leh mikh shvahkh
It hurts to urinate.	*Urinieren schmerzt.*	oo-rin-**eer**-ehn shmehrtst
I have body odor.	*Ich habe Körpergeruch.*	ikh **hah**-beh **kur**-per-geh-rookh
I'm going bald.	*Mir fallen die Haare aus.*	meer **fah**-lehn dee **hah**-reh ows
Is it serious?	*Ist es ernst?*	ist ehs ehrnst
Is it contagious?	*Ist es ansteckend?*	ist ehs **ahn**-shtehk-ehnt
Aging sucks.	*Altern stinkt.*	**ahl**-tern shtinkt
Take one pill	*Alle ___ Stunden*	**ah**-leh ___ **shtoon**-dehn

every __ hours	*eine Pille einnehmen*	**ī**-neh **pil**-leh **īn**-nay-mehn
for __ days.	*während ___ Tagen.*	**vehr**-ehnt ___**tah**-gehn
I need a receipt	*Ich brauche eine*	ikh **browkh**-eh **ī**-neh
for my insurance.	*Quittung für meine*	**kvit**-toong fewr **mī**-neh
	Versicherung.	fehr-**zikh**-eh-roong

Ailments

I have...	*Ich habe...*	ikh **hah**-beh
He / She has...	*Er / Sie hat...*	ehr / zee haht
I need / We need	*Ich brauche /*	ikh **browkh**-eh /
medication for...	*Wir brauchen*	veer **browkh**-ehn
	Medikament für...	meh-dee-kah-**mehnt** fewr
...arthritis.	*...Gelen-*	geh-**lehnk**-ehnt-
	kentzündung.	tsewn-doong
...asthma.	*...Asthma.*	**ahst**-mah
...athlete's foot.	*...Fußpilz.*	**foos**-pilts
...bad breath.	*...schlechten Atem.*	**shlehkh**-tehn **ah**-tehm
...blisters.	*...Blasen.*	**blah**-zehn
...bug bites.	*...Instektenstiche.*	in-**zehk**-tehn-shtikh-eh
...a burn.	*...eine Verbrennung.*	**ī**-neh fehr-**breh**-noong
...chest pains.	*...Schmerzen in*	**shmehrts**-ehn in
	der Brust.	dehr broost
...chills.	*...Kälteschauer.*	**kehl**-teh-show-ehr
...a cold.	*...eine Erkältung.*	**ī**-neh ehr-**kehl**-toong
...congestion.	*...Nasenver-*	**nah**-zehn-fehr-
	stopfung.	**shtohp**-foong
...constipation.	*...Verstopfung.*	fehr-**shtohp**-foong
...a cough.	*...einen Husten.*	**ī**-nehn **hoo**-stehn
...cramps.	*...Krämpfe.*	**krehmp**-feh
...diabetes.	*...Zuckerkrankheit.*	**tsoo**-ker-krahnk-hīt
...diarrhea.	*...Durchfall.*	**doorkh**-fahl
...dizziness.	*...Schwindel.*	**shvin**-dehl
...earache.	*...Ohrenschmerzen.*	**or**-ehn-shmehrts-ehn
...epilepsy.	*...Epilepsie.*	eh-pil-ehp-**see**
...a fever.	*...Fieber.*	**fee**-ber

...the flu.	...die Grippe.	dee **grip**-peh
...food poisoning.	...Lebensmittel-vergiftung.	**lay**-behns-mit-tehl-fehr-**gift**-oong
...giggles.	...einen Lachanfall.	**ī**-nehn **lahkh**-ahn-fahl
...hay fever.	...Heuschnupfen.	**hoysh**-nup-fehn
...a headache.	...Kopfschmerzen.	**kohpf**-shmehrts-ehn
...a heart condition.	...Herzbeschwerden.	**hayrts**-beh-shvehr-dehn
...hemorrhoids.	...Hämorrhoiden.	heh-mor-oh-**ee**-dehn
...high blood pressure.	...Bluthochdruck.	**bloot**-hohkh-drook
...indigestion.	...Verdauungs-störung.	fehr-**dow**-oongs-shtur-oong
...an infection.	...eine Infektion.	**ī**-neh in-fehk-tsee-**ohn**
...a migraine.	...Migräne.	mee-**gray**-neh
...nausea.	...Übelkeit.	**ew**-behl-kī t
...inflammation.	... eine Entzündung.	**ī**-neh ehnt-**tsewn**-doong
...pneumonia.	...Lungenent-zündung.	**loong**-ehn-ehnt-**tsewn**-doong
...a rash.	...einen Ausschlag.	**ī**-nehn **ows**-shlahg
...sinus problems.	...Schleimhaut-entzündung.	**shlī m**-howt-ehnt-**tsewn**-doong
...a sore throat.	...Halsschmerzen.	**hahls**-shmehrts-ehn
...a stomach ache.	...Magenschmerzen.	**mah**-gehn-shmehrts-ehn
...sunburn.	...Sonnenbrand.	**zoh**-nehn-brahnt
...a swelling.	...eine Schwellung.	**ī**-neh **shvehl**-loong
...a toothache.	...Zahnschmerzen.	**tsahn**-shmehrts-ehn
...urinary infection.	...Harnröhren-entzündung.	**harn**-rur-rehn-ehnt-**tsewn**-doong
...a venereal disease.	...eine Geschlechts-krankheit.	**ī**-neh geh-**shlehkhts**-krahnk-hī t
...vicious sunburn.	...üblen Sonnenbrand.	**ew**-behln **zoh**-nehn-brahnt
...vomiting.	...Übergeben.	ew-ber-**gay**-behn
...worms.	...Würmer.	**vewr**-mer

HEALTH

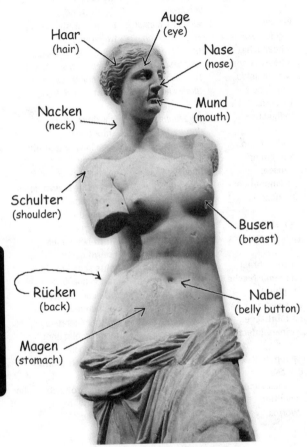

Haar
(hair)

Auge
(eye)

Nase
(nose)

Mund
(mouth)

Nacken
(neck)

Schulter
(shoulder)

Busen
(breast)

Rücken
(back)

Nabel
(belly button)

Magen
(stomach)

HEALTH

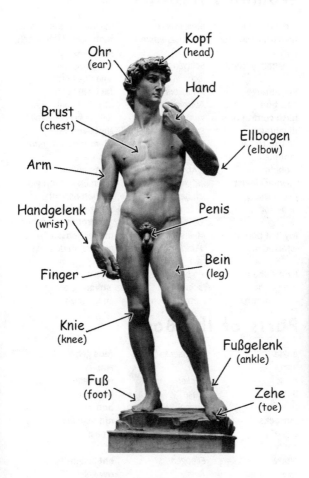

Kopf (head)
Ohr (ear)
Hand
Brust (chest)
Ellbogen (elbow)
Arm
Handgelenk (wrist)
Penis
Finger
Bein (leg)
Knie (knee)
Fußgelenk (ankle)
Fuß (foot)
Zehe (toe)

HEALTH

Women's Health

menstruation	*Menstruieren*	mehn-stroo-**eer**-ehn
menstrual cramps	*Monatskrämpfe*	**moh**-nahts-krehmp-feh
period	*Periode*	pehr-ee-**oh**-deh
pregnancy (test)	*Schwanger-schaft(-stest)*	**shvahng**-er-shahft(-stehst)
miscarriage	*Fehlgeburt*	**fayl**-geh-boort
abortion	*Abtreibung*	**ahp**-trī-boong
birth control pills	*Verhütungspille*	fehr-**hewt**-oongs-pil-leh
diaphragm	*Spirale*	shpee-**rah**-leh
I'd like to see a female...	*Ich möchte gern zu einer...*	ikh **murkh**-teh gehrn tsoo **ī**-ner
...doctor.	*...Ärztin.*	**ayrts**-tin
...gynecologist.	*...Gynäkologin.*	gewn-eh-koh-**loh**-gin
I've missed a period.	*Ich habe meine Tage nicht bekommen.*	ikh **hah**-beh **mī**-neh **tahg**-eh nikht beh-**kohm**-mehn
My last period started on ___.	*Meine letzte Periode fing am ___ an.*	**mī**-neh **lehts**-teh pehr-ee-**oh**-deh fing ahm ___ ahn
I am / She is... pregnant.	*Ich bin / Sie ist... schwanger.*	ikh bin / zee ist... **shvahng**-er
...___ months	*...im ___ Monat*	im ___ **moh**-naht

Parts of the Body

ankle	*Fußgelenk*	**foos**-geh-lehnk
arm	*Arm*	arm
back	*Rücken*	**rew**-kehn
bladder	*Blase*	**blah**-zeh
breast	*Busen*	**boo**-sehn
buttocks	*Hinterbacken*	**hin**-ter-bahk-ehn
chest	*Brust*	broost
ear	*Ohr*	or
elbow	*Ellbogen*	**ehl**-boh-gehn
eye	*Auge*	**ow**-geh

face	Gesicht	geh-**zikht**
finger	Finger	**fing**-er
foot	Fuß	foos
hair	Haar	har
hand	Hand	hahnt
head	Kopf	kohpf
heart	Herz	hayrts
hip	Hüfte	**hewf**-teh
intestines	Därme	**dayr**-meh
knee	Knie	kuh-**nee**
leg	Bein	bīn
lung	Lunge	**loong**-eh
mouth	Mund	moont
neck	Nacken	**nahk**-ehn
nose	Nase	**nah**-zeh
penis	Penis	**peh**-nees
rectum	Anus	**ah**-noos
shoulder	Schulter	**shool**-ter
stomach	Magen	**mah**-gehn
teeth	Zähne	**tsay**-neh
testicles	Hoden	**hoh**-dehn
throat	Hals	hahls
toe	Zehe	**tsay**-heh
urethra	Harnröhre	**harn**-rur-eh
uterus	Gebärmutter	geh-**bayr**-moo-ter
vagina	Vagina	vah-**gee**-nah
waist	Bund	boont
wrist	Handgelenk	**hahnt**-geh-lehnk

Medical Words

24-hour pharmacy	Vierundzwanzig-Stunden-Apotheke	**feer**-oont-tsvahn-tsig-**shtoon**-dehn-ah-poh-**tay**-keh
bleeding	bluten	**bloot**-ehn
blood	Blut	bloot
contraceptives	Verhütungsmittel	fehr-**hewt**-oongs-mit-tehl

HEALTH

dentist	Zahnarzt	**tsahn**-artst
doctor	Arzt	artst
health insurance	Krankenver-sicherung	**krahn**-kehn-fehr-**zikh**-eh-roong
hospital	Krankenhaus	**krahn**-kehn-hows
medical clinic	Klinik	**klee**-nik
medicine	Medikament	meh-dee-kah-**mehnt**
nurse	Krankenschwester	**krahn**-kehn-shvehs-ter
pain	Schmerz	shmehrts
pharmacy	Apotheke	ah-poh-**tay**-keh
pill	Pille	**pil**-leh
prescription	Rezept, Verschreibung	reh-**tsehpt**, fehr-**shrī**-boong
refill	Erneuerung	ehr-**noy**-er-oong
unconscious	bewußtlos	beh-**voost**-lohs
x-ray	Röntgenbild	**rurnt**-gehn-bilt

First-Aid Kit

antacid	Mittel gegen Magenbrennen	**mit**-tehl **gay**-gehn **mah**-gehn-breh-nehn
antibiotic	Antibiotika	ahn-tee-bee-**oh**-tee-kah
aspirin	Aspirin	ah-spir-**een**
non-aspirin substitute	Ben-u-ron	**behn**-oo-rohn
bandage	Verband	fehr-**bahnt**
Band-Aids	Pflaster	**pflahs**-ter
cold medicine	Grippemittel	**grip**-eh-mit-tehl
cough drops	Hustenbonbons	**hoo**-stehn-bohn-bohns
decongestant	Abführmittel	**ahp**-fewr-mit-tehl
disinfectant	Desinfektions-mittel	dehs-in-fehk-tsee-**ohns**-mit-tehl
first-aid cream	Erste-Hilfe-Salbe	**ehrst**-eh-**hil**-feh-**zahl**-beh
gauze / tape	Verband	fehr-**bahnt**
laxative	Laxativ	lahks-ah-**teef**
medicine for diarrhea	Durchfall-medikament	**doorkh**-fahl-meh-dee-kah-**mehnt**

HEALTH

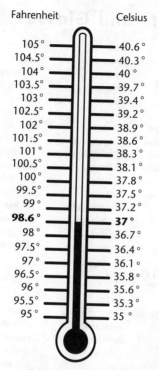

	Fahrenheit	Celsius
	105°	40.6°
	104.5°	40.3°
	104°	40°
	103.5°	39.7°
	103°	39.4°
	102.5°	39.2°
	102°	38.9°
	101.5°	38.6°
	101°	38.3°
	100.5°	38.1°
	100°	37.8°
	99.5°	37.5°
	99°	37.2°
	98.6°	**37°**
	98°	36.7°
	97.5°	36.4°
	97°	36.1°
	96.5°	35.8°
	96°	35.6°
	95.5°	35.3°
	95°	35°

HEALTH

moleskin	Pflaster gegen Blasen	**pflahs**-ter **gay**-gehn **blah**-zehn
pain killer	Schmerzmittel	**shmehrts**-mit-tehl
Preparation H	Hämorrhoiden Salbe	heh-mor-oh-**ee**-dehn **zahl**-beh
support bandage	Stützverband	**shtewts**-fehr-bahnt
thermometer	Thermometer	tehr-moh-**may**-ter
Vaseline	Vaseline, Mineralsalbe	vah-zeh-**lee**-neh, min-eh-**rahl**-zahl-beh
vitamins	Vitamine	vee-tah-**mee**-neh

Contacts and Glasses

glasses	Brille	**bril**-leh
sunglasses	Sonnenbrille	**zoh**-nehn-bril-leh
prescription	Rezept,	reh-**tsehpt**,
	Verschreibung	fehr-**shrī**-boong
soft...	weiche...	**vīkh**-eh
hard...	harte...	**har**-teh
...contact lenses	...Linsen	**lin**-zehn
cleaning solution	Reinigungslösung	**rī**-nee-goongs-lur-zoong
soaking solution	Kontaktlinsenbad	kon-**tahkt**-lin-zehn-baht
all-purpose solution	Salzlösung	**zahlts**-lur-zoong
20/20 vision	perfekte	pehr-**fehk**-teh
	Dioptrie	dee-ohp-**tree**
I've... a	Ich habe meine	ikh **hah**-beh **mī**-neh
contact lens.	Kontaktlinse...	kohn-**tahkt**-lin-zeh
...lost	...verloren.	fehr-**lor**-ehn
...swallowed	...verschluckt.	fehr-**shlookt**

Toiletries

comb	Kamm	kahm
conditioner for hair	Haarfestiger	**har**-fehs-tig-er
condoms	Kondome	kohn-**doh**-meh
dental floss	Zahnseide	**tsahn**-zī-deh
deodorant	Deodorant	deh-oh-doh-**rahnt**
facial tissue	Papiertuch	pah-**peer**-tookh
hairbrush	Haarbürste	**har**-bewr-steh
hand lotion	Handlotion	**hahnt**-loh-tsee-ohn
lip salve	Lippenbalsam	**lip**-pehn-bahl-zahm
mirror	Spiegel	**shpee**-gehl
nail clipper	Nagelschere	**nah**-gehl-sheh-reh
razor	Rasierapparat	rah-**zeer**-ahp-ar-aht
sanitary napkins	Damenbinden	**dah**-mehn-bin-dehn
scissors	Schere	**sheh**-reh
shampoo	Shampoo	**shahm**-poo
shaving cream	Rasierschaum	rah-**zeer**-showm

soap	Seife	**zī**-feh
sunscreen	Sonnenschutz	**zoh**-nehn-shoots
suntan lotion	Sonnenöl	**zoh**-nehn-url
tampons	Tampons	**tahm**-pohns
tissues	Taschentücher	**tah**-shehn-tewkh-er
toilet paper	Klopapier	kloh-pah-**peer**
toothbrush	Zahnbürste	**tsahn**-bewr-steh
toothpaste	Zahnpasta	**tsahn**-pah-stah
tweezers	Pinzette	pin-**tseh**-teh

Makeup

blush	Wangenröte	**vahng**-ehn-rur-teh
eye shadow	Augenschatten	**ow**-gehn-shah-tehn
eyeliner	Augenkontour	**ow**-gehn-kohn-toor
face cleanser	Gesichtsseife	geh-**zikhts**-zī-feh
face powder	Gesichtspulver	geh-**zikhts**-pool-ver
foundation	Grundlage	**groont**-lah-geh
lipstick	Lippenstift	**lip**-pehn-shtift
makeup	Makeup	"makeup"
mascara	Maskara	mahs-**kah**-rah
moisturizer...	Feuchtigkeitscreme...	**foykh**-tig-kīts-**kreh**-meh
...with sun block	...mit Sonnenschutz	mit **zoh**-nehn-shoots
nail polish	Nagellack	**nah**-gehl-lahk
nail polish remover	Nagellack-entferner	**nah**-gehl-lahk-ehnt-**fehr**-ner
perfume	Parfum	par-**foom**

For Babies

baby	Baby	**bay**-bee
baby food	Babynahrung	**bay**-bee-nah-roong
bib	Latz	lahts
bottle	Flasche	**flah**-sheh
diaper...	Windel...	**vin**-dehl
...wipes	...Feuchtigkeitstuch	**foykh**-tig-kīts-tookh

...ointment	...Salbe	**zahl**-beh
diapers	Windeln	**vin**-dehln
formula...	Babynahrung...	**bay**-bee-nah-roong
...powdered	...in Pulver	in **pool**-ver
...liquid	...flüssig	**flew**-sig
...soy	...mit Soya	mit **zoh**-yah
medication for...	Medikament für...	meh-dee-kah-**mehnt** fewr
...diaper rash	...Windelscheuern	**vin**-dehl-shoy-ehrn
...teething	...Zahnen	**tsahn**-ehn
nipple	Nippel	**nip**-pehl
pacifier	Nuggel	**noog**-gehl
Will you refrigerate this?	Können Sie das kühl stellen?	**kurn**-nehn zee dahs kewl **shteh**-lehn
Will you warm... for a baby?	Können Sie ... fürs Baby wärmen?	**kurn**-nehn zee... fewrs **bay**-bee **vayrm**-ehn
...this	...das	dahs
...some water	...etwas Wasser	**eht**-vahs **vah**-ser
...some milk	...etwas Milch	**eht**-vahs milkh
Not too hot, please.	Nicht zu heiß, bitte.	nikht tsoo hīs **bit**-teh

More Baby Things

backpack to carry baby	Rucksack-Babyträger	**rook**-zahk-**bay**-bee-**tray**-ger
booster seat	Kindersitz	**kin**-der-zits
car seat	Sicherheitssitz	**zikh**-er-hīts-zits
high chair	Kinderstuhl	**kin**-der-shtool
playpen	Babygitter	**bay**-bee-git-ter
stroller	Kinderwagen	**kin**-der-**vah**-gehn

CHATTING

My name is ___.	Ich heiße ___.	ikh **hī**-seh ___
What's your name?	Wie heißen Sie?	vee **hī**-sehn zee
Pleased to meet you.	Freut mich.	froyt mikh
This is ___.	Das ist ___.	dahs ist ___
How are you?	Wie geht's?	vee gayts
Very well, thanks.	Sehr gut, danke.	zehr goot **dahng**-keh
Where are you from?	Woher kommen Sie?	**voh**-hehr **koh**-mehn zee
What...?	Von welcher...?	fohn **vehlkh**-er
...city	...Stadt	shtaht
...country	...Land	lahnt
...planet	...Planet	plahn-**ayt**
I'm from...	Ich bin aus...	ikh bin ows
...America.	...Amerika.	ah-**mehr**-ee-kah
...Canada.	...Kanada.	**kah**-nah-dah
Where are you going?	Wo hin gehen Sie?	voh hin **gay**-hehn zee
I'm going to ___.	Ich gehe nach ___.	ikh **gay**-heh nahkh ___
We're going to ___.	Wir gehen nach ___.	veer **gay**-hehn nahkh ___
Will you take my / our photo?	Machen Sie ein Foto von mir / uns?	**mahkh**-ehn zee īn **foh**-toh fohn meer / oons

186

| Can I take a photo of you? | *Kann ich ein Foto von Ihnen machen?* | kahn ikh īn **foh**-toh fohn **ee**-nehn **mahkh**-ehn |
| Smile! | *Lächeln!* | **laykh**-ehln |

Nothing More Than Feelings...

I am / You are...	*Ich bin / Sie sind...*	ikh bin / zee zint
He / She is...	*Er / Sie ist...*	ehr / zee ist
...happy.	*...glücklich.*	**glewk**-likh
...sad.	*...traurig.*	**trow**-rig
...tired.	*...müde.*	**mew**-deh
...hungry.	*...hungrig.*	**hoon**-grig
...thirsty.	*...durstig.*	**door**-stig
I'm hot.	*Mir ist zu warm.*	meer ist tsoo varm
I'm cold.	*Mir ist kalt.*	meer ist kahlt
I'm homesick.	*Ich habe Heimweh.*	ikh **hah**-beh **hīm**-vay
I'm lucky.	*Ich habe Glück.*	ikh **hah**-beh glewk

KEY PHRASES: CHATTING

My name is ___.	*Ich heiße ___.*	ikh **hī**-seh ___
What's your name?	*Wie heißen Sie?*	vee **hī**-sehn zee
Pleased to meet you.	*Freut mich.*	froyt mikh
Where are you from?	*Woher kommen Sie?*	**voh**-hehr **koh**-mehn zee
I'm from ___.	*Ich bin aus ___.*	ikh bin ows ___
Where are you going?	*Wo hin gehen Sie?*	voh hin **gay**-hehn zee
I'm going to ___.	*Ich gehe nach ___.*	ikh **gay**-heh nahkh ___
I like...	*Ich mag...*	ikh mahg
Do you like...?	*Mögen Sie...?*	**mur**-gehn zee
Thank you very much.	*Vielen Dank.*	**fee**-lehn dahngk
Have a good trip!	*Gute Reise!*	**goo**-teh **rī**-zeh

CHATTING

Who's Who

This is...of mine.	Das ist... von mir.	dahs ist... fohn meer
...a male friend	...ein Freund	**īn froynt**
...a female friend	...eine Freundin	**ī**-neh **froyn**-din
This is my...	Das ist mein / meine...	dahs ist mīn / **mī**-neh
(male / female)		
...boy- / girlfriend.	...Freund / Freundin.	froynt / **froyn**-din
...husband / wife.	...Mann / Frau.	mahn / frow
...son / daughter.	...Sohn / Tochter.	zohn / **tohkh**-ter
...brother / sister.	...Bruder / Schwester.	**broo**-der / **shvehs**-ter
...father / mother.	...Vater / Mutter.	**fah**-ter / **moo**-ter
...uncle / aunt.	...Onkel / Tante.	**ohn**-kehl / **tahn**-teh
...nephew / niece.	...Neffe / Nichte.	**nehf**-feh / **neekh**-teh
...male / female cousin.	...Vetter / Base.	**feh**-ter / **bah**-zeh
...grandfather / grandmother.	...Großvater / Großmutter.	**grohs**-fah-ter / **grohs**-moo-ter
...grandson / granddaughter.	...Enkel / Enkelin.	**ehn**-kehl / **ehn**-kehl-in

Family

Are you married?	Sind Sie verheiratet?	zint zee fehr-**hī**-rah-teht
Do you have children?	Haben Sie Kinder?	**hah**-behn zee **kin**-der
How many boys / girls?	Wie viele Jungen / Mädchen?	vee **fee**-leh **yoong**-ehn / **mayd**-khehn
Do you have photos?	Haben Sie Fotos?	**hah**-behn zee **foh**-tohs
How old is your child?	Wie alt ist Ihr Kind?	vee ahlt ist eer kint
Beautiful child!	Schönes Kind!	**shur**-nehs kint
Beautiful children!	Schöne Kinder!	**shur**-neh **kin**-der

Work

What is your occupation?	Was machen Sie beruflich?	vahs **mahkh**-ehn zee beh-**roof**-likh
Do you like your work?	Gefällt Ihnen Ihre Arbeit?	geh-**fehlt** ee-nehn **eer**-eh ar-bīt
I'm a student (male / female).	Ich bin Student / Studentin.	ikh bin shtoo-**dehnt** / shtoo-**dehnt**-in
I'm studying to work in...	Ich studiere, um in... zu arbeiten.	ikh shtoo-**deer**-eh oom in... tsoo **ar**-bīt-ehn
I work in...	Ich arbeite in...	ikh **ar**-bīt-eh in
I used to work in...	Ich habe in... gearbeitet.	ikh **hah**-beh in... geh-**ar**-bīt-eht
I want a job in...	Ich möchte eine Stelle in...	ikh **murkh**-teh **ī**-neh **shteh**-leh in
...accounting.	...Buchhaltung	**bookh**-hahl-toong
...the medical field.	...Medizin	meh-deh-**tseen**
...social services.	...Sozialwesen	zoh-tsee-**ahl**-vay-zehn
...the legal profession.	...Rechtswesen	**rehkhts**-vay-zehn
...banking.	...Finanz	fee-**nahnts**
...business.	...Management	"management"
...government.	...Verwaltung	fehr-**vahl**-toong
...engineering.	...Technik	tehkh-**neek**
...public relations.	...Öffentlichkeits-arbeit	**urf**-ehnt-likh-kīts-**ar**-bīt
...science.	...Wissenschaft	**vis**-sehn-shahft
...teaching.	...Schulwesen	**shool**-vay-zehn
...the computer field.	...Informatik	in-for-**mah**-teek
...the travel industry.	...Reiseindustrie	**rī**-zeh-in-doos-**tree**
...the arts.	...Kunstgewerbe	**koonst**-geh-vehr-beh
...journalism.	...Journalismus	yorn-ahl-**ees**-moos
...a restaurant.	...einem Restaurant	**ī**-nehm rehs-tow-**rahnt**
...a store.	...einem Laden	**ī**-nehm **lah**-dehn
...a factory.	...einer Fabrik	**ī**-ner fah-**breek**

I am...	*Ich bin...*	ikh bin
...unemployed.	*...arbeitslos.*	**ar**-bīts-lohs
...retired.	*...pensioniert.*	pehn-zee-ohn-**eert**
...a professional traveler.	*...professioneller Reisender.*	proh-fehs-see-ohn-**neh**-ler **rī**-zehn-der
Do you have a...?	*Haben Sie eine...?*	**hah**-behn zee **ī**-neh
Here is my / our...	*Hier ist meine / unsere...*	heer ist **mī**-neh / **oon**-zer-eh
...business card.	*...Visitenkarte.*	vi-**zee**-tehn-kar-teh
...e-mail address.	*...E-Mail-Adresse.*	**ee**-mayl ah-**dreh**-seh

Chatting with Children

What's your name?	*Wie heißt du?*	vee hīst doo
My name is ___.	*Ich heiße ___.*	ikh **hī**-seh ___
How old are you?	*Wie alt bist du?*	vee ahlt bist doo
How old am I?	*Wie alt bin ich?*	vee ahlt bin ikh
I'm ___ years old.	*Ich bin ___ Jahre alt.*	ikh bin ___ **yah**-reh ahlt
Do you have siblings?	*Hast du Geschwister?*	hahst doo geh-**shvis**-ter
Do you like school?	*Magst du die Schule?*	mahgst doo dee **shoo**-leh
What are you studying?	*Was studierst du?*	vahs shtoo-**deerst** doo
What's your favorite subject?	*Was ist dein Lieblingsfach?*	vahs ist dīn **lee**-blings-fahkh
What is this?	*Was ist das?*	vahs ist dahs
Will you teach me / us some German words?	*Bringst du mir / uns einige deutsche Wörter bei?*	bringst doo meer / oons **ī**-nig-eh **doy**-cheh **vur**-ter bī
Will you teach me / us a simple German song?	*Kannst du mir / uns ein einfaches deutsches Lied beibringen?*	kahnst doo meer / oons īn **īn**-fahkh-ehs **doy**-chehs leet **bī**-bring-ehn
Guess which country I live / we live in.	*Rate mal, in welchem Land ich wohne / wir wohnen.*	**rah**-teh mahl in **vehlkh**-ehm lahnt ikh **voh**-neh / veer **voh**-nehn

Do you have pets?	Hast du Haustiere?	hahst doo **hows**-teer-eh
I have...	Ich habe...	ikh **hah**-beh
We have...	Wir haben...	veer **hah**-behn
...a cat / a dog / a fish / a bird	...eine Katze / einen Hund / einen Fisch / einen Vogel	**ī**-neh **kaht**-seh / **ī**-nehn / hoont / **ī**-nehn fish / **ī**-nehn **voh**-gehl
Want to hear me burp?	Willst du meinen Rülpser hören?	vilst doo **mī**-nehn **rewlp**-zer **hur**-ehn
Teach me a fun game.	Bringe mir ein lustiges Spiel bei.	**bring**-eh meer īn **loo**-shtig-ehs shpeel bī
Got any candy?	Hast du Süßigkeiten?	hahst doo **zew**-sig-kī-tehn
Want to thumb-wrestle?	Willst du Daumenziehen?	vilst doo **dow**-mehn-tsee-hehn
Give me a handshake.	Handschlag.	**hahnt**-shlahg

If you do break into song, you'll find the words for "Happy Birthday" on page 24, and words to more songs beginning on page 269.

German kids usually shake hands instead of doing a "high five," but teaching them can be a fun icebreaker. Just say *"So machen wir das in Amerika"* ("This is how we do it in America") and give 'em five!

Travel Talk

I am / Are you...?	Ich bin / Sind Sie...?	ikh bin / zint zee
...on vacation	...auf Urlaub	owf **oor**-lowp
...on business	...auf Geschäftsreise	owf geh-**shehfts**-rī-zeh
How long have you been traveling?	Wie lange sind Sie schon unterwegs?	vee **lahng**-eh zint zee shohn oont-er-**vehgs**
day / week	Tag / Woche	tahg / **vohkh**-eh
month / year	Monat / Jahr	**moh**-naht / yar
When are you going home?	Wann fahren Sie zurück?	vahn **far**-ehn zee tsoo-**rewk**
This is my first time in ___.	Ich bin zum ersten Mal in ___.	ikh bin tsoom **ehr**-stehn mahl in ___

This is our first time in ___.	Wir sind zum ersten Mal in ___.	veer zint tsoom **ehr**-stehn mahl in ___
It's (not) a tourist trap.	Es ist (nicht) nur für Touristen.	ehs ist (nikht) noor fewr too-**ris**-tehn
This is paradise.	Das ist das Paradies.	dahs ist dahs **pah**-rah-dees
This is a wonderful country.	Dies ist ein wunderbares Land.	deez ist īn **voon**-dehr-bah-rehs lahnt
The Germans / Austrians / Swiss...	Die Deutschen / Österreicher / Schweizer...	dee **doy**-chehn / **urs**-teh-rī kh-er / **shvī t**-ser
...are friendly / boring / rude.	...sind freundlich / langweilig / unhöflich.	zint **froynd**-likh / **lahng**-vī -lig / oon-**hurf**-likh
So far...	Bis jetzt...	bis yehtst
Today...	Heute...	**hoy**-teh
...I have seen ___ and ___.	...habe ich ___ und ___ gesehen.	**hah**-beh ikh ___ oont ___ geh-**zay**-hehn
...we have seen ___.	...haben wir ___ gesehen.	**hah**-behn veer ___ geh-**zay**-hehn
Next...	Nächste...	**nehkh**-steh
Tomorrow...	Morgen...	**mor**-gehn
...I will see ___.	...werde ich ___ sehen.	**vehr**-deh ikh ___ **zay**-hehn
...we will see ___.	...werden wir ___ sehen.	**vehr**-dehn veer ___ **zay**-hehn
Yesterday...	Gestern...	**geh**-stern
...I saw ___.	...habe ich ___ gesehen.	**hah**-beh ikh ___ geh-**zay**-hehn
...we saw ___.	...haben wir ___ gesehen.	**hah**-behn veer ___ geh-**zay**-hehn
My / Our vacation is ___ days long, starting in ___ and ending in ___.	Meine / Unsere Ferien dauern ___ Tage, fangen in ___ an und enden in ___.	**mī**-neh / **oon**-zer-eh **fay**-ree-ehn **dow**-ern ___ **tah**-geh **fahng**-ehn in ___ ahn oont **ehn**-dehn in ___
Travel is enlightening.	Reisen ist aufschlußreich.	**rī**-zehn ist **owf**-schloos-rī kh
I wish all	Ich wünschte alle	ikh **vewnsh**-teh **ah**-leh

(American)	(amerikanischen)	(ah-mehr-i-**kahn**-ish-ehn)
politicians traveled.	Politiker würden reisen.	poh-**lee**-tik-er vewr-dehn **rī**-zehn
Have a good trip!	Gute Reise!	**goo**-teh **rī**-zeh
To travel is to live.	Reisen heißt leben.	**rī**-zehn hī st **lay**-behn

Map Musings

These phrases and maps will help you delve into family history and explore travel dreams.

I live here.	Ich wohne hier.	ikh **voh**-neh heer
We live here.	Wir wohnen hier.	veer **voh**-nehn heer
I was born here.	Ich bin hier geboren.	ikh bin heer geh-**boh**-rehn
My ancestors came from ___.	Meine Vorfahren kamen aus ___.	**mī**-neh **for**-far-ehn **kah**-mehn ows ___
I'd like/We'd like to go to ___.	Ich möchte / Wir möchten nach ___ gehen.	ich **murkh**-teh / veer **murkh**-tehn nahhk ___ **gay**-hehn
I've / We've traveled to ___.	Ich bin / Wir sind in ___ gewesen.	ikh bin / veer zint in ___ geh-**vay**-zehn
Next I'll go to ___.	Als Nächstes gehe ich nach ___.	als **nehkh**-stehs **gay**-heh ikh nahhk ___
Next we'll go to ___.	Als Nächstes gehen wir nach ___.	als **nehkh**-stehs **gay**-hehn veer nahhk ___
Where do you live?	Wo wohnen Sie?	voh **voh**-nehn zee
Where were you born?	Wo sind Sie geboren?	voh zint zee geh-**boh**-rehn
Where did your ancestors come from?	Wo her kommen Ihre Vorfahren?	voh hehr **koh**-mehn **ee**-reh **for**-far-ehn
Where have you traveled?	Wo sind Sie schon gewesen?	voh zint zee shohn geh-**vay**-zehn
Where are you going?	Wo hin gehen Sie?	voh hin **gay**-hehn zee
Where would you like to go?	Wo hin möchten Sie?	voh hin **murkh**-tehn zee

GERMANY

AUSTRIA

SWITZERLAND

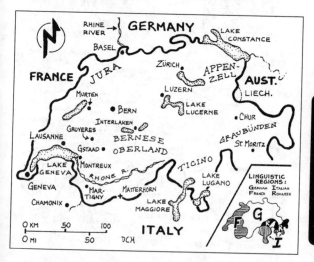

EUROPE

THE UNITED STATES

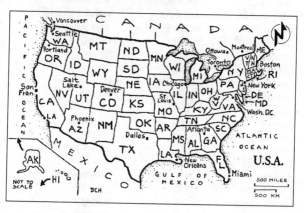

THE WORLD

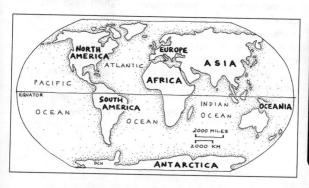

Favorite Things

What is your favorite...?	Was ist Ihr Lieblings...?	vahs ist eer **lee**-bleengs
What kind of... do you like?	Welche Art... mögen Sie?	**wehlkh**-eh art... **mur**-gehn zee
...art	...Kunst	koonst
...book	...Buch	bookh
...hobby	...Hobby	"hobby"
...ice cream	...Eis	īs
...food	...Essen	**eh**-sehn
...movie	...Film	"film"
...music	...Musik	moo-**zeek**
...sport	...Sport	shport
...vice	...Sünde	**zewn**-deh
Who is your favorite...?	Wer ist Ihr Lieblings...?	vayr ist eer **lee**-bleengs
...movie star	...Filmstar	"filmstar"
...male singer	...Sänger	**zehng**-er
...male artist	...Künstler	**kewnst**-ler
...male author	...Schriftsteller	**shrift**-shteh-ler
...female singer	...Sängerin	**zehng**-er-in
...female artist	...Künstlerin	**kewnst**-ler-in
...female author	...Schriftstellerin	**shrift**-shteh-ler-in
Can you recommend a good German CD?	Können Sie eine gute deutsche CD empfehlen?	**kurn**-nehn zee ī-neh **goo**-teh **doy**-cheh say-day ehmp-**fay**-lehn
Can you recommend a good German book translated in English?	Können Sie ein gutes deutsches Buch, in Englisch übersetzt empfehlen?	**kurn**-nehn zee īn **goo**-tehs **doy**-chehs bookh in **ehng**-lish ew-ber-**zehtst** ehmp-**fay**-lehn

Weather

What's the weather tomorrow?	*Wie wird das Wetter morgen?*	vee virt dahs **veh**-ter **mor**-gehn
sunny / cloudy	*sonnig / bewölkt*	**zoh**-nig / beh-**vurlkt**
hot / cold	*heiß / kalt*	hīs / kahlt
muggy / windy	*schwül / windig*	shvewl / **vin**-dig
rain / snow	*Regen / Schnee*	**ray**-gehn / shnay
Should I bring a jacket?	*Soll ich eine Jacke mitbringen?*	zohl ikh ī-neh **yah**-keh **mit**-bring-ehn

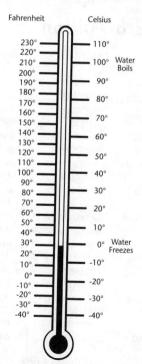

It's raining buckets.	Es regnet wie aus Kübeln.	ehs **rayg**-neht vee ows **kew**-behln
The fog is like milk soup.	Das ist eine Milchsuppe.	dahs ist **ī**-neh **milkh**-zoo-peh
It's so hot you can boil an egg on the sidewalk.	Es ist so heiß, daß man Eier auf dem Gehsteig braten kann.	es ist zo hīs dahs mahn **ī**-er owf daym **geh**-shtīg **brah**-tehn kahn
The wind could blow your ears off.	Der Wind könnte mir die Ohren wegblasen.	dehr vint **kurn**-teh meer dee **or**-ehn **vehg**-blah-zehn

Thanks a Million

Thank you very much.	Vielen Dank.	**fee**-lehn dahngk
This is great fun.	Das ist ein Riesenspaß.	dahs ist īn **ree**-zehn-shpahs
You are...	Sie sind...	zee zint
...helpful.	...hilfreich.	**hilf**-rīkh
...wonderful.	...wunderbar.	**voon**-der-bar
...generous.	...großzügig.	**grohs**-tsew-gig
You spoil me / us.	Sie verwöhnen mich / uns.	zee fehr-**vur**-nehn mikh / oons
You've been a great help.	Sie waren sehr hilfreich.	zee **vah**-rehn zehr **hilf**-rīkh
You are an angel from God.	Sie sind ein Engel, von Gott gesandt.	zee zint īn **ehng**-ehl fohn goht geh-**zahndt**
I will remember you...	Ich werde Sie... in Erinnerung behalten.	ikh **vehr**-deh zee... in eh-**rin**-er-oong beh-**hahl**-tehn
We will remember you...	Wir werden Sie... in Erinnerung behalten.	veer **vehr**-dehn zee... in eh-**rin**-er-oong beh-**hahl**-tehn
...always.	...immer	**im**-mer
...till Tuesday.	...bis Dienstag	bis **deen**-stahg

Smoking

Do you smoke?	*Rauchen Sie?*	**rowkh**-ehn zee
Do you smoke pot?	*Rauchen Sie Haschisch?*	**rowkh**-ehn zee hah-**sheesh**
I (don't) smoke.	*Ich rauche (nicht).*	ikh **rowkh**-eh (nikht)
We (don't) smoke.	*Wir rauchen (nicht).*	veer **rowkh**-ehn (nikht)
I haven't any.	*Ich habe keine.*	ikh **hah**-beh **kī**-neh
lighter	*Feuerzeug*	**foy**-er-tsoyg
cigarettes	*Zigaretten*	tsig-ah-**reh**-tehn
marijuana	*Marihuana*	mah-ri-**wah**-nah
hash	*Haschisch*	hah-**sheesh**
joint	*Joint, Kiffe*	"joint," **ki**-feh
stoned	*benebelt*	beh-**nay**-behlt
Wow!	*Woah!*	woh-**ah**

Responses for All Occasions

I like that.	*Das gefällt mir.*	dahs geh-**fehlt** meer
We like that.	*Das gefällt uns.*	dahs geh-**fehlt** oons
I like you.	*Sie gefallen mir.*	zee geh-**fah**-lehn meer
We like you.	*Sie gefallen uns.*	zee geh-**fah**-lehn oons
That's cool!	*Hey, cool! Toll!*	"hey, cool," tohl
Excellent!	*Ausgezeichnet!*	ows-geh-**tsīkh**-neht
What a nice place.	*Was für ein herrlicher Ort.*	vahs fewr īn **hehr**-likh-er ort
Perfect.	*Perfekt.*	pehr-**fehkt**
Funny.	*Komisch.*	**koh**-mish
Interesting.	*Interessant.*	in-tehr-eh-**sahnt**
Really?	*Wirklich?*	**virk**-likh
Wow!	*Woah!*	woh-**ah**
Congratulations!	*Herzlichen Glückwunsch!*	**hehrts**-likh-ehn **glewk**-vunsh
Well done!	*Gut gemacht!*	goot geh-**mahkht**
You're welcome.	*Bitte schön.*	**bit**-teh shurn
Bless you! (after sneeze)	*Gesundheit!*	geh-**zoond**-hīt

What a pity.	Wie schade.	vee **shah**-deh
That's life.	So geht's eben.	zoh gayts **ay**-behn
No problem.	Kein Problem.	kīn proh-**blaym**
O.K.	O.K.	"O.K."
This is the good life!	So läßt es sich leben!	zoh lehst ehs zikh **lay**-ben
Have a good day!	Schönen Tag!	**shurn**-ehn tahg
Good luck!	Viel Glück!	feel glewk
Let's go!	Auf geht's!	owf gayts

Conversing with Animals

rooster / cock-a-doodle-doo	Hahn / kikeriki	hahn / kee-keh-ree-**kee**
bird / tweet tweet	Vogel / piep piep	**foh**-gehl / peep peep
cat / meow	Katze / miau	**kaht**-seh / mee-**ow**
dog / woof woof	Hund / wuff wuff	hoont / vuff vuff
duck / quack quack	Ente / quak quak	**ehn**-teh / kvahk kvahk
cow / moo	Kuh / muh	koo / moo
pig / oink oink	Schwein / nöff nöff	shvīn / nurf nurf

Profanity

People make animal noises too. These words will help you understand what the more colorful locals are saying...

Go to hell!	Geh zur Hölle!	gay tsur **hurl**-leh
Damn it.	Verdammt.	fehr-**dahmt**
bastard (pig-dog)	Schweinehund	**shvī**-neh-hoont
bitch (goat)	Ziege	**tsee**-geh
breasts (colloq.)	Titten	**tit**-ehn
penis (colloq.)	Schwanz	shvahnts
butthole	Arschloch	**arsh**-lohkh
drunk	besoffen	beh-**zohf**-fehn
idiot	Idiot	id-ee-**oht**
imbecile	Trottel	**troh**-tehl

jerk	Blödmann	**blurd**-mahn
stupid (dumb head)	Dummkopf	**doom**-kohpf
Did someone fart?	Hat jemand gefurzt?	haht **yay**-mahnt geh-**foortst**
I burped.	Ich habe gerülpst.	ikh **hah**-beh geh-**rewlpst**
This sucks.	Das ödet an.	dahs **ur**-deht ahn
Shit.	Scheiße.	**shī**-seh
Bullshit.	Blödsinn.	**blurd**-zin
Sit on it.	Am Arsch.	ahm arsh
Shit on it.	Scheiß drauf.	shīs drowf
You are...	Du bist...	doo bist
Don't be...	Sei kein...	zī kīn
...a "shit guy."	...Scheißkerl.	**shīs**-kehrl
...an asshole.	...Arschloch.	**arsh**-lohkh
...an idiot.	...Idiot.	id-ee-**oht**
...a creep.	...Psychopath.	**psew**-koh-paht
...a cretin.	...Blödmann.	**blurd**-mahn
...a pig.	...Schwein.	shvīn

Sweet Curses

My goodness.	Meine Güte.	**mī**-neh **gew**-teh
Goodness gracious.	Ach du liebe Zeit.	ahkh doo **lee**-beh tsīt
Oh, my gosh.	Oh, Jemine.	oh **yeh**-mee-neh
Shoot.	Scheibenkleister.	**shī**-behn-klī-ster
Darn it!	Verflixt!	fehr-**flikst**

Create Your Own Conversation

You can mix and match these words into a conversation. Make it as deep or silly as you want.

Who

I / you	*ich / Sie*	**ikh** / zee
he / she	*er / sie*	ehr / zee
we / they	*wir / sie*	veer / zee
my / your...	*mein / Ihr...*	mīn / eer
...parents / children	*...Eltern / Kinder*	**ehl**-tern / **kin**-der
men / women	*Männer / Frauen*	**mehn**-ner / **frow**-ehn
rich / poor	*Reichen / Armen*	**rīkh**-ehn / **ar**-mehn
young / old	*Junge / Alte*	**yoong**-eh / **ahl**-teh
middle-aged	*Mittelalterliche*	**mit**-ehl-ahl-ter-likh-eh
Germans	*Deutschen*	**doy**-chehn
Austrians	*Österreicher*	**urs**-teh-rīkh-er
Swiss	*Schweizer*	**shvīt**-ser
Czechs	*Tschechen*	**chehkh**-ehn
French	*Franzosen*	frahn-**tsoh**-zehn
Italians	*Italiener*	i-tah-lee-**ehn**-er
Europeans	*Europäer*	ay-oo-roh-**pay**-er
EU (European Union)	*EU*	ay oo
Americans	*Amerikaner*	ah-mehr-ee-**kahn**-er
liberals	*Liberale*	lib-eh-**rah**-leh
conservatives	*Konservative*	kohn-zehr-vah-**teev**-eh
radicals	*Radikale*	rah-di-**kah**-leh
terrorists	*Terroristen*	tehr-or-**ist**-ehn
politicians	*Politiker*	poh-**lee**-tik-er
big business	*Großkapital*	**grohs**-kahp-i-**tahl**

CHATING

multinational corporations	*Multis*	**mool**-tees
military	*Militär*	mil-ee-**tehr**
mafia	*Mafia*	**mah**-fee-ah
Neo-Nazis	*Neonazis*	"Neo-Nazis"
eastern Germany	*Ostdeutschland*	**ohst**-doych-lahnt
western Germany	*Westen von Deutschland*	**vehs**-tehn fohn **doych**-lahnt
eastern / western Germans	*Ostdeutscher/ Westdeutscher*	**ohst**-doy-cher/ **vehst**-doy-cher
refugees	*Flüchtlinge*	**flewkht**-ling-eh
travelers	*Reisende*	**rī**-zehn-deh
God	*Gott*	goht
Christians	*Christen*	**kris**-tehn
Catholics	*Katholiken*	kah-**toh**-li-kehn
Protestants	*Protestanten*	proh-tehs-**tahn**-tehn
Jews	*Juden*	**yoo**-dehn
Muslims	*Moslems*	**mohz**-lehms
everyone	*alle Leute*	**ah**-leh **loy**-teh

What

buy / sell	*kaufen / verkaufen*	**kow**-fehn / fehr-**kow**-fehn
have / lack	*haben / haben nicht*	**hah**-behn / **hah**-behn nikht
help / abuse	*helfen / mißbrauchen*	**hehl**-fehn / mis-**browkh**-ehn
learn / fear	*lernen / fürchten*	**lehrn**-ehn / **fewrkh**-tehn
love / hate	*lieben / hassen*	**lee**-behn / **hah**-sehn
prosper / suffer	*florieren / leiden*	floh-**ree**-rehn / **lī**-dehn
take / give	*nehmen / geben*	**nay**-mehn / **gay**-behn
want / need	*wollen / brauchen*	**vol**-lehn / **browkh**-ehn
work / play	*arbeiten / spielen*	**ar**-bī t-ehn / **shpeel**-ehn

Why

(anti-)	(Anti-)	(**ahn**-tee-)
globalization	Globalisierung	gloh-bahl-is-**eer**-oong
class warfare	Klassenkampf	**klahs**-ehn-kahmpf
corruption	Korruption	kor-rupt-see-**ohn**
democracy	Demokratie	day-moh-krah-**tee**
education	Ausbildung	**ows**-bil-doong
family	Familie	fah-**mee**-lee-eh
food	Essen	**eh**-sehn
guns	Waffen	**vah**-fehn
happiness	Glück	glewk
health	Gesundheit	geh-**zoond**-hīt
hope	Hoffnung	**hohf**-noong
imperialism	Kolonisation	koh-loh-nee-saht-see-**ohn**
lies	Lügen	**lew**-gehn
love / sex	Liebe / Sex	**lee**-beh / zehx
marijuana	Marihuana	mah-ri-**wah**-nah
money / power	Geld / Macht	gehlt / mahkht
pollution	Umweltver- schmutzung	**oom**-vehlt-fehr- **shmut**-tsoong
racism	Rassimus	rah-**sis**-moos
regime change	Regimewechsel	reh-**zheem**-vehkh-sehl
relaxation	Entspannung	ehnt-**shpah**-noong
religion	Religion	reh-leeg-ee-**ohn**
respect	Respekt	rehs-**pehkt**
reunification	Wiedervereinigung	**vee**-dehr-fehr-īn-i-goong
taxes	Steuern	**shtoy**-ern
television	Fernsehen	**fehrn**-zay-hehn
violence	Gewalt	geh-**vahlt**
war / peace	Krieg / Frieden	kreeg / **free**-dehn
work	Arbeit	**ar**-bīt
global perspective	Gesamt- perspektive	geh-**zahmt**- per-spehk-**tee**-veh

CHATING

You be the Judge

(no) problem	(kein) Problem	(kīn) proh-**blaym**
(not) good	(nicht) gut	(nikht) goot
(not) dangerous	(nicht) gefährlich	(nikht) geh-**fayr**-likh
(not) fair	(nicht) fair	(nikht) "fair"
(not) guilty	(nicht) schuldig	(nikht) **shool**-dig
(not) powerful	(nicht) mächtig	(nikht) **mehkh**-tig
(not) stupid	(nicht) dumm	(nikht) doom
(not) happy	(nicht) glücklich	(nikht) **glewk**-likh
because / for	weil / wegen	vīl / **vay**-gehn
and / or / from	und / oder / von	oont / **oh**-dehr / fohn
too much	zu viel	tsoo feel
(never) enough	(nie) genug	(nee) geh-**noog**
same	gleich	glīkh
better / worse	besser / schlechter	**behs**-ser / **shlehkh**-ter
here / everywhere	hier / überall	heer / ew-ber-**ahl**

Beginnings and Endings

I like...	Ich mag...	ikh mahg
We like...	Wir mögen...	veer **mur**-gehn
I don't like...	Ich mag... nicht.	ikh mahg... nikht
We don't like...	Wir mögen... nicht.	veer **mur**-gehn... nikht
Do you like...?	Mögen Sie...?	**mur**-gehn zee
In the past...	Früher...	**frew**-her
When I was younger, I thought...	Als ich jünger war, dachte ich...	ahls ikh **yewng**-er var **dahkh**-teh ikh
Now, I think...	Jetzt denke ich...	yetst **dehnk**-eh ikh
I am / Are you...?	Ich bin / Sind Sie...?	ikh bin / zint zee
...an optimist / pessimist	...ein Optimist / Pessimist	īn **ohp**-ti-meest / **pehs**-i-meest
I believe in...	Ich glaube an...	ikh **glow**-beh ahn
I don't believe in...	Ich glaube nicht an...	ikh **glow**-beh nikht ahn
Do you believe in...?	Glauben Sie an...?	**glow**-behn zee ahn

CHATING

...God	...Gott	goht
...life after death	...Leben nach dem Tod	**lay**-behn nahkh daym tohd
...extraterrestrial life	...Leben im Weltall	**lay**-behn im **vehlt**-ahl
...Santa Claus	...Weihnachtsmann	**vī**-nahkhts-mahn
Yes. / No.	Ja. / Nein.	yah / nīn
Maybe. / I don't know.	Vielleicht. / Ich weiß nicht.	fee-**līkht** / ikh vīs nikht
What is most important in life?	Was ist das Wichtigste im Leben?	vahs ist dahs **vikh**-tig-steh im **lay**-behn
The problem is...	Das Problem ist...	dahs proh-**blaym** ist
The answer is...	Die Antwort ist...	dee **ahnt**-vort ist
We have solved the world's problems.	Wir haben die Probleme der Welt gelöst.	veer **hah**-behn dee proh-**blay**-meh dehr vehlt geh-**lurst**

A German Romance

Words of Love

CHATING

I / me / you / we	ich / mich / dich / wir	ikh / mikh / dikh / veer
flirt	flirten	**flir**-tehn
kiss	Kuß	kus
hug	Umarmung	oom-**arm**-oong
love	Liebe	**lee**-beh
make love (sleep together)	miteinander schlafen	mit-ī n-**ahn**-dehr **shlah**-fehn
condom	Kondom, Präservativ	**kon**-dohm, pray-zehr-fah-**tif**
contraceptive	Verhütungs- mittel	fehr-**hew**-toongs- **mit**-tehl
safe sex	safe sex	"safe sex"

sexy	sexy	"sexy"
cozy	gemütlich	geh-**mewt**-likh
romantic	romantisch	roh-**mahn**-tish
cupcake	Schnuckel	**shnook**-ehl
little rabbit	Häschen	**hays**-khehn
little sugar mouse	Zuckermäuschen	tsoo-ker-**moys**-khehn
pussy cat	Miezekatze	**meets**-eh-**kaht**-seh
baby	Baby	**bay**-bee

Ah, Liebe

What's the matter?	Was ist los?	vahs ist lohs
Nothing.	Nichts.	nikhts
I am / Are you...?	Ich bin / Sind Sie...?	ikh bin / zint zee
...straight	...hetero	**hay**-ter-oh
...gay	...schwul	shvul
...bisexual	...bisexual	bee-zeks-oo-**ahl**
...undecided	...mir nicht sicher	meer nikht **zikh**-er
...prudish	...verklemmt	fehr-**klehmt**
...horny	...geil	gīl
We are on our honeymoon.	Wir sind auf unserer Hochzeitsreise.	veer zint owf **oon**-zer-er **hohkh**-tsī ts-rī-zeh
I have...	Ich habe...	ikh **hah**-beh
...a boyfriend.	...einen Freund.	**ī**-nehn froynt
...a girlfriend.	...eine Freundin.	**ī**-neh **froyn**-din
I'm married, but...	Ich bin verheiratet. aber...	ikh bin fehr-**hī**-rah-teht **ah**-ber
I'm not married.	Ich bin nicht verheiratet.	ikh bin nikht fehr-**hī**-rah-teht
Do you have a boyfriend / a girlfriend?	Haben Sie einen Freund / eine Freundin?	**hah**-behn zee **ī**-nehn froynt / **ī**-neh **froyn**-din
I'm adventurous.	Ich bin auf Abenteuer aus.	ikh bin owf **ah**-behn-toy-er ows
I'm lonely (tonight).	Ich bin einsam (heut' Nacht).	ikh bin **īn**-zahm (hoyt nahkht)

I'm rich and single.	*Ich bin reich und zu haben.*	ikh bin rī kh oont tsoo **hah**-behn
Do you mind if I sit here?	*Stört es Sie, wenn ich hier sitze?*	shturt ehs zee vehn ikh heer **zit**-seh
Would you like a drink?	*Möchten Sie einen Drink?*	**murkh**-tehn zee **ī**-nehn drink
Will you go out with me?	*Gehen Sie mit mir aus?*	**gay**-hehn zee mit meer ows
Would you like to go out tonight for...?	*Möchten Sie heute ausgehen für...?*	**murkh**-tehn zee **hoy**-teh **ows**-gay-hehn fewr
...a walk	*...einen Spaziergang*	**ī**-nehn shpaht-**seer**-gahng
...dinner	*...ein Abendessen*	ī n **ah**-behnt-eh-sehn
...a drink	*...einen Drink*	ī n drink
Where's the best place to dance nearby?	*Wo geht man hier am besten Tanzen?*	voh gayt mahn heer ahm **beh**-stehn **tahn**-tsehn
Do you want to dance?	*Möchten Sie tanzen?*	**murkh**-tehn zee **tahn**-tsehn
Again?	*Noch einmal?*	nokh **ī n**-mahl
Let's party!	*Feiern wir!*	**fī**-ern veer
Let's have fun like idiots!	*Feiern wir wie blöd!*	**fī**-ern veer vee blurd
Let's have a wild and crazy night!	*Machen wir einen 'drauf!*	**mahkh**-ehn veer **ī**-neh drowf
I have no diseases.	*Ich habe keine Krankheiten.*	ikh **hah**-behh **kī**-neh **krahnk**-hī -tehn
I have many diseases.	*Ich habe viele Krankheiten.*	ikh **hah**-beh **fee**-leh **krahnk**-hī -tehn
I have only safe sex.	*Mit mir nur safe sex.*	mit meer noor "safe sex"
Can I take you home?	*Kann ich Sie nach Hause bringen?*	kahn ikh zee nahkh **how**-zeh **bring**-ehn
Why not?	*Warum nicht?*	vah-**room** nikht
How can I change your mind?	*Wie kann ich Sie umstimmen?*	vee kahn ikh zee **oom**-shtim-mehn

Kiss me.	*Küß mich.*	kews mikh
May I kiss you?	*Darf ich dich*	darf ikh dikh
	küssen?	**kews**-ehn
Can I see you	*Können wir uns*	**kurn**-nehn veer oons
again?	*wiedersehen?*	**vee**-der-zayn
Your place or mine?	*Bei dir oder bei mir?*	bī deer **oh**-der bī meer
How does this feel?	*Wie fühlt sich das an?*	vee fewlt zikh dahs ahn
Is this an	*Ist dies ein*	ist deez īn
aphrodisiac?	*Aphrodisiakum?*	ah-froh-dee-zee-**ahk**-oom
This is (not) my	*Dies ist für mich*	deez ist fewr mikh
first time.	*(nicht) das*	(nikht) dahs
	erste Mal.	**ehr**-steh mahl
You are my most	*Du bist mein*	doo bist mīn
beautiful	*schönstes*	**shurn**-stehs
souvenir.	*Andenken.*	**ahn**-dehnk-ehn
Do you do	*Machst du das oft?*	mahkhst doo dahs oft
this often?		
Do I have bad	*Habe ich*	**hah**-beh ikh
breath?	*Mundgeruch?*	**moont**-geh-rookh
Let's just be	*Wir können doch*	veer **kurn**-nehn dohkh
friends.	*einfach*	**īn**-fahkh
	Freunde sein.	**froyn**-deh zīn
I'll pay for	*Ich bezahle*	ikh beht-**sah**-leh
my share.	*meinen Anteil.*	**mī**-nehn **ahn**-tīl
Would you like a...	*Darf ich dir den...*	darf ikh deer dayn...
massage?	*massieren?*	mah-**see**-rehn
...back	*...Rücken*	**rew**-kehn
...foot	*...Fuß*	foos
Why not?	*Warum nicht?*	vah-**room** nikht
Try it.	*Versuch's*	fehr-**zookhs**
	doch mal.	dohk mahl
That tickles.	*Das kitzelt.*	dahs **kit**-sehlt
Oh my God!	*Oh mein Gott!*	oh mīn goht
I love you.	*Ich liebe dich.*	ikh **lee**-beh dikh
Darling,	*Liebling,*	**lee**-bleeng
marry me!	*heirate mich!*	**hī**-rah-teh mikh

DICTIONARY

German/English

A

German	English
A-Affenschwanz	at sign (@)
Abend	evening
Abendessen	dinner
aber	but
abfahren	depart
Abfahrten	departures
Abflußstöpsel	sink stopper
Abführmittel	decongestant
Abschleppwagen	tow truck
abschließen	lock (v)
abstempeln	validate
abstrakt	abstract
Abtreibung	abortion
Adresse	address
Afrika	Africa
aggressiv	aggressive
agnostisch	agnostic
ähnlich	similar
AIDS	AIDS
Alkohol	alcohol
allein	alone
Allergien	allergies
allergisch	allergic
alles	everything
alt	old
Altar	altar
Alter	age
altertümlich	ancient
am besten	best
Ampel	stoplight
anderes	other
ändern	change (v)
anfangen	begin
ängstlich	shy, afraid
Anhalter fahren	hitchhike
ankommen	arrive
Ankunften	arrivals
annullieren	cancel

Anschluß	connection (train)	**Ausfahrt**	exit (road)
anstatt	instead	**Ausgang**	exit (door)
ansteckend	contagious	**ausgeben**	spend
Antibiotika	antibiotic	**ausgezeichnet**	excellent
Antiquitäten	antiques	**Ausschlag**	rash
Antiquitäten-	antiques shop	**außer**	except
laden		**Aussprache**	pronunciation
Antwort	answer	**Ausverkauf**	sale
Anus	rectum	**Auto**	car
Anwalt	lawyer		
Apfel	apple	**B**	
Apfelsine	orange (fruit)	**B. H. (Büstenhalter)**	bra
Apotheke	pharmacy	**Baby**	baby
April	April	**Babygitter**	playpen
Arbeit	work (n)	**Babynahrung**	baby formula
arbeiten	work (v)	**Babypuder**	talcum powder
arbeitslos	unemployed	**Babysitter**	babysitter
Arm	arm	**Bäckerei**	bakery
arm	poor	**Bad**	bath; bathroom
Armband	bracelet	**Badeanzug**	swimsuit
Ärmel	sleeves	**Badehose**	swim trunks
Arzt	doctor	**Badelatschen**	thongs
Aschenbecher	ashtray	**Bademantel**	bathrobe
Atem	breath	**Badetuch**	bath towel
atheistisch	atheist	**Badewanne**	bathtub
attraktiv	attractive	**Bahnsteig**	platform (train)
auf	on	**bald**	soon
auf dem Land	countryside	**Balkon**	balcony
auf Wiedersehen	goodbye	**Ball**	ball
aufwachen	wake up	**Banane**	banana
aufwarmen	heat (v)	**Bank**	bank
Auge	eye	**Bankomat**	cash machine
Augenkontour	eyeliner	**Bargeld**	cash
Augenschatten	eye shadow	**Bart**	beard
August	August	**Batterie**	battery
Ausbildung	education	**Bauer**	farmer
Ausblick	view	**Bauernhof**	farm

Baum	tree
Baumwolle	cotton
Baustelle	construction (sign)
bearbeiten	edit
Bedienung	service
beeilen (sich)	hurry (v)
beenden	finish (v)
beendet	over (finished)
Beerdigung	funeral
behalten	keep
behindert	handicapped
bei	at
Bein	leg
Beispiel	example
Beleg	receipt
belegt	no vacancy
belegtes Brot	sandwich
Belgien	Belgium
benebelt	stoned
Ben-u-ron	non-aspirin substitute
Benzin	gas
beobachten	watch (v)
beraubt	robbed
bereit	ready
Berg	mountain
Beruf	job, profession
berühmt	famous
beschweren (sich)	complain
besetzt	occupied
besitzen	own (v)
Besitzer	owner
besonders	especially
besser	better
bestätigen	confirm
besten, am	best
Besuch	visit (n)
besuchen	visit (v)
betrunken	drunk
Bett	bed
bewölkt	cloudy
bewußtlos	unconscious
bezahlen	pay
bezaubernd	charming
Bier	beer
Bildhauer	sculptor
billig	cheap
Bindestrich	hyphen (-)
Birne	bulb
bitte	please
Blase	bladder
Blasen	blisters
Blasen, Pflaster gegen	moleskin
blau	blue
Bleistift	pencil
Blick	view
Blinker	turn signal
Blitz	flash (camera)
Blume	flower
Blumenmarkt	flower market
Bluse	blouse
Blut	blood
bluten	bleeding
Bluthochdruck	high blood pressure
Boden	bottom
Bombe	bomb
Bonbons	candy
Botschaft	embassy
brauchen	need
braun	brown
Bremsen	brakes
Brief	letter
Briefmarke	stamp

Brieftasche	wallet
Briefumschlag	envelope
Brille	glasses (eye)
Brosche	brooch
Brot	bread
Brücke	bridge
Bruder	brother
Brunnen	fountain
Brust	chest
Brust,	chest pains
Schmerzen in der	
Buch	book
Buchhalter	accountant
Buchladen	book shop
Bund	waist
Burg	castle
Burggraben	moat
Burgmauer	wall, fortified
Büro	office
Bürobedarf	office supplies store
Büroklammer	paper clip
Busbahnhof	bus station
Busen	breast
Bushaltestelle	bus stop
Büstenhalter	bra

C

Chef	boss, manager
chinesisch	Chinese (adj)
Chor	choir
christlich	Christian (adj)

D

Dach	roof
Damen	women, ladies
Damenbinden	sanitary napkins
danke	thanks

Därme	intestines
Decke	blanket
Deckel	cap
deklarieren	declare (customs)
Demokratie	democracy
denken	think
Denkmal	monument
Desinfektionsmittel	disinfectant
Deutschland	Germany
Dezember	December
Dia	slide (photo)
diabetisch	diabetic
Diamant	diamond
dick	thick; fat
Dieb	thief
Dienstag	Tuesday
Dienstleistung, mit	full-service
Ding	thing
direkt	direct
Dom	cathedral
Donau	Danube
Donnerstag	Thursday
doppel	double
Dorf	village
Dose	can (n)
Dosenöffner	can opener
dringend	urgent
drucken	print
drücken	push
du	you (informal)
dumm	stupid
dunkel	dark
dünn	thin, skinny
durch	through
Durchfall	diarrhea
Durchfall-	diarrhea medicine
medikament	

German	English
durchgehen	go through
durstig	thirsty
Dusche	shower
Dutzend	dozen

E

echt	genuine
Ecke	corner
Ehefrau	wife
Ehemann	husband
ehrlich	honest
Eimer	bucket
ein, noch	another
Einbahnstraße	one-way street
einfach	easy; plain; one way (street)
Einfahrt	entrance (road)
Eingang	entrance (door)
eingeschlossen	included
einige	some
einkaufen	shopping
Einkaufszentrum	shopping mall
Einladung	invitation
einmal	once
einmal, noch	again; repeat
Eintrittskarte	ticket (show)
einverstanden	agree
Eis	ice; ice cream
Eisenbahn	railway
Eisenwarengeschäft	hardware store
Eislaufen	ice skating
Ellbogen	elbow
Eltern	parents
E-Mail-Adresse	e-mail address
Empfangsperson	receptionist
empfehlen	recommend

eng	tight
Englisch	English
Enkel	grandson
Enkelin	granddaughter
Entschuldigung	excuse me; sorry
Entspannung	relaxation
Entzündung	infection, inflammation
Epilepsie	epilepsy
er	he
Erde	earth
erhalten	receive
erholen (sich)	relax (v)
erinnern (sich)	remember
Erkältung	cold (n)
erklären	explain
Ermäßigung	discount
Erneuerung	refill (n)
ernsthaft	serious
erschöpft	exhausted
erst	first
Erste Hilfe	first aid
erste Klasse	first class
Erste-Hilfe-Salbe	first-aid cream
Erwachsener	adult
Esel	donkey
essen	eat
Essen	food
etwas	something
Europa	Europe
evangelisch	Protestant

F

Fabrik	factory
Faden	thread
Fahne	flag

German	English
Fähre	ferry
fahren	drive (v)
fahren per Anhalter	hitchhike
Fahrer	driver
Fahrkarte	ticket (train)
Fahrplan	timetable
Fahrrad	bicycle
Fahrstuhl	elevator
Fahrt	trip
fair	fair (just)
fallen	fall (v)
falsch	false
Familie	family
fangen	catch (v)
Farbe	color
farbenfest	color-fast
faul	lazy
Februar	February
Fehler	mistake
Fehlgeburt	miscarriage
Feiertag	holiday
Feinkostgeschäft	delicatessen
Feld	field
Fels	rock (n)
Fenster	window
Fernbus	long-distance bus
Fernsehen	television
Festival	festival
festsitzen	stuck
fett	fat (adj)
Fett	fat (n)
fettig	greasy
Feuchtigkeits-creme	moisturizer
Feuer	fire
Feuerwerk	fireworks
Feuerzeug	lighter (n)
Fieber	fever
Film	movie
Finger	finger
Fisch	fish (n)
fischen	fish (v)
Flasche	bottle
Fleisch	meat
fliegen	fly
Floh	flea
Flohmarkt	flea market
florieren	prosper
Floß	raft
Flüchtlinge	refugees
Flug	flight
Flügel	wing
Fluggesellschaft	airline
Flughafen	airport
Flugkarte	ticket (plane)
Flugzeug	plane
Flur	corridor
Fluß	river; stream (n)
Football	American, football
Fotokopie	photocopy
Frage	question (n)
fragen	ask
Frankreich	France
Frau	Mrs.
Fräulein	Miss
frei	vacant
Freitag	Friday
fremd	foreign
Fremden-zimmer	bed & breakfast
Freund	friend
freundlich	kind
Freundschaft	friendship
Frieden	peace

frisch	fresh	**Gefrierbeutel**	zip-lock bag
Frisiersalon	beauty salon	**Geheimnis**	secret (n)
Frisör	barber	**Geheimnummer**	PIN code
Frisur	haircut	**gehen**	go; walk (v)
früh	early	**gekocht**	boiled
Frühling	spring	**gelb**	yellow
Frühstück	breakfast	**Geld**	money
Führer	guide	**Gelenkentzündung**	arthritis
Führung	guided tour	**Gemälde**	painting
für	for	**gemütlich**	cozy
fürchten	fear (v)	**genau**	exactly
Fuß	foot	**genießen**	enjoy
Fußball	soccer	**genug**	enough
Fußgänger	pedestrian	**geöffnet**	open (adj)
Fußgelenk	ankle	**Gepäck**	baggage
Fußpilz	athlete's foot	**Gepäckaufgabe**	baggage check
		Gepäckausgabe	baggage claim
G		**geradeaus**	straight
Gabel	fork	**Geruch**	smell (n)
Galerie	gallery	**Geschäft**	business; store
Gang	aisle	**Geschäftsführer**	manager
Garage	garage	**Geschenk**	gift
Garantie	guarantee	**Geschichte**	history
Garten	garden	**geschieden**	divorced
Gärtnern	gardening	**Geschlechts-**	venereal disease
Gast	guest	**krankeit**	
Gästezimmer	bed & breakfast	**geschlossen**	closed
Gasthaus	country inn	**Geschmack**	taste (v), flavor (n)
Gasthof	country inn	**Geschwindigkeit**	speed
Gebärmutter	uterus	**Gesicht**	face
Gebäude	building	**Gesichtspulver**	face powder
geben	give	**Gesichtsseife**	face cleanser
Gebühr	toll	**gestern**	yesterday
gebührenfrei	toll-free	**gesund**	healthy
Geburtstag	birthday	**Gesundheit**	health
Gefahr	danger	**Getränk**	drink (n)
gefährlich	dangerous	**getrennt**	separate (adj)

German	English
Getriebeöl	transmission fluid
Gewalt	violence
Gewehr	gun
Gewicht	weight
Gitarre	guitar
Glas	glass
glatt	slippery
gleiche	same
Gleis	train track
Glocken	bells
Glück	happiness; luck
glücklich	happy
Glückwünsche	congratulations
Gold	gold
gothisch	Gothic
Gott	God
Gottesdienst	church service
Grammatik	grammar
grau	gray
Grenze	border
Griechenland	Greece
Griff	handle (n)
Grippe	flu
Grippemittel	cold medicine
groß	big
Großbritannien	Great Britain
Größe	size
Großmutter	grandmother
Großstrich	underscore (_)
Großvater	grandfather
großzügig	generous
grün	green
Grundlage	foundation
gucken	look
gültig	valid
Gürtel	belt
gut	good
gutaussehend	handsome
guten Tag	good day
Gymnastik	gymnastics
Gynäkologin	gynecologist

H

Haarbürste	hairbrush
Haare	hair
Haarfestiger	conditioner (hair)
Haarsalon	beauty salon
haben	have
Hafen	harbor
Hähnchen	chicken
hallo	hello
Hals	throat
Halsband	necklace
Halsbonbon	lozenges
Halsschmerzen	sore throat
Halt	stop (n)
haltbar	sturdy
halten	stop (v)
Hämorrhoiden Salbe	Preparation H
Hämorrhoiden	hemorrhoids
Hand	hand
Handarbeiten	handicrafts
Handgelenk	wrist
Handgepäck	carry-on luggage
Handlotion	hand lotion
Handschuhe	gloves
Handtasche	purse
Handtuch	towel
Handy	cell phone
Harnröhre	urethra
Harnröhrenentzündung	urinary infection
hart	hard

German	English
Haschisch	hash
Hase	rabbit
hassen	hate (v)
häßlich	ugly
Haupt	main
Hauptbahnhof	main train station
Haus	house
Häuserblock	block (street)
hausgemacht	homemade
Haustier	pet (n)
Haut	skin
Heiliger	saint
Heimweh	homesickness
heiß	hot
Helm	helmet
Hemd	shirt
Herbst	autumn
Herr	gentleman; Mr.
Herren	men
Herrenfrisör	barber shop
herunterladen	download
Herz	heart
Herzbeschwerden	heart condition
Heuschnupfen	hay fever
heute	today
heute abend	tonight
hier	here
Hilfe	help (n)
Hilfe, Erste	first aid
hilfen	help (v)
hilfreich	helpful
Himmel	heaven; sky
Hinfahrkarte	one way (ticket)
hinter	behind
Hinterbacken	buttocks

German	English
Hitze	heat (n)
hoch	high; tall; up
Hochzeit	wedding
Hochzeitsreise	honeymoon
Hoden	testicles
Hoffnung	hope
Höhle	cave
Holz	wood
hören	hear
Hosen	pants
hübsch	pretty
Hüfte	hip
Hügel	hill
Hund	dog
hungrig	hungry
Husten	cough (n)
husten	cough (v)
Hustenbonbons	cough drops
Hut	hat

I

German	English
ich	I
ihr	her; their
Ihr	your (formal)
im Freien	outdoors
Imbiß	snack
immer	always
importiert	imported
impressionistisch	Impressionist
in	in
Industrie	industry
Infektion	infection
Information	information
Ingenieur	engineer
inklusive	included
innen	inside
Insekt	insect

Insel	island
interessant	interesting
Internet	Internet
Internet-anschluß	Internet access
Internetcafé	Internet café
Internetseite	Web site
Irland	Ireland
ist	is
Italien	Italy

J

ja	yes
Jacke	jacket
Jahr	year
Jahrhundert	century
Januar	January
jede	each; every
Jeton	token
jetzt	now
Jod	iodine
Joint	joint (marijuana)
jüdisch	Jewish
Jugendherberge	youth hostel
Jugendliche	youths
Jugendlicher	teenager
Jugendstil	Art Nouveau
Juli	July
jung	young
Junge	boy
Juni	June

K

Kaffee	coffee
Kaffeeladen	coffee shop
Kaiser	emperor
Kaiserin	empress
Kakerlake	cockroach
Kalender	calendar
Kalorie	calorie
kalt	cold (adj)
Kälteschauer	chills
Kamm	comb (n)
Kanada	Canada
Kanal	canal
Kanu	canoe
Kanzel	pulpit
Kapelle	chapel
Kapitän	captain
kaputt	broken
Karaffe	carafe
Karte	card; map
Karten	cards (deck)
Karton	box
Käse	cheese
Käserei	cheese shop
Kassette	cassette (tape)
Kassierer	cashier
Kathedrale	cathedral
katholisch	Catholic (adj)
Katze	cat
kaufen	buy
Kaufhaus	department store
Kaugummi	gum
Kaution	deposit
Keilriemen	fan belt
kein	no
Keller	basement
Kellner	waiter
Kellnerin	waitress
Keramik	ceramic
Kerze	candle
Kessel	kettle
Kiefer	jaw

Kiffe	joint (marijuana)	**kochen**	cook (v)
Kinder	children	**Koffer**	suitcase
Kinderaufsicht	babysitting service	**Kohlensäure**	carbon dioxide
Kinderbett	crib	**Kojen**	bunk beds
Kindereinteiler	sleeper (for baby)	**komfortabel**	comfortable
		komisch	funny
Kindersitz	booster seat	**kommen**	come
Kinderstuhl	highchair	**kompliziert**	complicated
Kinderwagen	stroller	**Komputer**	computer
Kino	cinema	**Konditorei**	pastry shop
Kiosk	newsstand	**Kondom**	condom
Kirche	church	**König**	king
Kirchenkonzert	church concert	**Königin**	queen
Kissen	pillow	**können**	can (v)
Klammeraffe	stapler	**Konzert**	concert
klar	clear	**Kopf**	head
Klasse	class	**Kopfschmerzen**	headache
Klasse, erste	first class	**Kopie**	copy
Klasse, zweiter	second class	**Kopierladen**	photocopy shop
klassisch	classical (music)	**Korb**	basket
klassizistisch	classical (period)	**Korbballspiel**	basketball
Klebeband	tape (adhesive)	**Korken**	cork
Kleid	dress (n)	**Korkenzieher**	corkscrew
Kleider	clothes	**Körper**	body
Kleiderbügel	coat hanger	**Korruption**	corruption
Kleiderladen	clothing boutique	**kosten**	cost (v)
klein	small	**kostenlos**	free (no cost)
Kleinküche	kitchenette	**kostet, wie viel**	how much ($)
Kliff	cliff	**Krämpfe**	cramps
Klimaanlage	air conditioning	**krank**	sick
Klinik	medical clinic	**Krankenhaus**	hospital
Klopapier	toilet paper	**Krankenschwester**	nurse
Kloster	cloister, monastery	**Kranken-versicherung**	health insurance
klug	intelligent	**Krankenwagen**	ambulance
Knie	knee	**Krankheit**	disease
Knopf	button	**Kreditkarte**	credit card

Kreisel	roundabout
Kreuz	cross
Kreuzung	intersection
Krieg	war
Krypte	crypt
Küche	kitchen
Kugelschreiber	pen
Kuh	cow
kühl	cool
Kühler	radiator
Kunst	art
Kunstgalerie	art gallery
Kunstgewerbe	crafts
Künstler	artist
künstlich	artificial
Kupfer	copper
Kuppel	dome
kurz	short
kurze Hosen	shorts
Küß	kiss
Küste	coast

L

Lächeln	smile (n)
lachen	laugh (v)
Laden	store
Laken	bedsheet
Lamm	lamb
Lampe	lamp
Land	country
Land, auf dem	countryside
Landstraße	highway
langsam	slow
Latz	bib
Lätzchen	bib
lau	lukewarm
laufen	run (v)

laut	loud
Laxativ	laxative
Leben	life
leben	live
Lebensmittel	food
Lebensmittelgeschäft	grocery store
Lebensmittelvergiftung	food poisoning
lecker	delicious
Leder	leather
ledig	single
leer	empty
Lehrer	teacher
leiden	suffer
Leihbücherei	library
leihen	borrow; lend
Leine	string
Leinen	linen
Leiter	ladder
Leitungswasser	tap water
lernen	learn
letzte	last
Leuchtbirne	light bulb
Leute	people
Licht	light (n)
Liebe	love (n)
lieben	love (v)
Liebhaber	lover
Lied	song
Liege	cot
Liegewagen	sleeper car (train)
Liegewagenplatz	berth (train)
Linienbus	city bus
links	left
Linsen	contact lenses
Lippe	lip

Lippenbalsam	lip salve
Lippenstift	lipstick
Liste	list
Liter	liter
Loch	hole
Löffel	spoon
löschen	delete
Luft	air
Luftpost	air mail
Lügen	lies
Lungen	lungs
Lungenentzündung	pneumonia

M

machen	make (v)
macho	macho
Macht	power
mächtig	powerful
Mädchen	girl
Magen	stomach
Magenbrennen, Mittel gegen	antacid
Magenschmerzen	stomachache
Mai	May
Mann	man
männlich	male
Marihuana	marijuana
Markt	market
Marmor	marble (material)
März	March
Maskara	mascara
Maximum	maximum
Mechaniker	mechanic
Medikament	medicine
Meer	ocean, sea
Meeresfrüchte	seafood

German	English
mehr	more
mein	my
mein Herr	sir
Meisterschaft	championship
Menge	crowd (n)
Menstruieren	menstruation
merkwürdig	strange
Messer	knife
Messing	brass
Metall	metal
mieten	rent (to rent)
Migräne	migraine
Militär	military
Mineralsalbe	Vaseline
Mineralwasser	mineral water
Minuten	minutes
Mischung	mix (n)
mißbrauchen	abuse (v)
Mißverständnis	misunderstanding
mit	with; by (via)
mitnehmen	take out (food)
Mittag	noon
Mitteilung	message (e-mail)
mittel	medium
Mittel gegen Magenbrennen	antacid
mittelalterlich	medieval
Mitternacht	midnight
Mittwoch	Wednesday
Möbel	furniture
möchte	want
Mode	fashion
Modem	modem
mögen	like (v)
möglich	possible
Monat	month

Monatskrämpfe	menstrual cramps
Mond	moon
Montag	Monday
Moped	motor scooter
Morgen	morning
morgen	tomorrow
Moschee	mosque
Motorrad	motorcycle
Mücke	mosquito
Mückenspray	insect repellant
müde	tired
Mund	mouth
Münzen	coins
muselmanisch	Muslim
Musik	music
Muskel	muscle
Mutter	mother

N

nabel	navel
nach	after; to
nachher	afterwards
Nachmittag	afternoon
Nachricht	message
nachschenken	refill (v)
nächste	next
Nacht	night
Nachthemd	nightgown
Nachtisch	dessert
Nacken	neck
nackt	naked
Nadel	needle, pin
Nagel	fingernail
Nagellack	nail polish
Nagellackentferner	nail polish remover

Nagelschere	nail clipper
nahe	near
Name	name
Nase	nose
Nasenverstopfung	congestion (sinus)
naß	wet
Natel	cell phone
Natelladen	cell phone shop
Nationalität	nationality
Natur	nature
natürlich	natural
Nebel	fog
Neffe	nephew
nehmen	take
nein	no
neoklassizistisch	neoclassical
nervös	nervous
nett	nice
neu	new
nicht	not
Nichte	niece
Nichtraucher	non-smoking
nichts	nothing
nie	never
Niederlande	Netherlands
niedrig	low
Niesen	sneeze (n)
noch ein	another
noch einmal	again; repeat
Norden	north
normal	normal
Notausgang	emergency exit
Notfall	emergency
Notfallaufnahme	emergency room
Notizbuch	notebook

notwendig	necessary
November	November
Nuggel	pacifier
null	zero
nur	only
nutzen	use
Nylon	nylon (material)

O

ob	if
oben	upstairs
Obst	fruit
oder	or
Ofen	oven
offen	open (adj)
öffentlich	public
öffnen	open (v)
Öffnungszeiten	opening hours
ohne	without
Ohr	ear
Ohrenschmerzen	earache
Ohrenschützer	earplugs
Ohrringe	earrings
Oktober	October
Öl	oil
Olympiade	Olympics
Onkel	uncle
Oper	opera
Optiker	optician
orange	orange (color)
Ordner	folder (computer)
Orgel	organ
örtlich	local
Ostdeutschland	eastern Germany
Osten	east
Ostern	Easter
Österreich	Austria

P

Paket	package
Pantoffeln	slippers
Papa	dad
Papier	paper
Papiertuch	facial tissue
Parfum	perfume
Park	park (garden)
parken	park (v)
Parkplatz	parking lot
Paß	passport
peinlich	embarrassing
Pension	small hotel
pensioniert	retired
per Anhalter fahren	hitchhike
perfekt	perfect
Periode	period (woman's)
Pferd	horse
Pflanze	plant
Pflaster	band-aid
Pflaster gegen Blasen	moleskin
phantastisch	fantastic
Photoapparat	camera
Photoladen	camera shop
Picknick	picnic
Pille	pill
Pinzette	tweezers
Plastik	plastic
Plastiktüte	plastic bag
Platz	square (town); seat
plötzlich	suddenly
Politiker	politicians
Polizei	police
Porzellan	porcelain
Post	mail (n)
Poster	poster

German	English
Postkarte	postcard
Postleitzahl	zip code
praktisch	practical
Präservativ	condom
Preis	price
Priester	priest
privat	private
probieren	taste (v)
Prost!	Cheers!
Prozent	percent
Pullover	sweater
Puls	pulse
Pumpe	pump (n)
Punkt	dot (computer)
pünktlich	on time
Puppe	doll

Q
Qualität	quality

R
Rad	wheel
Radiergummi	eraser
Rasierapparat	razor
Rasiercreme	shaving cream
Rasierwasser	aftershave
Rassimus	racism
Rauch	smoke
Rauchen	smoking
Rechnung	bill (payment)
rechts	right
reden	talk
Regen	rain (n)
Regenbogen	rainbow
Regenmantel	raincoat
Regenschirm	umbrella
Regionalbus	long-distance bus

German	English
reich	rich
reif	ripe
Reifen	tire
Reise	trip, journey
Reisebüro	travel agency
Reiseführer	guidebook
reisen	travel
Reisende	passenger, traveler
Reisescheck	traveler's check
Reißverschluß	zipper
reiten	horse riding
Religion	religion
Reliquie	relic
Renaissance	Renaissance
reparieren	repair (v)
reservieren	reserve
Reservierung	reservation
Respekt	respect
Rezept	prescription; recipe
Richtung	direction
Rindfleisch	beef
Ring	ring (n)
Ringstraße	ring road
Ritter	knights
Rock	skirt
roh	raw
Rollschuhe	roller skates
rollstuhlgängig	wheelchair-accessible
romanisch	Romanesque
Romantik	Romantic (art)
romantisch	romantic
Röntgenbild	X-ray
rosa	pink
rot	red
Rücken	back
Rückfahrt	round-trip

German	English
Rückgabe	refund (n)
Rücklichtern	tail lights
Rucksack	backpack
Ruderboot	rowboat
Ruhe	silence
ruhig	quiet
Ruine	ruins
runter	down
Rußland	Russia

S

Saal	hall
Saft	juice
Sahne	cream
Samstag	Saturday
Samt	velvet
Sandalen	sandals
Sänger	singer
sauber	clean (adj)
sauer	sour
schade, wie	It's a pity
Schaffner	conductor
Schal	scarf
Schale	bowl; shell
Schatzkammer	treasury
Scheck	check
Scheibe	slice
Scheibenwischern	windshield wipers
Scheinwerfern	headlights
Schenkel	thigh
Schere	scissors
schicken	ship (v)
Schiff	boat
Schild	sign
schlafen	sleep (v)
schläfrig	sleepy

German	English
Schlafsaal	dormitory
Schlafsack	sleeping bag
Schlafwagenplatz	sleeper (train)
Schlagsahne	whipped cream
schlecht	bad
schlechter	worse
schlechteste	worst
Schleimhautentzündung	sinus problems
Schließfächer	lockers
Schloß	palace; lock (n)
schlucken	swallow (v)
Schlüssel	key
schmal	narrow
Schmerz	pain
Schmerzen in der Brust	chest pains
Schmerzmittel	pain killer
Schmuck	jewelry
Schmuckladen	jewelry shop
schmutzig	dirty
schnarchen	snore
Schnee	snow
Schnorchel	snorkel
Schnuller	pacifier
Schnur	string
Schnurrbart	moustache
Schnürsenkel	shoelaces
Schokolade	chocolate
schon	already
schön	beautiful
Schraubenzieher	screwdriver
schrecklich	terrible
schreiben	write
Schuhe	shoes
schuldig	guilty

Schule	school	Serviette	napkin
Schulter	shoulder	Shampoo	shampoo
schwanger	pregnant	sich beeilen	hurry (v)
Schwangerschaft	pregnancy	sich beschweren	complain
Schwangerschaftstest	pregnancy test	sich erholen	relax (v)
		sich erinnern	remember
Schwanz	tail	sich sonnen	sunbathe
schwarz	black	sich übergeben	vomit (v)
Schwein	pig	sicher	safe
Schweinefleisch	pork	Sicherheitsnadel	safety pin
Schweiz	Switzerland	Sicherheitssitz	car seat (baby)
Schwellung	swelling (n)	Sicherungen	fuses
schwer	heavy	sie	she; they
Schwester	sister	Sie	you (formal)
Schwiegermutter	mother-in-law	Silber	silver
Schwiegervater	father-in-law	singen	sing
schwierig	difficult	Skandinavien	Scandinavia
Schwierigkeiten	trouble	Skifahren	skiing
Schwimmbad	swimming pool	skilaufen	ski (v)
schwimmen	swim	Skulptur	sculpture
Schwindel	dizziness	Socken	socks
schwitzen	sweat (v)	sofort	immediately
schwul	gay	sofortig	instant
schwül	muggy	Sohn	son
See	lake	Sommer	summer
Segelboot	sailboat	Sonnabend	Saturday
segeln	sailing	Sonne	sun
sehen	see	sonnen (sich)	sunbathe
sehr	very	Sonnenaufgang	sunrise
Seide	silk	Sonnenbrand	sunburn
Seife	soap	Sonnenbräune	suntan (n)
Seil	rope	Sonnenbrille	sunglasses
Seite	page	Sonnenöl	suntan lotion
Selbstbedienung	self-service	Sonnenschein	sunshine
senden	send	Sonnenschutz	sunscreen
Senioren	seniors	Sonnenstich	sunstroke
September	September	Sonnenuntergang	sunset

sonnig	sunny	**Stimme**	voice
Sonntag	Sunday	**Stock**	story (floor)
Souvenirladen	souvenir shop	**Stoff**	cloth
Spanien	Spain	**stören**	disturb
Spaß	fun	**Strand**	beach
spät	late	**Strandsandalen**	flip-flops
später	later	**Straße**	street
speichern	save (computer)	**Streichhölzer**	matches
Speisekarte	menu	**Streik**	strike (no work)
Speisewagen	dining car (train)	**Streit**	fight (n)
Spezialität	specialty	**streiten**	fight (v)
Spiegel	mirror	**Strom-**	electrical adapter
Spiel	game	**wandler**	
spielen	play (v)	**Strümpfe**	nylons (panty hose)
Spielplatz	playground	**Stück**	piece
Spielzeug	toy	**Stuhl**	chair
Spielzeugladen	toy store	**Stunde**	hour
Spinne	spider	**Sturm**	storm
Spirale	diaphragm (birth control)	**Stützverband**	bandage, support
Spitze	lace	**Süden**	south
Spitzname	nickname	**sündig**	scandalous
Sportler	athlete	**super**	great
Sprache	language	**Supermarkt**	supermarket
sprechen	speak	**süß**	sweet
springen	jump (v)	**Süßwaren-**	sweets shop
sprudelnd	fizzy	**geschäft**	
Staat	state	**Synagoge**	synagogue
Stadt	city, town	**synthetisch**	synthetic
Stadtmitte	downtown		
stark	strong	**T**	
Station	station		
Stativ	tripod	**Tag**	day
sterben	die	**Tag, guten**	good day
Stern	star (in sky)	**Tal**	valley
Steuer	tax	**Tankstelle**	gas station
Stiefel	boots	**Tante**	aunt
Stil	style	**tanzen**	dance (v)
		Tasche	pocket

Taschendieb	pick-pocket
Taschenlampe	flashlight
Taschentuch	tissues
Taschentücher	facial tissue
Tasse	cup
Telefon	telephone
Telefonkabine	phone booth
Telefonkarte	telephone card
Teller	plate
Temperatur	temperature
Tennisschuhe	tennis shoes
Teppich	carpet, rug
Terroristen	terrorists
Tesafilm	scotch tape
teuer	expensive
Theater	theater; play (n)
Tier	animal
Tipp-Ex	white-out
Tisch	table
Tochter	daughter
Toilette	toilet
Tonbandführer	audioguide
tot	dead
töten	kill
Tour	tour
traditionell	traditional
tragen	carry
Tragflächenboot	hydrofoil
Traum	dream (n)
träumen	dream (v)
traurig	sad
Treppe	stairs
trinken	drink (v)
Trinkwasser	drinkable water
trocken	dry (adj)
trocknen	dry (v)
Trockner	dryer

Tschechische Republik	Czech Republic
Tür	door
Türkei	Turkey
Turm	tower
Tüte	bag

U

U-Bahn	subway
U-Bahn-Ausgang	subway exit
U-Bahn-Eingang	subway entrance
U-Bahn-Haltestelle	subway stop
U-Bahn-Station	subway station
U-Bahn-Streckenplan	subway map
Übelkeit	nausea
über	above
übergeben (sich)	vomit (v)
übermorgen	day after tomorrow
Überraschung	surprise (n)
übersetzen	translate
Uhr	clock, watch (n)
Umleitung	detour
umsonst	free (no cost)
umsteigen	transfer (v)
Umweltverschmutzung	pollution
umwickeln	wrap
unabhängig	independent
und	and
Unfall	accident
ungefähr	approximately
unglaublich	incredible
unglücklicherweise	unfortunately
Universität	university

unmöglich	impossible
uns	us
unschuldig	innocent
unter	under
Unterhose	underpants
Unterhosen	briefs; panties
Unterrock	slip
Unterschrift	signature
Unterwäsche	underwear
Urlaub	vacation

V

Vater	father
Vegetarier	vegetarian (n)
Verabredung	appointment
Verband	bandage, gauze
verboten	prohibited
Verbrennung	burn (n)
Verdauungsstörung	indigestion
verdorben	rotten
Vereinigte Staaten	United States
Vergangenheit	past
vergessen	forget
Vergewaltigung	rape (n)
verheiratet	married
Verhütungsmittel	contraceptives
Verhütungspille	birth control pills
verkaufen	sell
Verkehr	traffic
verletzt	injured
Verlies	dungeon
verloren	lost
vermieten	rent (to rent out)
Vermittlung	operator

versichert	insured
Versicherung	insurance
Verspätung	delay
verstehen	understand
Verstopfung	constipation
Vetter	cousin
Videogerät	video recorder
Videokamera	video camera
viel	much
viele	many
vielleicht	maybe
Viertel	quarter (1/4)
violett	purple
Virus	virus
Visitenkarte	business card
Vitamine	vitamins
Vogel	bird
Völlig	total
von	from; of
vor	before
Vorfahre	ancestor
Vorführung	show (n)
vorsichtig	careful
Vorspeise	appetizers

W

Waffe	gun
Wagen	train car
wandern	hike
Wangenröte	blush (makeup)
wann	when
Wanzen	bedbugs
warm	warm (adj)
warten	wait
Wartesaal	waiting room
warum	why
was	what

Waschbecken	sink
Wäscheklammern	clothes pins
Wäscheleine	clothesline
waschen	wash (v)
Waschmaschine	washer
Waschmittel	detergent (laundry)
Waschsalon	launderette
Wasser	water
Wasserfahrrad	paddleboat
Wasserfall	waterfall
Wasserhahn	faucet
Wasserskifahren	waterskiing
Wechsel	exchange (n)
wechseln	change (v, money)
Wecker	alarm clock
weiblich	female
Weihnachten	Christmas
Weihnachtsmann	Santa Claus
weil	because
Wein	wine
Weinberg	vineyard
weinen	cry (v)
Weinhandlung	wine shop
weiß	white
weit	far
Wellenreiter	surfer
Welt	world
wenig	few
wer	who
werfen	throw
Weste	vest
Westen	west
Westen von Deutschland	western Germany
Wetter	weather
Wettervorhersage	weather forecast

wichtig	important
wie	how
wie schade	it's a pity
wie viel kostet	how much ($)
wie viele	how many
Wiedersehen, auf	goodbye
Wiedervereinigung	reunification
wild	wild
willkommen	welcome
Wind	wind
Windel	diaper
Windelscheuern	diaper rash
windig	windy
Windsurfen	windsurfing
Winter	winter
wir	we
Wischtücher	handiwipes
wissen	know
Wissenschaft	science
Wissenschaftler	scientist
Witwe	widow
Witwer	widower
Witz	joke (n)
wo	where
Woche	week
Wohnung	apartment
Wohnwagen	R.V.
Wolle	wool
Wort	word
Wörterbuch	dictionary
wünschen	wish (v)
wütend	angry

Z

Zähler	taxi meter
Zahlmarke	token
Zahn	tooth

German	English
Zahnarzt	dentist
Zahnbürste	toothbrush
Zähne	teeth
Zahnen	teething (baby)
Zahnpasta	toothpaste
Zahnschmerzen	toothache
Zahnseide	dental floss
Zahnstocher	toothpick
Zange	pliers
zart	tender
Zehe	toe
zeigen	show (v); point (v)
Zeitabschnitt	period (of time)
Zeitschrift	magazine
Zeitung	newspaper
Zeitungsstand	newsstand
Zelt	tent
Zelthäringe	tent pegs
Zeltstelle	campsite
Zentrum	center; downtown
zerbrechlich	fragile
ziehen	pull
Zigarette	cigarette
Zimmer	room
Zimmer frei	vacancy (sign)
Zinn	pewter
Zoll	customs
zollfrei	duty free
zu	too
Zuckerbäcker	pastry shop
Zuckerkrankheit	diabetes
Zug	train
zuhören	listen
Zukunft	future
Zündkerzen	sparkplugs
zurück	back (return)
zurückgeben	return
zusammen	together
Zuschlag	supplement
zweite	second
zweiter Klasse	second class
Zwillinge	twins

English/German

A

abortion	Abtreibung	alone	allein
above	über	already	schon
abstract	abstrakt	altar	Altar
abuse (v)	mißbrauchen	always	immer
accident	Unfall	ambulance	Krankenwagen
accountant	Buchhalter	ancestor	Vorfahre
adapter, electrical	Stromwandler	ancient	altertümlich
		and	und
address	Adresse	angry	wütend
address, e-mail	E-Mail-Adresse	animal	Tier
adult	Erwachsener	ankle	Fußgelenk
afraid	ängstlich	another	noch ein
Africa	Afrika	answer	Antwort
after	nach	antacid	Mittel gegen Magenbrennen
afternoon	Nachmittag		
aftershave	Rasierwasser	antibiotic	Antibiotika
afterwards	nachher	antiques shop	Antiquitätenladen
again	noch einmal	antiques	Antiquitäten
age	Alter	apartment	Wohnung
aggressive	aggressiv	apology	Entschuldigung
agnostic	agnostisch	appetizers	Vorspeise
agree	einverstanden	apple	Apfel
AIDS	AIDS	appointment	Verabredung
air	Luft	approximately	ungefähr
air conditioning	Klimaanlage	April	April
air mail	Luftpost	arm	Arm
airline	Fluggesellschaft	arrivals	Ankunften
airport	Flughafen	arrive	ankommen
aisle	Gang	art	Kunst
alarm clock	Wecker	art gallery	Kunstgalerie
alcohol	Alkohol	Art Nouveau	Jugendstil
allergic	allergisch	arthritis	Gelenkentzündung
allergies	Allergien	artificial	künstlich

artist	Künstler	ball	Ball
ashtray	Aschenbecher	banana	Banane
ask	fragen	bandage	Verband
aspirin	Aspirin	bandage, support	Stützverband
asthma	Asthma		
at	bei	band-aid	Pflaster
at sign (@)	A-Affenschwanz	bank	Bank
atheist	atheistisch	barber	Frisör
athlete	Sportler	barber shop	Herrenfrisör
athlete's foot	Fußpilz	baseball	Baseball
attractive	attraktiv	basement	Keller
audioguide	Tonbandführer	basket	Korb
August	August	basketball	Basketball, Korbballspiel
aunt	Tante		
Austria	Österreich	bath	Bad
autumn	Herbst	bathrobe	Bademantel
		bathroom	Bad

B

		bathtub	Badewanne
baby	Baby	battery	Batterie
baby booster seat	Kindersitz	beach	Strand
baby car seat	Sicherheitssitz	beard	Bart
baby food	Babynahrung	beautiful	schön
baby formula	Babynahrung	beauty salon	Frisiersalon, Haarsalon
babysitter	Babysitter		
babysitting service	Kinderaufsicht	because	weil
		bed	Bett
back	Rücken	bedbugs	Wanzen
backpack	Rucksack	bedroom	Zimmer
bad	schlecht	bedsheet	Laken
bag	Tüte	beef	Rindfleisch
bag, plastic	Plastiktüte	beer	Bier
bag, zip-lock	Gefrierbeutel	before	vor
baggage	Gepäck	begin	anfangen
baggage check	Gepäckaufgabe	behind	hinter
baggage claim	Gepäckausgabe	Belgium	Belgien
bakery	Bäckerei	bells	Glocken
balcony	Balkon	below	unter

belt	Gürtel
berth (train)	Liegewagenplatz
best	am besten
better	besser
bib	Latz, Lätzchen
bicycle	Fahrrad
big	groß
bill (payment)	Rechnung
bird	Vogel
birth control pills	Verhütungspille
birthday	Geburtstag
black	schwarz
bladder	Blase
blanket	Decke
bleeding	bluten
blisters	Blasen
block (street)	Häuserblock
blond	blond
blood	Blut
blood pressure, high	Bluthochdruck
blouse	Bluse
blue	blau
blush (makeup)	Wangenröte
boat	Schiff
body	Körper
boiled	gekocht
bomb	Bombe
book	Buch
book shop	Buchladen
booster seat	Kindersitz
boots	Stiefel
border	Grenze
borrow	leihen
boss	Chef, Boss
bottle	Flasche

bottom	Boden
boutique, clothing	Kleiderladen
bowl	Schale
box	Karton
boy	Junge
bra	B. H. (Büstenhalter)
bracelet	Armband
brakes	Bremsen
brass	Messing
bread	Brot
breakfast	Frühstück
breast	Busen
breath	Atem
bridge	Brücke
briefs	Unterhosen
Britain	England
broken	kaputt
bronze	Bronze
brooch	Brosche
brother	Bruder
brown	braun
bucket	Eimer
building	Gebäude
bulb	Birne
bulb, light	Leuchtbirne
bunk beds	Kojen
burn (n)	Verbrennung
bus	Bus
bus station	Busbahnhof
bus stop	Bushaltestelle
bus, city	Linienbus
bus, long-distance	Regionalbus, Fernbus
business	Geschäft
business card	Visitenkarte
but	aber

buttocks	Hinterbacken	cash	Bargeld
button	Knopf	cash machine	Bankomat
buy	kaufen	cashier	Kassierer
by (via)	mit	cassette	Kassette
		castle	Burg
C		cat	Katze
calendar	Kalender	catch (v)	fangen
calorie	Kalorie	cathedral	Dom, Kathedrale
camera	Photoapparat	Catholic (adj)	katholisch
camera shop	Photoladen	cave	Höhle
camping	Camping	cell phone	Handy
campsite	Zeltstelle	cell phone shop	Natelladen
can (n)	Dose	cellar	Keller
can (v)	können	center	Zentrum
can opener	Dosenöffner	century	Jahrhundert
Canada	Kanada	ceramic	Keramik
canal	Kanal	chair	Stuhl
cancel	annullieren	championship	Meisterschaft
candle	Kerze	change (n)	Wechsel
candy	Bonbons	change (v)	ändern, wechseln
canoe	Kanu		(money)
cap	Deckel	chapel	Kapelle
captain	Kapitän	charming	bezaubernd
car	Auto	cheap	billig
car (train)	Wagen	check	Scheck
car seat (baby)	Sicherheitssitz	Cheers!	Prost!
car, dining (train)	Speisewagen	cheese	Käse
car, sleeper (train)	Liegewagen	cheese shop	Käserei
carafe	Karaffe	chest	Brust
carbon dioxide	Kohlensäure	chest pains	Schmerzen in der
card	Karte		Brust
card, telephone	Telefonkarte	chicken	Hähnchen
cards (deck)	Karten	children	Kinder
careful	vorsichtig	chills	Kälteschauer
carpet	Teppich	Chinese (adj)	chinesisch
carry	tragen	chocolate	Schokolade
carry-on luggage	Handgepäck	choir	Chor

Christian (adj)	christlich	comb (n)	Kamm
Christmas	Weihnachten	come	kommen
church	Kirche	comfortable	komfortabel
church concert	Kirchenkonzert	compact disc	C.D.
church service	Gottesdienst	complain	sich beschweren
cigarette	Zigarette	complicated	kompliziert
cinema	Kino	computer	Komputer
city	Stadt	concert	Konzert
class	Klasse	concert, church	Kirchenkonzert
classical (music)	klassisch	conditioner (hair)	Haarfestiger
classical (period)	klassizistisch	condom	Präservativ, Kondom
clean (adj)	sauber	conductor	Schaffner
clear	klar	confirm	bestätigen
cliff	Kliff	congestion	Nasenverstopfung
clinic, medical	Klinik	(sinus)	
clock	Uhr	congratulations	Glückwünsche
clock, alarm	Wecker	connection (train)	Anschluß
cloister	Kloster	constipation	Verstopfung
closed	geschlossen	construction (sign)	Baustelle
cloth	Stoff	contact lenses	Linsen
clothes	Kleider	contagious	ansteckend
clothes pins	Wäscheklammern	contra-	Verhütungsmittel
clothesline	Wäscheleine	ceptives	
clothing boutique	Kleiderladen	cook (v)	kochen
cloudy	bewölkt	cool	kühl
coast	Küste	copper	Kupfer
coat	Jacke	copy	Kopie
coat hanger	Kleiderbügel	copy shop	Kopierladen
cockroach	Kakerlake	cork	Korken
coffee	Kaffee	corkscrew	Korkenzieher
coffee shop	Kaffeeladen	corner	Ecke
coins	Münzen	corridor	Flur
cold (adj)	kalt	corruption	Korruption
cold (n)	Erkältung	cost (v)	kosten
cold medicine	Grippemittel	cot	Liege
color	Farbe	cotton	Baumwolle
color-fast	farbenfest	cough (n)	Husten

cough (v)	husten	**dead**	tot
cough drops	Hustenbonbons	**December**	Dezember
country	Land	**declare (customs)**	deklarieren
countryside	auf dem Land	**decongestant**	Abführmittel
cousin	Vetter	**delay**	Verspätung
cow	Kuh	**delete**	löschen
cozy	gemütlich	**delicatessen**	Feinkostgeschäft
crafts	Kunstgewerbe	**delicious**	lecker
cramps	Krämpfe	**democracy**	Demokratie
cramps,	Monatskrämpfe	**dental floss**	Zahnseide
menstrual		**dentist**	Zahnarzt
cream	Sahne	**deodorant**	Deodorant
cream,	Erste-Hilfe-Salbe	**depart**	abfahren
first-aid		**department store**	Kaufhaus
credit card	Kreditkarte	**departures**	Abfahrten
crib	Kinderbett	**deposit**	Kaution
cross	Kreuz	**dessert**	Nachtisch
crowd (n)	Menge	**detergent**	Waschmittel
cry (v)	weinen	**detour**	Umleitung
crypt	Krypte	**diabetes**	Zuckerkrankheit
cup	Tasse	**diabetic**	diabetisch
customs	Zoll	**diamond**	Diamant
Czech	Tschechische Republik	**diaper**	Windel
Republic		**diaper rash**	Windelscheuern
		diaphragm	Spirale
		(birth control)	

D

dad	Papa	**diarrhea**	Durchfall
dance (v)	tanzen	**diarrhea**	Durchfallmedikament
danger	Gefahr	**medicine**	
dangerous	gefährlich	**dictionary**	Wörterbuch
Danube	Donau	**die**	sterben
dark	dunkel	**difficult**	schwierig
dash (-)	Bindestrich	**dining car (train)**	Speisewagen
daughter	Tochter	**dinner**	Abendessen
day	Tag	**direct**	direkt
day after	übermorgen	**direction**	Richtung
tomorrow		**dirty**	schmutzig

discount	Ermäßigung
disease	Krankheit
disease, venereal	Geschlechtskrankheit
disinfectant	Desinfektionsmittel
disturb	stören
divorced	geschieden
dizziness	Schwindel
doctor	Arzt
dog	Hund
doll	Puppe
dome	Kuppel
donkey	Esel
door	Tür
dormitory	Schlafsaal
dot (computer)	Punkt
double	doppel
down	runter
download	herunterladen
downtown	Stadtmitte, Zentrum
dozen	Dutzend
dream (n)	Traum
dream (v)	träumen
dress (n)	Kleid
drink (n)	Getränk
drink (v)	trinken
drive (v)	fahren
driver	Fahrer
drunk	betrunken
dry (adj)	trocken
dry (v)	trocknen
dryer	Trockner
dungeon	Verlies
duty free	zollfrei

E

each	jede
ear	Ohr
earache	Ohrenschmerzen
early	früh
earplugs	Ohrenschützer
earrings	Ohrringe
earth	Erde
east	Osten
Easter	Ostern
eastern Germany	Ostdeutschland
easy	einfach
eat	essen
edit	bearbeiten
education	Ausbildung
elbow	Ellbogen
electrical adapter	Stromwandler
elevator	Fahrstuhl
e-mail	E-Mail
e-mail address	E-Mail-Adresse
embarrassing	peinlich
embassy	Botschaft
emergency	Notfall
emergency exit	Notausgang
emergency room	Notfallaufnahme
emperor	Kaiser
empress	Kaiserin
empty	leer
engineer	Ingenieur
English	Englisch
enjoy	genießen
enough	genug
entrance (door)	Eingang
entrance (road)	Einfahrt

entry	Eingang	fan belt	Keilriemen
envelope	Briefumschlag	fantastic	phantastisch
epilepsy	Epilepsie	far	weit
eraser	Radiergummi	farm	Bauernhof
especially	besonders	farmer	Bauer
Europe	Europa	fashion	Mode
evening	Abend	fat (adj)	fett
every	jede	fat (n)	Fett
everything	alles	father	Vater
exactly	genau	father-in-law	Schwiegervater
example	Beispiel	faucet	Wasserhahn
excellent	ausgezeichnet	fear (v)	fürchten
except	außer	February	Februar
exchange (n)	Wechsel	female	weiblich
excuse me	Entschuldigung	ferry	Fähre
exhausted	erschöpft	festival	Festival
exit (door)	Ausgang	fever	Fieber
exit (road)	Ausfahrt	few	wenig
exit, emergency	Notausgang	field	Feld
expensive	teuer	fight (n)	Streit
explain	erklären	fight (v)	streiten
eye	Auge	fine (good)	gut
eye shadow	Augenschatten	finger	Finger
eyeliner	Augenkontour	fingernail	Nagel
		finish (v)	beenden
F		fire	Feuer
face	Gesicht	fireworks	Feuerwerk
face cleanser	Gesichtsseife	first	erst
face powder	Gesichtspulver	first aid	Erste Hilfe
facial tissue	Papiertuch,	first class	erste Klasse
	Taschentücher	first-aid cream	Erste-Hilfe-Salbe
factory	Fabrik	fish (n)	Fisch
fair (just)	fair	fish (v)	fischen
fall (v)	fallen	fix (v)	reparieren
false	falsch	fizzy	sprudelnd,
family	Familie		mit Kohlensäure
famous	berühmt	flag	Fahne

flash (camera)	Blitz	Frisbee	Frisbee
flashlight	Taschenlampe	from	von
flavor (n)	Geschmack	fruit	Obst
flea	Floh	full-service	mit Dienstleistung
flea market	Flohmarkt	fun	Spaß
flight	Flug	funeral	Beerdigung
flip-flops	Strandsandalen	funny	komisch
floss, dental	Zahnseide	furniture	Möbel
flower	Blume	fuses	Sicherungen
flower market	Blumenmarkt	future	Zukunft
flu	Grippe		
fly	fliegen	**G**	
fog	Nebel	gallery	Galerie
folder (computer)	Ordner	game	Spiel
food	Essen, Lebensmittel	garage	Garage
food	Lebensmittelvergiftung	garden	Garten
poisoning		gardening	Gärtnern
foot	Fuß	gas	Benzin
football	Fußball	gas station	Tankstelle
football, American	Football	gauze	Verband
for	für	gay	schwul
forbidden	verboten	generous	großzügig
foreign	fremd	gentleman	Herr
forget	vergessen	genuine	echt
fork	Gabel	Germany	Deutschland
formula	Babynahrung	gift	Geschenk
(for baby)		girl	Mädchen
foundation	Grundlage	give	geben
fountain	Brunnen	glass	Glas
fragile	zerbrechlich	glasses (eye)	Brille
France	Frankreich	gloves	Handschuhe
free (no cost)	umsonst,	go	gehen
	kostenlos	go through	durchgehen
fresh	frisch	God	Gott
Friday	Freitag	gold	Gold
friend	Freund	golf	Golf
friendship	Freundschaft	good	gut

good day	guten Tag	handiwipes	Wischtücher
goodbye	auf Wiedersehen	handle (n)	Griff
Gothic	gothisch	handsome	gutaussehend
grammar	Grammatik	happiness	Glück
granddaughter	Enkelin	happy	glücklich
grandfather	Großvater	harbor	Hafen
grandmother	Großmutter	hard	hart
grandson	Enkel	hardware	Eisenwarengeschäft
gray	grau	store	
greasy	fettig	hash	Haschisch
great	super	hat	Hut
Great Britain	Großbritannien	hate (v)	hassen
Greece	Griechenland	have	haben
green	grün	hay fever	Heuschnupfen
grocery	Lebensmittelgeschäft	he	er
store		head	Kopf
guarantee	Garantie	headache	Kopfschmerzen
guest	Gast	headlights	Scheinwerfern
guide	Führer	health	Gesundheit
guidebook	Reiseführer	health	Krankenversicherung
guided tour	Führung	insurance	
guilty	schuldig	healthy	gesund
guitar	Gitarre	hear	hören
gum	Kaugummi	heart	Herz
gun	Waffe, Gewehr	heart	Herzbeschwerden
gymnastics	Gymnastik	condition	
gynecologist	Gynäkologin	heat (n)	Hitze
		heat (v)	aufwarmen
H		heaven	Himmel
hair	Haare	heavy	schwer
hairbrush	Haarbürste	hello	hallo
haircut	Frisur	helmet	Helm
hall	Saal	help (n)	Hilfe
hand	Hand	help (v)	hilfen
hand lotion	Handlotion	helpful	hilfreich
handicapped	behindert	hemorrhoids	Hämorrholden
handicrafts	Handarbeiten	her	ihr

here	hier	hungry	hungrig
hi	hallo	hurry (v)	sich beeilen
high	hoch	husband	Ehemann
high blood pressure	Bluthochdruck	hydrofoil	Tragflächenboot
		hyphen (-)	Bindestrich
highchair	Kinderstuhl		
highway	Landstraße	**I**	
hike	wandern	I	ich
hill	Hügel	ice	Eis
hip	Hüfte	ice cream	Eis
history	Geschichte	if	ob
hitchhike	per Anhalter fahren	ill	krank
hobby	Hobby	immediately	sofort
hockey	Hockey	important	wichtig
hole	Loch	imported	importiert
holiday	Feiertag	impossible	unmöglich
homemade	hausgemacht	Impressionist	impressionistisch
homesickness	Heimweh	in	in
honest	ehrlich	included	inklusive, eingeschlossen
honeymoon	Hochzeitsreise		
hope	Hoffnung	incredible	unglaublich
horrible	schrecklich	independent	unabhängig
horse	Pferd	indigestion	Verdauungsstörung
horse riding	reiten	industry	Industrie
hospital	Krankenhaus	infection	Infektion, Entzündung
hot	heiß		
hotel	Hotel	infection, urinary	Harnröhrenentzündung
hotel, bed & breakfast	Gästezimmer, Fremdenzimmer		
		inflammation	Entzündung
hotel, country inn	Gasthaus, Gasthof	information	Information
		injured	verletzt
hotel, small	Pension	innocent	unschuldig
hour	Stunde	insect	Insekt
house	Haus	insect repellant	Mückenspray
how	wie	inside	innen
how many	wie viele	instant	sofortig
how much ($)	wie viel kostet	instead	anstatt

insurance	Versicherung	**K**	
insurance,	Krankenver-		
health	sicherung	keep	behalten
insured	versichert	kettle	Kessel
intelligent	klug	key	Schlüssel
interesting	interessant	kill	töten
Internet	Internet	kind	freundlich
Internet	Internetanschluß	king	König
access		kiss	Küß
Internet café	Internetcafé	kitchen	Küche
intersection	Kreuzung	kitchenette	Kleinküche
intestines	Därme	knee	Knie
invitation	Einladung	knife	Messer
iodine	Jod	knights	Ritter
Ireland	Irland	know	wissen
is	ist		
island	Insel	**L**	
Italy	Italien	lace	Spitze
		ladder	Leiter
J		ladies	Damen
jacket	Jacke	lake	See
January	Januar	lamb	Lamm
jaw	Kiefer	lamp	Lampe
jeans	Jeans	language	Sprache
jewelry	Schmuck	large	groß
jewelry shop	Schmuckladen	last	letzte
Jewish	jüdisch	late	spät
job	Beruf	later	später
jogging	Jogging	laugh (v)	lachen
joint (marijuana)	Joint, Kiffe	launderette	Waschsalon
joke (n)	Witz	laundry soap	Waschmittel
journey	Reise	lawyer	Anwalt
juice	Saft	laxative	Laxativ
July	Juli	lazy	faul
jump (v)	springen	learn	lernen
June	Juni	leather	Leder
		leave	gehen

English	German	English	German
left	links	lukewarm	lau
leg	Bein	lungs	Lungen
lend	leihen		
lenses, contact	Linsen	**M**	
letter	Brief	macho	macho
library	Leihbücherei	mad	wütend
lies	Lügen	magazine	Zeitschrift
life	Leben	mail (n)	Post
light (n)	Licht	main	Haupt
light bulb	Leuchtbirne	make (v)	machen
lighter (n)	Feuerzeug	makeup	Makeup
like (v)	mögen	male	männlich
linen	Leinen	man	Mann
lip	Lippe	manager	Chef, Geschäftsführer
lip salve	Lippenbalsam	many	viele
lipstick	Lippenstift	map	Karte
list	Liste	marble (material)	Marmor
listen	zuhören	March	März
liter	Liter	marijuana	Marihuana
little (adj)	klein	market	Markt
live	leben	market, flea	Flohmarkt
local	örtlich	market, flower	Blumenmarkt
lock (n)	Schloß	market, open-air	Markt
lock (v)	abschließen	married	verheiratet
lockers	Schließfächer	mascara	Maskara
look	gucken	matches	Streichhölzer
lost	verloren	maximum	Maximum
lotion, hand	Handlotion	May	Mai
loud	laut	maybe	vielleicht
love (n)	Liebe	meat	Fleisch
love (v)	lieben	mechanic	Mechaniker
lover	Liebhaber	medicine	Medikament
low	niedrig	medicine for a cold	Grippemittel
lozenges	Halsbonbon	medicine, non-aspirin substitute	Ben-u-ron
luck	Glück		
luggage	Gepäck	medieval	mittelalterlich
luggage, carry-on	Handgepäck		

medium	mittel	more	mehr
men	Herren	morning	Morgen
menstrual cramps	Monatskrämpfe	mosque	Moschee
		mosquito	Mücke
menstruation	Menstruieren	mother	Mutter
menu	Speisekarte	mother-in-law	Schwieger-
message	Nachricht,		mutter
	Mitteilung (e-mail)	motor scooter	Moped
metal	Metall	motorcycle	Motorrad
meter, taxi	Zähler	mountain	Berg
midnight	Mitternacht	moustache	Schnurrbart
migraine	Migräne	mouth	Mund
military	Militär	movie	Film
mineral water	Mineralwasser	Mr.	Herr
minimum	Minimum	Mrs.	Frau
minutes	Minuten	much	viel
mirror	Spiegel	muggy	schwül
miscarriage	Fehlgeburt	muscle	Muskel
Miss	Fräulein	museum	Museum
mistake	Fehler	music	Musik
misunder- standing	Mißverständnis	Muslim	muselmanisch
		my	mein
mix (n)	Mischung		
moat	Burggraben	**N**	
modem	Modem		
modern	modern	nail clipper	Nagelschere
moisturizer	Feuchtigkeits- creme	nail polish	Nagellack
		nail polish remover	Nagellack- entferner
moleskin	Pflaster gegen Blasen	nail, finger	Nagel
		naked	nackt
moment	Moment	name	Name
monastery	Kloster	napkin	Serviette
Monday	Montag	narrow	schmal
money	Geld	nationality	Nationalität
month	Monat	natural	natürlich
monument	Denkmal	nature	Natur
moon	Mond	nausea	Übelkeit

near	nahe	nurse	Krankenschwester
necessary	notwendig	nylon (material)	Nylon
neck	Nacken	nylons (panty hose)	Strümpfe
necklace	Halsband		
need	brauchen	**O**	
needle	Nadel	O.K.	O.K.
neoclassical	neoklassizistisch	occupation	Beruf
Neo-Nazis	Neonazis	occupied	besetzt
nephew	Neffe	ocean	Meer
nervous	nervös	October	Oktober
Netherlands	Niederlande	of	von
never	nie	office	Büro
new	neu	office supplies	Bürobedarf
newspaper	Zeitung	store	
newsstand	Kiosk,	oil	Öl
	Zeitungsstand	old	alt
next	nächste	Olympics	Olympiade
nice	nett	on	auf
nickname	Spitzname	on time	pünktlich
niece	Nichte	once	einmal
night	Nacht	one way (street)	einfach
nightgown	Nachthemd	one way (ticket)	Hinfahrkarte
no	nein, kein	one-way street	Einbahnstraße
no vacancy	belegt	only	nur
noisy	laut	open (adj)	offen, geöffnet
non-aspirin	Ben-u-ron	open (v)	öffnen
substitute		open-air market	Markt
non-smoking	Nichtraucher	opening hours	Öffnungszeiten
noon	Mittag	opera	Oper
normal	normal	operator	Vermittlung
north	Norden	optician	Optiker
nose	Nase	or	oder
not	nicht	orange (color)	orange
notebook	Notizbuch	orange (fruit)	Apfelsine
nothing	nichts	organ	Orgel
November	November	original	Original
now	jetzt	other	anderes

outdoors	im Freien
oven	Ofen
over (finished)	beendet
own (v)	besitzen
owner	Besitzer

P

pacifier	Nuggel, Schnuller
package	Paket
paddleboat	Wasserfahrrad
page	Seite
pail	Eimer
pain	Schmerz
pain killer	Schmerzmittel
pains, chest	Schmerzen in der Brust
painting	Gemälde
pajamas	Pyjama
palace	Schloß
panties	Unterhosen
pants	Hosen
paper	Papier
paper clip	Büroklammer
parents	Eltern
park (garden)	Park
park (v)	parken
parking lot	Parkplatz
party	Party
passenger	Reisende
passport	Paß
past	Vergangenheit
pastry shop	Zuckerbäcker, Konditorei
pay	bezahlen
peace	Frieden
pedestrian	Fußgänger
pen	Kugelschreiber

pencil	Bleistift
penis	Penis
people	Leute
percent	Prozent
perfect	perfekt
perfume	Parfum
period (of time)	Zeitabschnitt
period (woman's)	Periode
person	Person
pet (n)	Haustier
pewter	Zinn
pharmacy	Apotheke
phone booth	Telefonkabine
phone, mobile	Handy
photo	Photo
photocopy	Fotokopie
photocopy shop	Kopierladen
pick-pocket	Taschendieb
picnic	Picknick
piece	Stück
pig	Schwein
pill	Pille
pillow	Kissen
pills, birth control	Verhütungspille
pin	Nadel
PIN code	Geheimnummer
pink	rosa
pity, it's a	wie schade
pizza	Pizza
plain	einfach
plane	Flugzeug
plant	Pflanze
plastic	Plastik
plastic bag	Plastiktüte
plate	Teller
platform (train)	Bahnsteig

play (n)	Theater	problem	Problem
play (v)	spielen	profession	Beruf
playground	Spielplatz	prohibited	verboten
playpen	Babygitter	pronunciation	Aussprache
please	bitte	prosper	florieren
pliers	Zange	Protestant	evangelisch
pneumonia	Lungenentzündung	public	öffentlich
pocket	Tasche	pull	ziehen
point (v)	zeigen	pulpit	Kanzel
police	Polizei	pulse	Puls
politicians	Politiker	pump (n)	Pumpe
pollution	Umweltver-schmutzung	punctual	pünktlich
		purple	violett
polyester	Polyester	purse	Handtasche
poor	arm	push	drücken
porcelain	Porzellan		
pork	Schweinefleisch	**Q**	
Portugal	Portugal	quality	Qualität
possible	möglich	quarter (1/4)	Viertel
postcard	Postkarte	queen	Königin
poster	Poster	question (n)	Frage
power	Macht	quiet	ruhig
powerful	mächtig		
practical	praktisch	**R**	
pregnancy	Schwangerschaft	R.V.	Wohnwagen
pregnancy test	Schwanger-schaftstest	rabbit	Hase
		racism	Rassimus
pregnant	schwanger	radiator	Kühler
Preparation H	Hämorrhoiden Salbe	radio	Radio
		raft	Floß
prescription	Rezept	railway	Eisenbahn
present (gift)	Geschenk	rain (n)	Regen
pretty	hübsch	rainbow	Regenbogen
price	Preis	raincoat	Regenmantel
priest	Priester	rape (n)	Vergewaltigung
print	drucken	rash	Ausschlag
private	privat	rash, diaper	Windelscheuern

raw	roh	robbed	beraubt
razor	Rasierapparat	rock (n)	Fels
ready	bereit	roller skates	Rollschuhe
receipt	Beleg	Romanesque	romanisch
receive	erhalten	Romantic (art)	Romantik
receptionist	Empfangsperson	romantic	romantisch
recipe	Rezept	roof	Dach
recommend	empfehlen	room	Zimmer
rectum	Anus	rope	Seil
red	rot	rotten	verdorben
refill (n)	Erneuerung	roundabout	Kreisel
refill (v)	nachschenken	round-trip	Rückfahrt
refugees	Flüchtlinge	rowboat	Ruderboot
refund (n)	Rückgabe	rucksack	Rucksack
relax (v)	sich erholen	rug	Teppich
relaxation	Entspannung	ruins	Ruine
relic	Reliquie	run (v)	laufen
religion	Religion	Russia	Rußland
remember	sich erinnern		
Renaissance	Renaissance	**S**	
rent (to rent out)	vermieten	sad	traurig
rent (to rent)	mieten	safe	sicher
repair (v)	reparieren	safety pin	Sicherheitsnadel
repeat	noch einmal	sailboat	Segelboot
reservation	Reservierung	sailing	segeln
reserve	reservieren	saint	Heiliger
respect	Respekt	sale	Ausverkauf
retired	pensioniert	same	gleiche
return	zurückgeben	sandals	Sandalen
reunification	Wiederver-	sandwich	belegtes Brot
	einigung	sanitary napkins	Damenbinden
rich	reich	Santa Claus	Weihnachtsmann
right	rechts	Saturday	Samstag, Sonnabend
ring (n)	Ring		
ring road	Ringstraße	save (computer)	speichern
ripe	reif	scandalous	sündig
river	Fluß		

DICTIONARY

English / German

Scandinavia	Skandinavien
scarf	Schal
school	Schule
science	Wissenschaft
scientist	Wissenschaftler
scissors	Schere
scotch tape	Tesafilm
screwdriver	Schraubenzieher
sculptor	Bildhauer
sculpture	Skulptur
sea	Meer
seafood	Meeresfrüchte
seat	Platz
second	zweite
second class	zweiter Klasse
secret	Geheimnis
see	sehen
self-service	Selbstbedienung
sell	verkaufen
send	senden
seniors	Senioren
separate (adj)	getrennt
September	September
serious	ernsthaft
service	Bedienung
service, church	Gottesdienst
sex	Sex
sexy	sexy
shampoo	Shampoo
shaving cream	Rasiercreme
she	sie
sheet	Laken
shell	Schale
ship (n)	Schiff
ship (v)	schicken
shirt	Hemd
shoelaces	Schnürsenkel

shoes	Schuhe
shoes, tennis	Tennisschuhe
shop (n)	Laden, Geschäft
shop, antique	Antiquitäten-laden
shop, barber	Herrenfrisör
shop, camera	Photoladen
shop, cell phone	Natelladen
shop, cheese	Käserei
shop, coffee	Kaffeeladen
shop, jewelry	Schmuckladen
shop, pastry	Zuckerbäcker / Konditorei
shop, photocopy	Kopierladen
shop, souvenir	Souvenirladen
shop, sweets	Süßwarengeschäft
shop, wine	Weinhandlung
shopping	einkaufen
shopping mall	Einkaufszentrum
short	kurz
shorts	kurze Hosen
shoulder	Schulter
show (n)	Vorführung
show (v)	zeigen
shower	Dusche
shy	ängstlich
sick	krank
sign	Schild
signature	Unterschrift
silence	Ruhe
silk	Seide
silver	Silber
similar	ähnlich
simple	einfach
sing	singen

singer	Sänger
single	ledig
sink	Waschbecken
sink stopper	Abflußstöpsel
sinus problems	Schleimhautentzündung
sir	mein Herr
sister	Schwester
size	Größe
skating (ice)	Eislaufen
ski (v)	skilaufen
skiing	Skifahren
skin	Haut
skinny	dünn
skirt	Rock
sky	Himmel
sleep (v)	schlafen
sleeper (for baby)	Kindereinteiler
sleeper (train)	Schlafwagenplatz
sleeper car (train)	Liegewagen
sleeping bag	Schlafsack
sleepy	schläfrig
sleeves	Ärmel
slice	Scheibe
slide (photo)	Dia
slip	Unterrock
slippers	Pantoffeln
slippery	glatt
slow	langsam
small	klein
smell (n)	Geruch
smile (n)	Lächeln
smoke	Rauch
smoking	Rauchen
snack	Imbiß

sneeze (n)	Niesen
snore	schnarchen
snorkel	Schnorchel
snow	Schnee
soap	Seife
soap, laundry	Waschmittel
soccer	Fußball
socks	Socken
some	einige
something	etwas
son	Sohn
song	Lied
soon	bald
sore throat	Halsschmerzen
sorry	Entschuldigung
sour	sauer
south	Süden
souvenir shop	Souvenirladen
Spain	Spanien
sparkplugs	Zündkerzen
speak	sprechen
specialty	Spezialität
speed	Geschwindigkeit
spend	ausgeben
spider	Spinne
spoon	Löffel
sport	Sport
spring	Frühling
square (town)	Platz
stairs	Treppe
stamp	Briefmarke
stapler	Klammeraffe
star (in sky)	Stern
state	Staat
station	Station
stomach	Magen
stomach-ache	Magenschmerzen

stoned	benebelt
stop (n)	Halt
stop (v)	halten
stoplight	Ampel
stopper, sink	Abflußstöpsel
store	Laden, Geschäft
store, department	Kaufhaus
store, hardware	Eisenwarengeschäft
store, office supplies	Bürobedarf
store, toy	Spielzeugladen
storm	Sturm
story (floor)	Stock
straight	geradeaus
strange	merkwürdig
stream (n)	Fluß
street	Straße
strike (no work)	Streik
string	Schnur
string	Leine
stroller	Kinderwagen
strong	stark
stuck	festsitzen
student	Student
stupid	dumm
sturdy	haltbar
style	Stil
subway	U-Bahn
subway entrance	U-Bahn-Eingang
subway exit	U-Bahn-Ausgang
subway map	U-Bahn-Streckenplan
subway station	U-Bahn-Station
subway stop	U-Bahn-Haltestelle

suddenly	plötzlich
suffer	leiden
suitcase	Koffer
summer	Sommer
sun	Sonne
sunbathe	sich sonnen
sunburn	Sonnenbrand
Sunday	Sonntag
sunglasses	Sonnenbrille
sunny	sonnig
sunrise	Sonnenaufgang
sunscreen	Sonnenschutz
sunset	Sonnenuntergang
sunshine	Sonnenschein
sunstroke	Sonnenstich
suntan (n)	Sonnenbräune
suntan lotion	Sonnenbräune
supermarket	Supermarkt
supplement	Zuschlag
surfboard	Surfboard
surfer	Wellenreiter
surprise (n)	Überraschung
swallow (v)	schlucken
sweat (v)	schwitzen
sweater	Pullover
sweet	süß
sweets shop	Süßwaren-geschäft
swelling (n)	Schwellung
swim	schwimmen
swim trunks	Badehose
swimming pool	Schwimmbad
swimsuit	Badeanzug
Switzerland	Schweiz
synagogue	Synagoge
synthetic	synthetisch

T

table	Tisch
tail	Schwanz
tail lights	Rücklichtern
take	nehmen
take out (food)	mitnehmen
talcum powder	Babypuder
talk	reden
tall	hoch
tampons	Tampons
tape (adhesive)	Klebeband
tape (cassette)	Kassette
taste (n)	Geschmack
taste (v)	probieren
tax	Steuer
taxes	Steuern
taxi meter	Zähler
teacher	Lehrer
team	Team
teenager	Jugendlicher
teeth	Zähne
teething (baby)	Zahnen
telephone	Telefon
telephone card	Telefonkarte
television	Fernsehen
temperature	Temperatur
tender	zart
tennis	Tennis
tennis shoes	Tennisschuhe
tent	Zelt
tent pegs	Zelthäringe
terrible	schrecklich
terrorists	Terroristen
testicles	Hoden
thanks	danke
theater	Theater
thermometer	Thermometer
they	sie
thick	dick
thief	Dieb
thigh	Schenkel
thin	dünn
thing	Ding
think	denken
thirsty	durstig
thongs	Badelatschen
thread	Faden
throat	Hals
through	durch
throw	werfen
Thursday	Donnerstag
ticket (plane)	Flugkarte
ticket (show)	Eintrittskarte
ticket (train)	Fahrkarte
tight	eng
time, on	pünktlich
timetable	Fahrplan
tire	Reifen
tired	müde
tires	Reifen
tissue, facial	Papiertuch, Taschentuch
tissues	Taschentücher
to	nach, zu
today	heute
toe	Zehe
together	zusammen
toilet	Toilette
toilet paper	Klopapier
token	Zahlmarke, Jeton
toll	Gebühr
toll-free	gebührenfrei
tomorrow	morgen

tomorrow, day after	übermorgen	T-shirt	T-Shirt
tonight	heute abend	Tuesday	Dienstag
too	zu	tunnel	Tunnel
tooth	Zahn	Turkey	Türkei
toothache	Zahnschmerzen	turn signal	Blinker
toothbrush	Zahnbürste	tweezers	Pinzette
toothpaste	Zahnpasta	twins	Zwillinge
toothpick	Zahnstocher		
total	Völlig	**U**	
tour	Tour	ugly	häßlich
tour, guided	Führung	umbrella	Regenschirm
tourist	Tourist	uncle	Onkel
tow truck	Abschleppwagen	unconscious	bewußtlos
towel	Handtuch	under	unter
towel, bath	Badetuch	underpants	Unterhose
tower	Turm	underscore (_)	Großstrich
town	Stadt	understand	verstehen
toy	Spielzeug	underwear	Unterwäsche
toy store	Spielzeugladen	unemployed	arbeitslos
track (train)	Gleis	unfortunately	unglückliche- weise
traditional	traditionell		
traffic	Verkehr	United States	Vereinigte Staaten
train	Zug		
train car	Wagen	university	Universität
transfer (v)	umsteigen	up	hoch
translate	übersetzen	upstairs	oben
transmission fluid	Getriebeöl	urethra	Harnröhre
travel	reisen	urgent	dringend
travel agency	Reisebüro	urinary infection	Harnröhrenentzündung
travelers	Reisende		
traveler's check	Reisescheck	us	uns
treasury	Schatzkammer	use	nutzen
tree	Baum	uterus	Gebärmutter
trip	Reise, Fahrt		
tripod	Stativ	**V**	
trouble	Schwierigkeiten	vacancy (sign)	Zimmer frei
		vacant	frei

vacation	Urlaub
vagina	Vagina
valid	gültig
validate	abstempeln
valley	Tal
Vaseline	Vaseline, Mineralsalbe
vegetarian (n)	Vegetarier
velvet	Samt
venereal disease	Geschlechtskrankeit
very	sehr
vest	Weste
vest	Weste
video	Video
video camera	Videokamera
video recorder	Videogerät
view	(Aus-)Blick
village	Dorf
vineyard	Weinberg
violence	Gewalt
virus	Virus
visit (n)	Besuch
visit (v)	besuchen
vitamins	Vitamine
voice	Stimme
vomit (v)	sich übergeben

W

waist	Bund
wait	warten
waiter	Kellner
waiting room	Wartesaal
waitress	Kellnerin
wake up	aufwachen
walk (v)	gehen
wall, fortified	Burgmauer

wallet	Brieftasche
want	möchte
war	Krieg
warm (adj)	warm
wash (v)	waschen
washer	Waschmaschine
watch (n)	Uhr
watch (v)	beobachten
water	Wasser
water, drinkable	Trinkwasser
water, tap	Leitungswasser
waterfall	Wasserfall
waterskiing	Wasserskifahren
we	wir
weather	Wetter
weather forecast	Wettervorhersage
Web site	Internetseite
wedding	Hochzeit
Wednesday	Mittwoch
week	Woche
weight	Gewicht
welcome	willkommen
west	Westen
western Germany	Westen von Deutschland
wet	naß
what	was
wheel	Rad
wheelchair-accessible	rollstuhlgängig
when	wann
where	wo
whipped cream	Schlagsahne
white	weiß
white-out	Tipp-Ex
who	wer

why	warum
widow	Witwe
widower	Witwer
wife	Ehefrau
wild	wild
wind	Wind
window	Fenster
windshield wipers	Scheibenwischern
windsurfing	Windsurfen
windy	windig
wine	Wein
wine shop	Weinhandlung
wing	Flügel
winter	Winter
wipers, windshield	Scheibenwischern
wish (v)	wünschen
with	mit
without	ohne
women	Damen
wood	Holz
wool	Wolle
word	Wort
work (n)	Arbeit
work (v)	arbeiten
world	Welt
worse	schlechter
worst	schlechteste
wrap	umwickeln
wrist	Handgelenk
write	schreiben

X

X-ray	Röntgenbild

Y

year	Jahr
yellow	gelb
yes	ja
yesterday	gestern
you (formal)	Sie
you (informal)	du
young	jung
youth hostel	Jugendherberge
youths	Jugendliche

Z

zero	null
zip code	Postleitzahl
zip-lock bag	Gefrierbeutel
zipper	Reißverschluß
zoo	Zoo

TIPS FOR HURDLING
The Language Barrier

Don't be Afraid to Communicate

Even the best phrase book won't satisfy your needs in
every situation. To really hurdle the language barrier, you
need to leap beyond the printed page, and dive into contact with the locals. Never allow your lack of foreign language skills to isolate you from the people and cultures
you traveled halfway around the world to experience.
Remember that in every country you visit, you're sur-
rounded by expert, native-speaking tutors. Spend bus
and train rides letting them teach you.

Start conversations by asking politely in the local
language, "Do you speak English?" When you speak
English with someone from another country, talk slowly,
clearly, and with carefully chosen words. Use what the
Voice of America calls "simple English." You're talking to
people who are wishing it was written down, hoping to
see each letter as it tumbles out of your mouth.
Pronounce each letter, avoiding all contractions and
slang. For bad examples, listen to other tourists.

Keep things caveman-simple. Make single nouns
work as entire sentences ("Photo?"). Use internationally-

262

understood words ("auto kaput" works in Bordeaux). Butcher the language if you must. The important thing is to make the effort. To get air mail stamps, you can flap your wings and say "tweet, tweet." If you want milk, moo and pull two imaginary udders. Risk looking like a fool.

If you're short on words, make your picnic a potluck. Pull out a map and point out your journey. Draw what you mean. Bring photos from home and introduce your family. Play cards or toss a Frisbee. Fold an origami bird for kids or dazzle 'em with sleight-of-hand magic.

Go ahead and make educated guesses. Many situations are easy-to-fake multiple choice questions. Practice. Read timetables, concert posters, and newspaper headlines. Listen to each language on a multilingual tour. Be melodramatic. Exaggerate the local accent. Self-consciousness is the deadliest communication-killer.

Choose multilingual people to communicate with, such as students, business people, urbanites, young well-dressed people, or anyone in the tourist trade. Use a small note pad to jot down handy phrases and to help you communicate more clearly with the locals by scribbling down numbers, maps, and so on. Some travelers carry important messages written on a small card: allergic to nuts, strict vegetarian, your finest ice cream.

International Words

As our world shrinks, more and more words hop across their linguistic boundaries and become international. Savvy travelers develop a knack for choosing words most likely to be universally understood ("auto" instead of "car," "kaput" instead of "broken," "photo" instead of "picture"). Internationalize your pronunciation. "University," if you play around with its sound (oo-neevehr-see-tay), will be understood anywhere. Practice speaking English with a heavy German accent. Wave your arms a lot. Be creative.

Here are a few internationally understood words. Remember, cut out the Yankee accent and give each word a pan-European sound.

auto	picnic	amigo	autobus
chocolate	moment	sexy	Disneyland
ciao	bank	hotel	bye-bye
Europa	self-service	toilet	information
Michelangelo	beer	oo la la	coffee
nuclear	macho	tourist	English
pardon	university	fascist	U.S. profanity
rock'n roll	post	camping	OK
stop	kaput	vino	restaurant
super	taxi	central	Rambo
tea	Coca-Cola®	no problem	passport
telephone	photo	photocopy	police
yankee	Americano	mama mia	Casanova

German Verbs

These conjugated verbs will help you assemble a caveman sentence in a pinch.

Many Americans are confused and dismayed by German sentence structure, which sometimes tacks verbs onto the end of a sentence. Mark Twain joked that German newspaper writers, under deadline, often didn't even get around to writing the verb before they had to go to press. Actually, this verb placement usually occurs only when the sentence has two verbs–most often when you're saying that you want or like to do something, or when you're saying that something will or would happen. In these sentences, the main verb is exactly where we'd expect it to be in English, and only the secondary verb is sent to the end. To keep things simple, you can say "*Ich gehe nach Deutschland"* ("I'm going to Germany")–and the verb (*gehe*) is right there where Americans like it, after the pronoun. But if you say, *"Ich möchte nach Deutschland gehen"* ("I would like to go to Germany"), then the two verbs split up. The main verb (*möchte*, or "would like") stays where it is in English–right after the pronoun. But the secondary verb (*gehen*, or "go") moves to the end. So the German sentence order is literally, "I would like to Germany go."

There are also a handful of prepositions such as *weil* (because) or *wenn* (if) that push the verb to the end of the sentence: "I'm going to Germany because it is so beautiful" is translated as *"Ich gehe nach Deutschland weil es so schön ist,"* which is literally "I'm going to Germany because it so beautiful is."

My favorite German teacher insisted, *"Deutsch ist leicht und logisch"*–German is easy and logical. And it is, if you know the rules.

TO GO	*GEHEN*	**gay**-hehn
I go	*ich gehe*	ikh **gay**-heh
you go	*Sie gehen*	zee **gay**-hehn
(formal, singular or plural)		
you go	*du gehst*	doo gayst
(informal, singular)		
he / she goes	*er / sie geht*	ehr / zee gayt
we go	*wir gehen*	veer **gay**-hehn
they go	*sie gehen*	zee **gay**-hehn

TO BE	*SEIN*	zīn
I am	*ich bin*	ikh bin
you are	*Sie sind*	zee zint
(formal, singular or plural)		
you are	*du bist*	doo bist
(informal, singular)		
he / she is	*er / sie ist*	ehr / zee ist
we are	*wir sind*	veer zint
they are	*sie sind*	zee zint

TO DO, TO MAKE	*MACHEN*	**mahkh**-ehn
I do	*ich mache*	ikh **mahkh**-eh
you do	*Sie machen*	zee **mahkh**-ehn
(formal, singular or plural)		
you do	*du macht*	doo mahkht
(informal, singular)		
he / she does	*er / sie macht*	ehr / zee mahkht
we do	*wir machen*	veer **mahkh**-ehn
they do	*sie machen*	zee **mahkh**-ehn

TO HAVE	*HABEN*	**hah**-behn
I have	*ich habe*	ikh **hah**-beh
you have	*Sie haben*	zee **hah**-behn
(formal, singular or plural)		
you have	*du hast*	doo hahst
(informal, singular)		
he / she has	*er / sie hat*	ehr / zee haht
we have	*wir haben*	veer **hah**-behn
they have	*sie haben*	zee **hah**-behn

TO SEE	*SEHEN*	**zay**-hehn
I see	*ich sehe*	ikh **zay**-heh
you see	*Sie sehen*	zee **zay**-hehn
(formal, singular or plural)		
you see	*du siehst*	doo zeest
(informal, singular)		
he / she sees	*er / sie sieht*	ehr / zee zeet
we see	*wir sehen*	veer **zay**-hehn
they see	*sie sehen*	zee **zay**-hehn

TO SPEAK	*SPRECHEN*	**shprehkh**-ehn
I speak	*ich spreche*	ikh **shprehkh**-eh
you speak	*Sie sprechen*	zee **shprehkh**-ehn
(formal, singular or plural)		
you speak	*du sprichst*	doo shprikhst
(informal, singular)		
he / she speaks	*er / sie spricht*	ehr / zee shprikht
we speak	*wir sprechen*	veer **shprehkh**-ehn
they speak	*sie sprechen*	zee **shprehkh**-ehn

TO LIKE	*MÖGEN*	**mur**-gehn
I like	*ich mag*	ikh mahg
you like (informal, singular)	*du magst*	doo mahgst
you like (formal, singular or plural)	*Sie mögen*	zee **mur**-gehn
he / she likes	*er / sie mag*	ehr / zee mahg
we like	*wir mögen*	veer **mur**-gehn
they like	*sie mögen*	zee **mur**-gehn

TO WANT (literally "would like")	*MÖCHTEN*	**murkh**-tehn
I would like	*ich möchte*	ikh **murkh**-teh
you would like (formal, singular or plural)	*Sie möchten*	zee **murkh**-tehn
you would like (informal, singular)	*du möchtest*	doo **murkh**-tehst
he / she would like	*er / sie möchtet*	ehr / zee **murkh**-teht
we would like	*wir möchten*	veer **murkh**-tehn
they would like	*sie möchten*	zee **murkh**-tehn

TO NEED	*BRAUCHEN*	**browkh**-ehn
I need	*ich brauche*	ikh **browkh**-eh
you need (formal, singular or plural)	*Sie brauchen*	zee **browkh**-ehn
you need (informal, singular)	*du brauchst*	doo browkhst
he / she needs	*er / sie braucht*	ehr / zee browkht
we need	*wir brauchen*	veer **browkh**-ehn
they need	*sie brauchen*	zee **browkh**-ehn

German Tongue Twisters

Tongue twisters are a great way to practice a language and break the ice with the locals. Here are a few *Zungenbrecher* that are sure to challenge you, and amuse your hosts:

Zehn zahme Ziegen zogen Zucker zum Zoo.	Ten domesticated goats pulled sugar to the zoo.
Blaukraut bleibt Blaukraut und Brautkleid bleibt Brautkleid.	Bluegrass remains bluegrass and a wedding dress remains a wedding dress.
Fischers Fritze fischt frische Fische, frische Fische fischt Fischers Fritze.	Fritz Fischer catches fresh fish, fresh fish Fritz Fisher catches.
Die Katze trapst die Treppe rauf.	The cat is walking up the stairs.
Ich komme über Oberammergau, oder komme inch über Unterammergau?	I am coming via Oberammergau, or am I coming via Unterammergau?

English Tongue Twisters

After your German friends have laughed at you, let them try these tongue twisters in English:

If neither he sells seashells, nor she sells seashells, who shall sell seashells? Shall seashells be sold?	Wenn er keine Muscheln verkauft, und sie verkauft keine Muscheln, wer verkauft dann Muscheln? Werden Muscheln verkauft?
Peter Piper picked a peck of pickled peppers.	Peter Pfeiffer erntete einen Korb voll eingemachter Pfefferschoten.
Rugged rubber baby buggy bumpers.	Starke Gummistoßdämpfer am Kinderwagen.

The sixth sick sheik's sixth sheep's sick.	Das sechste Schaf vom sechsten Scheich ist krank.
Red bug's blood and black bug's blood.	Blut vom roten Käfer und Blut vom schwarzen Käfer.
Soldiers' shoulders.	Soldatenschultern.
Thieves seize skis.	Diebe klauen Schi.
I'm a pleasant mother pheasant plucker. I pluck mother pheasants. I'm the most pleasant mother pheasant plucker that ever plucked a mother pheasant.	Ich bin ein freundlicher Federrupfer von Fasanenhennen. Ich rupfe Federn von Fasanenhennen. Ich bin der freundlichste Federrupfer von Fasanenhennen, der je die Federn einer Fasanenhenne gerupft hat.

German Songs

Another way to connect with locals is to sing a song together. Most folks are familiar with *"Stille Nacht, Heilige Nacht"* ("Silent Night, Holy Night") and *"O Tannenbaum"* ("O Christmas Tree"). Here are the words to a few more German songs. Get a local to teach you the tunes.

First, a favorite folksong:

Du, Du Liegst Mir Im Herzen —Anonymous	**You Are in My Heart**
Du, du liegst mir im Herzen,	You are in my heart,
Du, du liegst mir in Sinn.	You are in my mind.
Du, du machst mir viel Schmertzen,	You cause me much pain,
Weißt nicht wie gut ich dir bin.	You do not know how good I am for you.
Ja, ja, ja, ja, weißt nicht wie gut ich dir bin.	Yes, you do not know how good I am for you.
So, so, wie ich dich liebe,	Just as I love you,
So, so, liebe auch mich.	So love me too.

Die, die zärtlichstenTriebe,	The most affectionate instincts,
Fühl' ich allein ewig für dich.	I feel lonesome always for you.
Doch, doch, darf ich dir trauen,	But yes, I may trust you,
Dir, dir, mit leichtem Sinn.	You, with light thoughts.
Du, du kannst auf mich bauen,	You can count on me,
Weißt ja, wie gut ich dir bin.	You do know how good I am for you.
Ja, ja, ja, ja, weißt ja, wie gut ich dir bin.	Yes, you do know how good I am for you.
Und, und, wenn in der Ferne,	And if in the distance,
Mir, mir, dein Bild erscheint,	Your image appears to me,
Dann, dann wünscht ich so gerne,	Then I will so gladly wish
Daß uns die Liebe vereint.	That love would unite us.
Ja, ja, ja, ja, daß uns die Liebe vereint.	Yes, that love would unite us.

Rollicking drinking songs (often accompanied by an oompah band and swaying locals) are an important part of German beer-hall culture. You'll likely hear this simple *Trinklied* (drinking song), especially during Oktoberfest in Munich:

Ein Prosit der Gemütlichkeit!	**A toast to Coziness!**
—Traditional	
Ein Prosit, ein Prosit	A toast, a toast
Der Gemütlichkeit!	To coziness!
Ein Prosit, ein Prosit	A toast, a toast
Der Gemütlichkeit!	To coziness!

And finally, here's a lovesong often played on Rhine cruises passing the infamous Loreley. This huge hulking cliff is steeped in the legend of a beautiful siren who lured sailors to their deaths.

Die Lorelei
—Lyrics by Heinrich Heine,
music by Friedrich Silcher, 1827

The Loreley

Ich weiß nicht, was soll es
bedeuten, daß ich so traurig bin;
ein Märchen aus alten Zeiten, das
kommt mir nicht aus dem Sinn.

I don't know what it should
mean that I'm so sad;
a tale from the olden times,
which does not come to me
from reason.

Die Luft ist kühl, es dunkelt,
und ruhig fließt der Rhein;
der Gipfel des Berges funkelt
im Abendsonnenschein.

The air is cool, it gets dark, and
gently flows the Rhine;
the peak of the mountain glistens
in afternoon sunshine.

Die schönste Jungfrau sitzet
dort oben wunderbar;
ihr goldnes Geschmeide blitzet,
sie kämmt ihr goldnes Haar.
Sie kämmt es mit goldnem
Kamme und singt ein Lied
dabei; das hat eine wunder-
same, gewaltige Melodei.

The prettiest maiden sits
up there wonderfully;
her golden jewelry twinkles,
she combs her golden hair.
She combs it with a golden comb
while she sings a song,
which has a wondrous,
overwhelming melody.

Den Schiffer im kleinen Schiffe
ergreift es mit wildem Weh;
er schaut nicht die Felsenriffe,
er schaut nur hinauf in die Höh'.
Ich glaube, die Wellen
verschlingen am Ende Schiffer
und Kahn;
und das hat mir ihrem
Singen die Lorelei getan.

The boatman in the small rowboat
seizes the song with a wild ache;
he looks not at the cliff's reef,
but only above to the sky.
I believe in the end the waves
will engulf the boatman and
his boat;
and the Loreley has
done this with her singing.

Numbers and Stumblers

- Europeans write a few of their numbers differently than we do. 1 = 1 , 4 = 4 , 7 = 7 . Learn the difference or miss your train.
- Europeans write the date in this order: day/month/year.
- Commas are decimal points, and decimals are commas. A dollar and a half is 1,50, and there are 5.280 feet in a mile.
- The European "first floor" isn't the ground floor but the first floor up.
- When counting with your fingers, start with your thumb. If you hold up only your first finger, you'll probably get two of something.

APPENDIX

Let's Talk
Telephones

Making Calls within a European Country: About half of all European countries use area codes (like we do); the other half uses a direct-dial system without area codes.

To make calls within a country that uses a direct-dial system (Belgium, Czech Republic, Denmark, France, Italy, Portugal, Norway, Spain, and Switzerland), you dial the same number whether you're calling across the country or across the street.

In countries that use area codes (such as Austria, Britain, Finland, Germany, Ireland, Netherlands, and Sweden), you dial the local number when calling within a city and you add the area code if calling long-distance within the country.

Making International Calls: You always start with the international access code (011 if you're calling from America or Canada, or 00 from Europe), then dial the country code of the country you're calling (see codes below).

What you dial next depends on the phone system of the country you're calling. If the country uses area codes, drop the initial zero of the area code, then dial the rest of the number.

Countries that use direct-dial systems (no area codes) vary in how they're accessed internationally by phone. You always start by dialing the international access code, followed by the country code. Then, if you're calling the Czech Republic, Denmark, Italy, Norway, Portugal, or Spain, simply dial the phone number in its entirety. But if you're calling Belgium, France, or Switzerland, drop the initial zero of the phone number.

Country Codes

After you've dialed the international access code, dial the code of the country you're calling.

Austria—43	Belgium—32
Britain—44	Canada—1
Czech Rep.—420	Denmark—45
Estonia—372	Finland—358
France—33	Germany—49
Gibraltar—350	Greece—30
Ireland—353	Italy—39
Morocco—212	Netherlands—31
Norway—47	Portugal—351
Spain—34	Sweden—46
Switzerland—41	United States—1

APPENDIX

Directory Assistance

	National	International	Train Information
Austria:	16	08	051717
Germany:	11833	11834	01805-996-633

German tourist offices—dial area code, then 19433

Switzerland:	111	191	0900-300-300

U.S. Embassies

Austria (in Vienna)
- Tel. 01/31339
- Marriott Building 4th floor, Gartenbaupromenade 2
- www.usembassy-vienna.at/consulate

Germany
- Tel. 089/28880
- Königinstrasse 5, **Munich**
  or
- Tel. 030/832-9233
- Clayallee 170, **Berlin**
- www.usembassy.de

Switzerland (in Bern)
- Tel. 031-357-7234
- Jubilaeumsstrasse 95
- www.us-embassy.ch/consul/consul.html

Tear-out Cheat Sheet

Keep this sheet of German survival phrases in your pocket, handy to memorize or use if you're caught without your phrase book.

Good day.	Guten Tag.	**goo**-tehn tahg
Do you speak English?	Sprechen Sie Englisch?	**shprehkh**-ehn zee **ehng**-lish
Yes. / No.	Ja. / Nein.	yah / nīn
I don't understand.	Ich verstehe nicht	ikh fehr-**shtay**-heh nikht
Please.	Bitte.	**bit**-teh
Thank you.	Danke.	**dahng**-keh
You're welcome.	Bitte.	**bit**-teh
I'm sorry.	Es tut mir leid.	ehs toot meer līt
Excuse me. (to pass- or to get attention)	Entschuldigung.	ehnt-**shool**-dig-oong
No problem.	Kein Problem.	kīn proh-**blaym**
Very good.	Sehr gut.	zehr goot
Goodbye.	Auf Wiedersehen.	owf **vee**-der-zayn
How much is it?	Wie viel kostet das?	vee feel **kohs**-teht dahs
Write it?	Aufschreiben?	**owf**-shrī-behn
euro (€)	Euro	**oy**-roh
one / two	eins / zwei	īns / tsvī
three / four	drei / vier	drī / feer
five / six	fünf / sechs	fewnf / zehx
seven / eight	sieben / acht	**zee**-behn / ahkht
nine / ten	neun / zehn	noyn / tsayn
20	zwanzig	**tsvahn**-tsig
30	dreißig	**drī**-sig
40	vierzig	**feer**-tsig
50	fünfzig	**fewnf**-tsig
60	sechzig	**zehkh**-tsig
70	siebzig	**zeeb**-tsig
80	achtzig	**ahkht**-tsig
90	neunzig	**noyn**-tsig
100	hundert	**hoon**-dert

I'd like...	Ich hätte gern...	ikh **heh**-teh gehrn
We'd like...	Wir hätten gern...	veer **heh**-tehn gehrn
...this.	...dies.	deez
...more.	...mehr.	mehr
...a ticket.	...eine Fahrkarte.	**Ī**-neh **far**-kar-teh
...a room.	...ein Zimmer.	**ī** **tsim**-mer
...the bill.	...die Rechnung.	dee **rehkh**-noong
Is it possible?	Ist es möglich?	ist ehs **mur**-glikh
Where is the toilet?	Wo ist die Toilette?	voh ist dee toh-**leh**-teh
men / women	Herren / Damen	**hehr**-ehn / **dah**-mehn
entrance / exit	Eingang / Ausgang	**īn**-gahng / **ows**-gahng
no entry	kein Zugang	**kīn** **tsoo**-gahng
open / closed	geöffnet / geschlossen	geh-**urf**-neht / geh-**shloh**-sehn
When does this open / close?	Wann ist hier geöffnet / geschlossen?	vahn ist heer geh-**urf**-neht / geh-**shloh**-sehn
Now.	Jetzt.	yehtzt
Soon.	Bald.	bahlt
Later.	Später.	**shpay**-ter
Today.	Heute.	**hoy**-teh
Tomorrow.	Morgen.	**mor**-gehn
Monday	Montag	**mohn**-tahg
Tuesday	Dienstag	**deen**-stahg
Wednesday	Mittwoch	**mit**-vohkh
Thursday	Donnerstag	**doh**-ner-stahg
Friday	Freitag	**frī**-tahg
Saturday	Samstag	**zahm**-stahg
Sunday	Sonntag	**zohn**-tahg

MAKING YOUR HOTEL RESERVATION

Most hotel managers know basic "hotel English." E-mailing or faxing are the preferred methods for reserving a room. They're clearer and more foolproof than telephoning. Photocopy and enlarge this form, or find it online at www.ricksteves.com/reservation.

One-Page Fax

To: _____ @ _____
　　　　　　　hotel　　　　　　　　　　　　　　　fax

From: _____ @ _____
　　　　　　　name　　　　　　　　　　　　　　　fax

Today's date: _____/_____/_____
　　　　　　　　　day　month　year

Dear Hotel_____

Please make this reservation for me:

Name: _____

Total # of people: _____ # of rooms: _____ # of nights: _____

Arriving: _____/_____/_____　　My arrival time: (24-hr clock): _____
　　　　　　day　month　year　　　　　　(I will telephone if later)

Departing: _____/_____/_____
　　　　　　day　month　year

Room(s): Single ____ Double ____ Twin ____ Triple ____ Quad ____ Quint ____

With: Toilet ____ Shower ____ Bathtub ____ Sink only ____

Special needs: View ____ Quiet ____ Cheapest ____ Ground floor ____

Please fax or e-mail your confirmation of my reservation, along with the type of room reserved and the price. Please also inform me of your cancellation policy. After I hear from you, I will quickly send my credit-card information as a deposit to hold the room. Thank you.

Signature _____

Name _____

Address _____

City _____ State ____ Zip Code _____ Country _____

E-mail address _____